Religion, Economy, and Cooperation

Religion and Reason

Founded by Jacques Waardenburg

Edited by
Gustavo Benavides and Michael Stausberg

Volume 49

De Gruyter

Religion, Economy, and Cooperation

Edited by

Ilkka Pyysiäinen

De Gruyter

ISBN 978-3-11-024632-2
e-ISBN 978-3-11-024633-9
ISSN 0080-0848

Library of Congress Cataloging-in-Publication Data

Religion, economy, and cooperation / [edited by] Ilkka Pyysiäinen.
p. cm. – (Religion and reason, ISSN 0080-0848 ; v. 49)
Includes bibliographical references and index.
ISBN 978-3-11-024632-2 (hardcover 23 × 15,5 : alk. paper)
1. Economics – Religious aspects. 2. Economics – Moral and ethical aspects. 3. Cooperation – Religious aspects. 4. Cooperation – Moral and ethical aspects. I. Pyysiäinen, Ilkka.
HB72.R453 2010
201'.633–dc22
2010021490

Bibliographic information published by the Deutsche Nationalbibliothek

The Deutsche Nationalbibliothek lists this publication in the Deutsche Nationalbibliografie; detailed bibliographic data are available in the Internet at http://dnb.d-nb.de.

Printing: Hubert & Co. GmbH & Co. KG, Göttingen
∞ Printed on acid-free paper

Printed in Germany

www.degruyter.com

Preface

Why do humans cooperate and show altruistic behavior? The topic has recently fascinated scholars from varying fields from evolutionary biology and economics to religious studies. In this volume, economists, philosophers and religion scholars analyze the many-fold interconnections between religion and economy from this perspective. The first chapter introduces the various views, questions, and hypotheses related to this theme. These include, first, the idea of humans as rational maximizers of utility, a view by and large contested by those who argue for a "bounded-rationality." In this latter view, human choices and judgments are largely intuitive and not based on a purely rational calculation. Second, several authors have noted the obvious analogy between the concepts of the 'market' and 'God.' Is there an invisible hand guiding evolution and development? Or, more appropriately, what might be the actual mechanisms in this way metaphorically represented? And, notably, what is it in human cognition that predisposes us to think in such terms? Finally, how has human cooperation actually evolved?

The first contributions are more theoretical in nature. Bulbulia and Schjoedt present a new model for analyzing the evolution of cooperation and the role of religion in that process. The model is based on the ideas of the creation of common knowledge and attempts at predicting the outcomes of one's selfish and cooperative actions in a hostile world. Bulbulia and Schjoedt argue that the classical Prisoner's Dilemma argument is misguided in that, although deception may seem like the winning strategy, in reality the focal problem is that the outcomes of deception are unknown and people thus must try to somehow predict the outcomes of cooperation versus deception. It is here that religion comes in: it is a means of coordinating common knowledge so that a reliable context for cooperation is created.

How economists actually use modeling and how representatives of the rational choice theory have responded to criticism from the supporters of the idea of bounded rationality is dealt with by Grüne-Yanoff. He argues that, although the idea of bounded rationality has increased social scientists' sensitivity to the cognitive mechanisms underlying choice, and to systematic behavioral deviations from the standard view, the significance of these experimental results and modeling efforts are sometimes overemphasized.

The idea of the market as a god-like imagined entity receives a systematic analysis in Kamppinen's contribution. Although Superior beings in archaic and modern contexts are analogous and share some functional properties that can be explicated by means of game-theoretical analysis, it does not follow that the superior beings of modern contexts are in any sense religious. By and large, people do not believe that the causal factors pertaining to market forces are supernatural agents in a religious sense. It is rather a question of a generic human phenomenon, that is, the idea of playing against superior beings. This can happen in different contexts, such as religion and economy.

The respective roles of psychology and sociology in explanations of human action and judgment, as in economic behavior, are discussed by Schmaus. He shows that, despite many arguments to the contrary, Durkheim's sociological theory was not anti-psychological, although it is anti-reductionist. Such disciplines as the sociology of knowledge, cultural anthropology, anthropological linguistics, and cognitive psychology can cooperate in analyzing the relationship between individual mental capacities and a culture's ways of representing concepts such as space, time, and causality, for example.

With North and Gwin's contribution we move to more concrete analyses of the coevolution of economics and religion in Europe. North and Gwin start from the observation that only in the last few centuries we have testified to a widespread accumulation of wealth typical in a modern developed economy. With this economic prosperity has also come improvement in quality of life in many measurable ways. North and Gwin then ask why it was in Western Europe that the modern wealth-generating economy first got its start. Why not elsewhere? They argue that the Roman Catholic Church was one of the primary producers of wealth in the medieval period (from 1000 to 1500 CE). This was because of the productivity of the monastic estates that was likely a direct result of greater cooperative behavior encouraged by the shared beliefs and social norms within the monastery. To protect monastic lands and other Church properties from appropriation by secular authorities, the Church tried to assert the power of the Pope over both the Church and the secular rulers. This led to the emergence of ecclesiastical courts as the creators and interpreters of the canon law, which laid the legal foundation for limitations on the authority of the state. The Church used its own court system to protect itself against the arbitrariness of the emerging states of the medieval period. The laws developed in ecclesiastical courts then had a lasting impact on the secular laws of property and contract, with effects still felt today.

Nelson continues where North and Gwin left, reevaluating Weber's theory of Protestantism and the rise of capitalism. Nelson emphasizes a point very much neglected by Weber and argues that the Protestant Reformation may have contributed to the rise of capitalism by triggering the Catholic counter-reformation. Counter-reformation may then have changed Catholicism in ways that undermined its prior flexibility and thus its compatibility with capitalism and the forces of the modern world. A newly energized Catholic Church looked backward rather than forward and now moved effectively to limit threats to its authority posed by modern ideas.

Finally, Goodchild argues that economy is an heir to ascetic life: the market is best considered neither as a means towards human fulfillment, nor as the end of human fulfillment; yet it regulates human life through self-determination. It, like the religious life, provides the collective goals of human behavior.

Helsinki, March 2010 Ilkka Pyysiäinen

Contents

Servants of Two Masters: Religion, Economy, and Cooperation

Ilkka Pyysiäinen

1. Rational Choice in Economics and Religion

Why do people give money to beggars? Why do we help complete strangers? Briefly, why do humans cooperate (Henrich and Henrich 2007)? There are two different ways of trying to answer this question. Scholars of religion usually favor an individualistic approach, trying to understand and interpret the noble motives of unselfish individuals (Gothóni 2005; see Alles 2005). Another option is to map and model the macro-level consequences of the various choices individuals make. In this latter alternative, it is possible to count the costs and benefits of various behaviors and then predict which types of behavior are more likely to endure in the long run (see Maynard-Smith 1982; Cavalli-Sforza and Feldman 1981; Richerson and Boyd 2005). Much confusion has resulted from not keeping these two approaches separate.

Here I focus mostly on the second approach that typifies evolutionary explanations and also very much the contributions to this volume. As I point out elsewhere, we must be clear on whether we wish to explain why some given individuals have the particular beliefs they do or why they perform the particular acts they do, *or* whether we want to explain why certain *types* of beliefs and practices are selected for cultural transmission (Pyysiäinen in press). The latter are explanations concerning population-level questions and do not target the deepest unconscious motives of specific individuals (Ariew 2003). Psychological, behavioral, and evolutionary altruism, for example, are all different phenomena. Wanting to help is an instance of psychological altruism, doing something that helps another person exemplifies behavioral altruism quite irrespective of the motives of the helper, and a sacrifice in terms of one's reproductive success in order to help others to survive and reproduce is evolutionary altruism.

Thus, it is possible to explain giving to beggars by referring to the psychological motives of individuals, behavioral norms of the society, or the long-term population-level effects of such giving. Take Jainism for example (Laidlaw 1995). It is one of the most ascetic and uncompromising religious traditions to date. Jain renouncers are homeless ascetics that filter the water they drink and the air they breathe; they even sweep the foot path in front of them in order not to crush small insects under their feet. Despite such an unpractical attitude towards life, the wealthiest merchants of India come from Jain communities. Only a fraction of Jains are renouncers who practice moral policing with regard to laity that feeds them. Religion provides lay merchants with an effective network that can be utilized in business interactions. Thus, it seems that the more uncompromising they come, the more they prosper (Wilson 2008).

Economist Laurence Iannaccone (1994, 1995) explains such costly sacrifices by rational choice theory, arguing that the "combined actions of religious consumers and religious producers form a religious market that, like all other markets, tends toward a steady-state equilibrium" (1995, 77). Costly sacrifices thus are rational in the sense of being based on a rational cost-benefit analysis, according to which, the benefits of sacrifices are greater than their costs. The positive effects of religions are not side-effects or by-products as they are in functionalist theories. Such rational choice theory (a variant of exchange theories) is basically borrowed from economics; Gary Becker (1976) characterizes it as the "combined assumptions of maximizing behavior, market equilibrium, and stable preferences, used relentlessly and unflinchingly" (see Nelson 2003, 166–89).

The idea of rational choice, in the sense of persons choosing actions in a manner consistent with their beliefs, is at the heart of the standard economic model (see Grüne-Yanoff, this volume). As Milton Friedman argued in 1953, a good economic theory makes accurate predictions if individuals seem to behave *as if* they follow the behavioral assumptions of the theory (Wilkinson 2008, 5–6; see Mäki 2009; Goodchild, this volume). The standard economic model includes the following assumptions (Wilkinson 2008, 5):

- Economic agents are rational
- They are motivated by expected utility maximization
- They have only selfish concerns
- They are Bayesian probability operators

– All income and assets are completely fungible

That people are rational maximizers of utility is not so much a psychological assumption as a methodological stance (as also Becker argued, see Nelson 2003, 168; Grüne-Yanoff, this volume). It is also said that markets average out individual behavioral differences. Thus, economic theories cannot be falsified on the basis of the unrealistic nature of their assumptions; at the most they can be shown to be unrealistic (Wilkinson 2008, 6–7, 15).

The rational choice approach has also been applied to explain religious choice. The most famous application is Rodney Stark and William Sims Bainbridge's (1987) theory of religion (see Stark 1997, 36–39, 167–184). According to them, religion is typified by compensators for desired rewards that seem to be absolutely unavailable in this life. On this premise they build a theory that consists of seven axioms, 104 definitions, and 344 theoretical propositions. The propositions have empirical content, are falsifiable in principle, and they follow purely logically from the axioms and definitions. Axioms and definitions are judged only on their theoretical fruitfulness. If these claims were valid, this would amount to a formal theory of religion. It would enable us to make predictions irrespective of empirical constraints, much as in the standard economic theory. Unfortunately all of the propositions do not logically follow from the axioms and definitions; instead, certain new, undefined concepts are introduced in the propositions, for example.

Theology, however, is truly formal. It can be understood as a model or a set of models depicting the relationship between humans and God. Theology yields predictions concerning the religious behavior of humans and the consequent response of God *quite apart from any empirical constraints*. It is not for example possible to examine a person in order to see whether he or she has been baptized. Such problems have led Protestant theologians to develop the distinction between the visible Church (*ecclesia visibilis*) that consists of sinners and of the righteous, and the invisible or hidden Church (*ecclesia invisibilis/abscondita*) only consisting of the righteous. Only God knows who belong to the invisible Church, and humans cannot know what God knows (see Härle 1989, 287–88).

Thus, theological beliefs about humans, God, creation, and redemption are not assumptions that could be empirically falsified; instead, they represent a specific stance on life (see Fusfeld 1994, 9–12). Much as the standard economic model, also theology is incapable of answering certain questions such as:

- How did the children of Adam and Eve reproduce?
- If some day we will find intelligent beings on another planet, should we treat them as God's creation?
- Etc.

Theology simply is not about such issues just as the standard economic theory is not about human psychology. To the extent that we can ask if economic theories can be said to be unrealistic, also theology may have to face the same criticism (see Goodchild, this volume).

2. Bounded Rationality and Intuitions

According to Nobel Laureate Amartya Sen (1977, 332), one reason for the egoist conception of humans in economic models is that it is possible to define a person's interests in such a way that no matter what a person does he or she can always be seen to be furthering her or his own interests. If a person is observed to choose *x* and reject *y*, he or she is said to have "revealed" a preference for *x* over *y*. Thus, one is apparently always maximizing her or his utility, unless one behaves in inconsistently. What may look like an empirical observation is actually a non-informative tautology. Behavior is explained in terms of preferences which are, in turn, defined with reference to observed behavior. By the same token, the idea of rational choice involves nothing more than internal consistency: one prefers *x* if and only if it is true that one prefers *x* (Sen 1977, 323, 325).

Problems with the idea of humans as rational calculators had been noticed also by Herbert Simon (1955, 1959) who presented the idea of "limited rationality" in the 1950's. At the end of the 1970 s the new discipline of behavioral economics was born when the psychologists Amos Tversky and Daniel Kahneman published their first papers. In the 1980's new evidence of economic decision making began to accumulate (Wilkinson 2008, 11–12). Guth et al. (1982), for instance, introduced the so-called "Ultimatum"[1] game and showed experimentally

1 In the Ultimatum game, a person is promised a certain amount of money; s/he then has to divide the sum between himself/herself and another player. The other player can either accept or reject the decision. If he or she accepts,

that in low-income countries persons will rather punish others for an unfair offer than accept a small amount of money. This finding has ever since been replicated in many different cultures. There is, however, considerable variation in cross-cultural variation on punishment and co-operation; in larger, more complex societies, people for example engage in significantly more third-party punishment than people in small-scale societies (Henrich et al. 2005; Henrich et al. 2006; Marlowe et al. 2008). Tversky and Kahneman (2002, 2003a,b) also provided more experimental evidence to support the claim that persons frame problems to be solved in different ways that cannot be accounted for by the rational choice model. The bounds of rationality are due to those tacit and often emotional intuitions that intrude on our calculating inferences (see Gilovich et al. 2005).

Behavioral economics attempts to provide a more realistic psychological foundation for economics. It is, for instance, emphasized that only by using real money in experimenting with such games as Ultimatum and Dictator, can reliable information be acquired (Wilkinson 2008, 16). Yet there is at least some evidence that people may bracket their cultural beliefs and tendencies during the experiment, although after the experiment they may use the money earned in culture-bound ways that contradict with their behavior in the games (Wiessner 2009). In mid-1990 s, the new idea of combining neurology and economics then emerged. Scholars had high hopes about the new possibility of monitoring biological responses to reward and punishment which then would not need to be inferred from observed behavior alone. Yet problems also emerged and the neoclassical economic model predicted many choices only poorly. It was soon realized that neuroeconomics had to be connected with psychology and behavioral economics (Politser 2008, 4–6; see Wilkinson 2008, 18–20). In principle, behavioral research can help economists to answer many such questions that the standard economic theory cannot explain (Wilkinson 2008, 4). These include:

- Why are people willing to drive across town to save $5 to purchase a $15 calculator but not to purchase a $125 jacket?

---

both get their money. If he or she rejects, neither one gets anything. Players often punish the decision maker and reject the offer if it is unfair (e.g. $ 9 to the first player, $ 1 to the other). A rational choice would of course be to accept $ 1 rather than nothing. In the Dictator, one person simply says how the money is divided between the two players (see Wiessner 2009).

- Why do people go to the ATM and withdraw only $50?
- Why do people prefer to postpone a treat luxury dinner rather than have it sooner?
- Why are people often willing to drive through a blizzard to go to see a ball game when
- they have paid for the ticket, but not when they have been given the ticket for free (Wilkinson 2008, 7–8)?

Such criticism also challenges the rational choice approach to religion. We may ask why people do not simply decide to form effective networks of trustworthy individuals where no one would cheat on others, if this is the rational thing to do and humans are rational. Why all the rather outlandish costly signaling to assure others that one is a cooperator (see Boyer and Bergstrom 2008)? The rational choice theory cannot explain this because it is a rather formal theory. It thus seems more plausible that enhanced cooperation follows from costly signaling without anyone's rational choice to do so (see Wilson 2002, 81–83, 163–65). The Jains do not give food to the renouncers in order to create a prosperous community of merchants; they rather do so because they feel that it is the right thing to do (Wilson 2002, 2008). Prosperity is a by-product of this. Such moral sentiments have emerged in evolution because they are adaptive. This is a population-level explanation, not a psychological argument at the level of the individual. The motives and emotions of individuals vary; evolutionary arguments are about statistically relevant regularities at the populational level (see Pyysiäinen in press).

Cognitive scientists of religion, indeed, argue that the spread and cultural success of religion can be explained by the nonconscious intuitions that drive spontaneous human behavior (Lawson and McCauley 1990; Boyer 1994, 2001; Boyer and Bergstrom 2008; Barrett 2004; Pyysiäinen 2001, 2009). Just as spontaneous intuitions intrude on our economic decision making, so also our religious decision making is influenced by tacit intuitions (see Barrett and Keil 1996). Anthropologists have known for long that literate religions involve two different levels or dimensions variously called "great" and "little" tradition, religion of the "elite" vs. "masses," and so forth (e.g. Redfield 1956; Geertz 1960; Spiro 1970; Sharot 2001; see Whitehouse 2000, 3–4). Yet such distinctions are not always taken into account and scholars can, for example, speculate on the evolution of religion as if written theological doctrines reflected people's actual beliefs and attitudes (see Boyer

1994, 260–61; 2004). "Mind-blind" theories of religion thus are psychologically just as implausible as the standard economic model (see Boyer 1994).

Such criticism notwithstanding, the standard economic model can be used to explore human behavior in the abstract (see Grüne-Yanoff 2007; this volume; Mäki 2009). It is possible to provide speculative scenarios of what would happen under certain specified initial conditions. Likewise, also the rational choice theory of Stark and Bainbridge is a rich source of ideas for scholars of religion. Although it partly fails as a general theory of religion, it includes claims, ideas, and results that can be profitably used in the study of religion. Even such evolutionary theories of religion which overlook the role of intuitions are useful in extending mere social scientific explanations and providing more robust explanatory theories (e.g. Wilson 2002).

3. Religion and Cooperation

The problem of intuitions versus rational choice is not the only point of contact between economics and the study of religion. The analogy goes much deeper as several authors have noticed. Theologian Harvey Cox (1999), for instance, notes the analogy between the market and God: both are often envisioned as an "invisible hand" that guides everything that happens, leading automatically to the best possible end result. That is, to the extent that people have faith, trusting the invisible agent. Yet it seems that the market is not enough as such. Economist Robert Nelson argues that, although neoclassical economics is based on the ideal of self-interest of the individual, this ideal does not apply indiscriminately. Self interest has its limits but economics cannot explain these limits. The successful working of an economic system depends on religious beliefs advancing the pursuit of self-interest in appropriate domains but restrains it in others, thus providing a normative foundation for the market. The market system works best when there is a clear limit to self-interest and there are institutions that encourage actions that benefit the whole community. Nelson does not speak of the empirical study of the economic dimension of religion but, instead, of "economic theology" in the sense of theology that provides arguments for the proper contextualization of the market (Nelson 2003, xviii, 7–9, 268; see Nelson this volume).

This again raises the problem that theology is not about the market but about God. Even if theology has consequences for economic activities theologians do not see this as their primary goal (but cf. Goodchild 2009; this volume). In other words, the economic effects of theology are not based on a rational choice. We must dig deeper in order to find the lowest common denominator of economy and religion and theology. Such functionalism Iannaccone was ready to overthrow may need to be revived. Religion is a very heterogeneous category and only by studying the functions of the various elements of religion we may be able to find a point of contact with it and economy (see Boyer and Bergstrom 2008; Wilson 2002, 6–7, 52–55, 65–79, 83–85).

Émile Durkheim (1925), for example, argues that (at least) in primitive societies religion was the source of within-group solidarity. Religion is a symbolic expression of reverence toward the group (*la société*), a system of ideas by which people represent the group (Durkheim 1925, 323). The action of the group is all that is needed to arouse the "sense of the divine" in people; God is the image of the group (Durkheim 1925, 295, 323). "The social" is a reality outside of individuals and the material world; it is in relation to the social that the kind of delusion or hallucination (*délire*) that all religion is, acquires meaning and objective value[2]. Religion necessitates psychological arousal and literally speaking erroneous beliefs; it is only the power of the social that is real (Durkheim 1925, 294–304, 320–25). Thus, religion is a symbolic expression of the reverence persons have towards the group. Although science can help reveal the psychological mechanisms behind apparently meaningless ritual acts, this is not an explanation of the ritual. Only the participants' belief in the power of the ritual to raise spiritual forces can be psychologically explained; the objective value of the ritual is based on the fact that by it the group is regenerated. This fact calls for a sociological explanation (Durkheim 1925, 496–97; see Schmaus, this volume).

However, religion may not be the only source of solidarity and social structure; economic exchange is another (see Alles 2000). In a functionally differentiated society, religion is just one functional subsystem among others, each of which has its own rationality. As economics

2 "En dehors de l'individu humain et du monde physique, il doit donc y avoir quelque autre réalité par rapport à laquelle cette espèce de delire qu'est bien, en un sense, toute religion, prend unde signification et une valeur objective" (Durkheim 1925, 124; see Pyysiäinen 2005a).

and science for example have their own standards of rationality, religion can no longer be the sole basis of all rationality. Therefore, within religion the existence of other subsystems is experienced as a problematic denial of religion (Luhman 1982, 190–225, 229–54).

Before publishing his *Elementary Forms of Religious Life*, also Durkheim (1926) had argued that "organic solidarity," as distinct from "mechanical," was based on division of labor. According to him, Adam Smith (1952, 3–12) was the first to attempt a theory of the division of labor (Durkheim 1926, 1–2, 26–27). In a primitive society, solidarity was mechanical in the sense that the group in a way owned its members who were all alike; they were not unique individuals. Only in more advanced societies, persons are individuals and have differing roles in food production and economy. Solidarity is "organic" in the sense that there are more complex relationships between different kinds of individuals. This, then, leads us to ask if Durkheim actually thought that within-group solidarity was based on religion only in primitive societies and that in modern societies division of labor in a way served the same function.

Although it may seem that in *The Elementary Forms of Religious Life* Durkheim wanted to generalize from primitive religion to all religion ever, he also suggests that in modern societies science will eventually take role of religion, and sociology (and socialism) will replace Catholicism (Durkheim 1925, 613). Religious belief necessitates such suspension of reason that is not possible in a modern society (Durkheim 1930, 430–31). When we cease to believe in supernatural beings, they actually no longer exist (Durkheim 1925, 121, 492). In a modern society, division of labor produces cohesion as spontaneously and organically as religion does in a primitive society (see Lukes 1977, 158). As such, division of labor is not merely an economic arrangement; for Durkheim (1926), it also brings along genuine morality.

Durkheim's "primitive society" is of course a caricature. People are individuals also in so-called primitive societies and also some kind of division of labor exists. Smith (1952) famously showed that even such an apparently simple task as making needles involved 18 different operations on which various workers could specialize, thus making the whole process more efficient. Similarly, religion is not absent from modern societies. The question now arises what might be the division of labor between religion and economics in creating solidarity.

The world expert on ants, Edward O. Wilson, once quipped about Marxism: "Wonderful theory. Wrong species" (quoted in Pinker 2002,

296), thus suggesting that human nature is ill fit for such collectivist society as envisioned in communism. Worker ants, however, sacrifice themselves for the sake of the collective; they do not reproduce but instead dedicate themselves for taking care of the offspring of the queen with which they share 75 % of their genes (Hölldobler and Wilson 1995; Ridley 1996). Such apparent altruism is actually reciprocal in the sense that by helping others the workers also enhance the spread of their own genes, a phenomenon William Hamilton (1964) referred to as "inclusive fitness," John Maynard-Smith as "kin selection," and Robert Trivers as "reciprocal altruism" (see Trivers 2002; Axelrod 1990, 89–91).

Notwithstanding the differences between ants and humans, it has been possible to model the evolution of altruism and cooperation in humans along the same lines (see Boyd et al. 2003; Henrich and Henrich 2007). The crucial question is how and why intra-group cooperation evolved as a characteristically human behavioral strategy, if it yet is the case that individual free-riders always do better than altruists, as for example the Prisoner's Dilemma suggests (Luce and Raiffa 1967, 94–102; Axelrod 1990; Table 1.1.). In this game theoretical model, one must choose between cooperation and defection; how one scores depends on the choice made by the other party. For an individual, it is always the best strategy to defect, although a group of two cooperators scores the best. It seems that groups can afford a certain number of free-riders that take benefits from altruists and do not give anything back. This, however, requires that there are those who do cooperate. So, how did cooperation evolve? (see Trivers 2002; Maynard-Smith 1982; Axelrod 1990; Ridley 1996; Nowak and Sigmund 2005; Nowak et al. 2004; Boyd and Richerson 2005; Richerson and Boyd 2005).

	Elwood does not confess	**Elwood confesses**
Jake does not confess	Jake: 1 year; Elwood: 1 year	Jake: 10 years; Elwood: 3 months
Jake confesses	Jake: 3 months; Elwood: 10 years	Jake: 8 years; Elwood: 8 years

Fig. 1.1. Prisoner's Dilemma. Adapted from Duncan & Raiffa 1967, 95. The best strategy for an individual is to let his pal down and confess, because then he will get a sentence of either 3 months or 8 years. This contrast with mutual cooperation (not confessing), which leads either to 1 or 10 years of im-

prisonment. Now, 1 year in the non-confessing option is of course less than 8 years in the confessing alternative, but non-confessing (cooperation) yet does not pay off because, in order to get only 1 year, it is necessary that the other party does not confess, and in such a situation the best strategy for oneself is to confess (and only get 3 months).

Recently, scholars from various disciplines have suggested that religion is what has made cooperation possible. If the group is held together by the costly signals by which people communicate to others that they are cooperators, there is the risk that others may try to take advantage of the potential cooperators. The ideas of spirits and of an all-seeing god effectively block such deception because they trigger the feeling that one is being watched and subsequently rewarded or punished (Wilson 2002; Johnson 2005; Bering and Johnson 2005; Johnson and Bering 2006; Johnson and Krüger 2004; Bering 2006; Bulbulia and Mahoney 2008; Norenzayan and Shariff 2008).

This is a prima facie plausible scenario (see Bateson et al. 2006). However, there is still the empirical problem that we do not know much about the earliest forms of "religion" (if such there was). Also religion as we now know it is a very heterogeneous category of beliefs and behaviors. There is no reason why all its different aspects should have evolved together; thus it is way too loose to say that *religion* is what made cooperation possible (see Boyer and Bergstrom 2008).

If we then try to pinpoint some single element of religion, such as belief in an all-seeing God, as the factor that helped cooperation to emerge, it may turn out to be difficult to find functional systems that support God beliefs and *only them*. And, if a system supports both God beliefs and other kinds of beliefs (about imaginary companions, for example), it cannot have evolved to support God beliefs only (see McKay and Dennett 2009). It is also evident that the relationship between morals and beliefs about spirits and gods is understood in differing ways and also is in no way a necessary one; it is perfectly possible to be moral without religious beliefs (see Sinnott-Armstrong 2009; Pyysiäinen and Hauser 2010; Beit-Hallahmi in press). There is a host of prosocial cognitive mechanisms in the human mind that bear no necessary relationship with religion: reputation monitoring, signaling commitment, coalitional psychology, strong reciprocity, and so forth (Boyer 2002, 2006).

It thus seems that god beliefs are a secondary add-on to pro-social cognition: they are compelling and have become widespread because they fit with the way the human mind works in representing social relationships (see Boyer 2001; Pyysiäinen 2009; see Schjoedt et al. 2009; Kapogiannis et al. 2009; Hari and Kujala 2009). Because of this fit, god beliefs have subsequently acquired the important role in social cognition they now have (cf. Bulbulia 2004, in this volume; Bulbulia and Mahoney 2008; Norenzayan and Shariff 2008). As Boyer and Bergstrom (2008) recognize, the issue of whether religion is a biological adaptation or a by-product has not been solved. However, it seems to me that the by-product view is more parsimonious and in line with the evidence (also McKay and Dennett 2009).

This is not to deny that after some kind of religious beliefs and behavior have emerged they may have been coopted for adaptive use in a manner predicted by the gene-culture coevolutionary theories (Richerson and Boyd 2005). We know, for example, that religious people tend to have more offspring than nonreligious people, and that religious communities live longer than their secular analogues (see Irons 2001; Sosis and Alcorta 2003). As I have pointed out elsewhere, this may involve a Baldwin effect in the sense that religious practices are a "good trick" (Dennett 1991, 184–87) that confers a reproductive advantage to the "believers" (Pyysiäinen 2006a; Weber and Depew 2003). Thus, those whose general cognitive and emotional capacities make them prone to religious belief and behavior may in due course outnumber the nonreligious. This does not mean a genetic assimilation of religion; it is rather that religious ideas and practices are shaped by our cognitive and emotional capacities: those forms of religion that are easy to acquire and hold will persist (see Deacon 1998, 322–39, 359–62).

Thus, my view is here a bit different from but not necessarily contradictory with the views of religion as a biological adaptation (cf. Wilson 2002; Bering 2006; Bulbulia in this volume). As Wilson (2008, 26–27) puts it, most elements of religion may be based on nonreligious genetic psychological adaptations and cultural evolution may have turned these "exaptations" into adaptations for collective action. The evolved cognitive-emotional capacities are not specifically religious and dedicated to support religious cognition and behavior only (Boyer 2006; Pyysiäinen 2006b). Instead, religion is a by-product of our evolved capacities (Boyer 1994, 2001; Atran 2002; Pyysiäinen 2009). Steven Brams (2007), for example, shows that it is possible to model human attempts at playing against a "Superior Being," analogous to the Prisoner's Dilemma, irrespective of the problem of God's existence and of whether this being is somehow religious or not (see Kamppinen this volume). The "central question" is that if a superior being who possessed the supernatural qualities of omniscience, omnipotency, immortality, and incomprehensibility existed, how would he or she act differently from us, and whether these differences would be knowable (Brams 2007, 157).

4. God and the Market

The idea of superior beings suggests that humans not only have psychological mechanisms that enable us to reason about others' beliefs and desires (so-called "theory of mind") but that we also can reason about the beliefs and desires of absent and imaginary agents as well as of whole groups. Understanding other minds is a special domain of cognition with at least two components: an early developing system of reasoning about goals, perceptions, and emotions, together with a system for representing the contents of beliefs that develops later (Saxe et al. 2004). An important part of this is the ability to understand that people may also have false beliefs and they can act on their basis (Bloom and German 2000). Leslie et al. (2004, 2005) argue that the theory of mind is partly a modular learning mechanism that only "kick-starts" the attribution of beliefs and desires. Just as color vision provides us with color concepts so theory of mind introduces belief and desire concepts. Reasoning about the contents of beliefs takes place through a selection process with inhibition. Selection, developing slowly from the preschool period onwards, acts by selecting a content for an agent's belief and an action for the agent's desire. As in everyday thinking taking a belief to be true is the default, understanding that people may act on the basis of false beliefs requires an ability to inhibit the default attribution and to select the erroneous belief for the character looking for the hidden object.

I have elsewhere tried to show that the capacity to reason about others' intentional states importantly includes what Dennett (1993, 243–46) calls "orders of intentionality" (Pyysiäinen 2009, 19–20). Without any external memory stores, adult humans are capable of fourth- or fifth-order intentionality in the sense of, for example, representing: "I know that John *wants* Mary to *understand* that Bill *believes* that Linda *loves* him" (see Dunbar 2003, 170; 2006, 171–72). "I know" here represents 0–order intentionality (unless it metarepresented as "I think I *know*"). Thus, there are altogether four embedded intentional attitudes. It is important that we are here dealing with *mental states*. For example the sentence "John *says* Mary to *claim* that Bill *wrote* her that Linda *sent* him a love letter," is not a case of degrees of intentionality. Even an autistic person incapable of mindreading might be able to understand this sentence.

However, in fast on-line cognition we do not usually operate with very long chains of intentional attitudes, representing every intermediate link separately. The limits of human working memory do not allow for this. In most cases it is enough to be able to represent four orders of intentionality: the rest comes for free, as it were (Cargile 1970). This is because information can be "chunked" to form wholes the detailed content of which can then be deduced by reasoning (see Cowan 2000; see Bulbulia and Schjoedt, this volume).

Think, for example, Pascal emailing Emma and Tom: "Shall we meet for lunch at Browns at 1 p.m.?" Emma then emails back: "Suits me." Now Pascal knows that it suits Emma but Emma does not know that Pascal knows. Pascal therefore emails Emma: "Okay, at Browns at 1 p.m." Now Pascal thinks that Emma knows that he knows that the lunch suits Emma. But Emma may be uncertain on whether Pascal knows for sure that she has received the confirmation. So she emails Pascal: "Okay with me." Emma then thinks that Pascal knows that she knows that Pascal knows that the lunch suits her. Theoretically, this could be continued forever because it is always possible to ask: "But does s/he know that I know that …" And once Tom joins the exchange of emails, things get still more complicated. Yet sane persons usually stop at the stage where one emails an "Okay" as a reply to another's message saying that the lunch suits her (see Perner 1993, 252–53). The further orders of intentionality are presupposed to be contained within the initial ones.

The same cognitive mechanisms also allow us to reason about groups and institutions as if they were rational agents: we say that "The Church wants," "The Parliament has decided," "The team fears," and so forth. In such cases, we do not think of the beliefs and desires of all the individuals that make up the group; instead, we think as if there were collective beliefs and desires that are not necessarily attributed to the individuals that form the relevant group. What the group "thinks" may, for example, be based on voting and many kinds of compromises on the part of the individuals.

Not just any group of persons is treated as an entity-like unit. An arbitrary group of people walking near each other on a sidewalk is normally not perceived as a single meaningful unit, for example. Only such groups as military platoons, religious sects, and the like are likely to be regarded as coherent units rather than as mere aggregates of individuals. When a collection of persons is perceived as being bonded together in a coherent unit, information about this group is processed in much the same way as information about individuals. Also the degree to which the group is perceived as having potency to act as a causal agent is increased. Across the studies Lickel et al. report, there was consistent evidence that perception of interaction, common goals, common outcomes, group-member similarity, and importance of the group were strongly intercorrelated and also highly correlated with perceptions of a group of people as being bonded together in a coherent unit (Lickel et al. 2000).

Huebner (2008, 91, 109–110) argues that many intentionally specified collective actions, such as the docking of a big ship by a large crew, can be explained as coordinated activity of persons; the various individuals involved ought to be seen as components of a cognitive system in the same sense as that the systems of face perception and affective response must be seen as components of an individual's representation of someone as her mother. Trying to reduce collective representational states to the representational states of individuals either proves too much or too little in the sense that either the individual level is reduced as well, or only continuity between individual and collective representations is established.

Thus, whether there really are irreducible collective representational states or not, it seems obvious that humans can "chunk" the beliefs and desires of many individuals together and by the same token to form ideas of agents that are not individual persons. States, clubs, teams, and unions are not the only examples of this. Also ideas of gods belong to this category although in Christian theology, for example, God is regarded as a person. Despite this, gods cannot be perceptually individuated in the same sense as human individuals. The idea of a god is an abstraction in the sense that in it are summarized the central norms and values of the group (see Boyer 2001, 2002). The often observed close connection between a god and a nation can be understood as testifying to the fact that the idea of a god is a way of representing the nation as an agent.

Here Durkheim's way of equating between a god and the group is basically to the point (Pyysiäinen 2009). It is only necessary to extend the argument using modern psychological knowledge concerning the representation of the mental states of others. This need not be a problem, as even Durkheim himself was in actual practice not such an anti-psychologist as he claimed in the *Les régles de la méthode sociologique*

(Durkheim 1968; Schmaus 2004, this volume). Ideas of gods only make sense on the condition that humans have the capacity to entertain beliefs about the beliefs of others and also to attribute beliefs to nonobserved agents (see Tomasello and Carpenter 2007). Any god is always the god of at least two persons; he is a "full-access strategic agent" that has an unlimited access to persons' minds and thus can act as a sort of collective conscience (Boyer 2001, 150–60).

This is not a place to elaborate more on this idea (see Pyysiäinen 2009). Instead, I only want to draw attention to Brams's (2007) idea that the gods of religions are one type superior beings and that the really interesting thing is the cognitive superiority of these beings, not other, more accidental features of supernatural agents (see Boyer 1996). By these lights, the idea of the market is one more instance of imagined superior beings. I say "imagined" because we tend to mentally represent the market a quasi-agent of sorts, although we are actually dealing with only different kinds of processes of exchange and their results in the area of economy (see Goodchild, this volume; Kamppinen this volume). Adam Smith's (1952) "invisible hand" is only a metaphor; nothing is explained by saying that an invisible hand guides the market so that common good is necessarily achieved when individuals only pursue their own self-interest (see Fusfeld 1994, 30–34). We should rather be able to describe the many micro-mechanisms that here operate. The idea of the market as a single agent is an idea of a "superior being" with such perfect knowledge that allows it to keep everything in balance.

Let me take an analogy from Indian beliefs (see Pyysiäinen 2009, 155–56). Within the old Vaiśesika school of thought the idea was developed that a creator god (*Īśvara*) is responsible for karmic retribution. God knows the future effects of the deeds of all living beings. He then creates everything according to the nature of the deeds of persons. God does not have any freedom of the will; he is rather like a book keeper that assigns each person the fate he or she deserves on the basis of karmic merit (Bronkhorst 2000, 37–38). Later, the Vedānta philosopher Śankara wrote in his *Brahmasūtra Bhāsya:* "For it is proper that He, who controls all, brings about the fruit in accordance with their actions for those who have acted, while ordering creation, preservation and destruction ..." (quoted in Bronkhorst 2000, 50). Thus, understanding how the myriads of mechanical processes work in karmic retribution is made easier to understand by positing a single agent – God – in whose mind all necessary information is represented (Bronkhorst

2000, 49–53). God reads off each person's karmic record, as it were, and then sees that the fate of the person matches her or his deeds.

The idea of the market is similar in the sense that the concept of market is used as a placeholder for whatever micro-processes it is that produce the varying situations of the market. Yet the market, of course, is not literally regarded as a personal agent with beliefs and desires. But neither is it merely a word for describing something figuratively; instead, it is a concept that triggers human intuitions about agents and agency and therefore makes it easy to think about the market *as if* it really were guided by an invisible hand of an invisible agent (see Pyysiäinen 2009, 6–8, 189–92; Evans 2008). Such anthropomorphism and animism are easy and natural ways of thinking for humans (Guthrie 1993; Barrett and Keil 1996; Barrett 1998). Thus, even if people consciously think that the market is only an abstract concept, they in fast on-line thinking may rely on intuitions about the market as an agent (see Pyysiäinen 2004a).

If we now forget about the motivations and capacities of specific individuals and look at the population-level effects of beliefs about superior beings, it is apparent that these could be modeled much as economic choices, irrespective of individual differences in belief. Games such as the Prisoner's Dilemma can be used to model various kinds of person-God dilemmas. The simplest example is belief in God and its consequences (Table 1.2.).

	God exists	**God does not exist**
Jake believes	10	-5
Jake does not believe	-10	0

Fig. 1.2. Belief in God as Prisoner's Dilemma

In the table, Jake scores 10 points as a reward for his belief in the case that God exists (Jake, e. g., gets into heaven). If God does not exist, Jake who believes gets -5 for wasted time. In the case Jake does not believe and God does exist, Jake gets -10 (he, e. g., goes to hell). If God does not exist and Jake does not believe, nothing follows. This can be turned into a repeated Prisoner's Dilemma by introducing doubt: faith and doubt alternate as Jake variously interprets various signs of God's existence.

However, a more realistic target would be the social effects of belief irrespective of whether God exists or not. This is analogous to the model of superstition developed by Foster and Kokko (2008); they define the condition under which natural selection will favor assigning causality between two events even when there is no such link. The model in a way combines Pascal's wager and Hamilton's (1964) rule which says that it is reasonable to perform a costly action if $br > c$. c is the cost paid by the actor, r is the genetic relatedness between the actor and the recipient and b is the fitness benefit to the recipient. Also costs are here measured in terms of fitness (i. e. the number of potential offspring). Helping genetic kin pays off in the sense that by so doing one also advances the spread of the genes one shares with the kin (evolutionary altruism). In Foster and Kokko's model, natural selection can favor strategies that lead to frequent errors in judgment as long as the occasional correct response carries larger fitness benefits.

Also belief in a god or some other variant of superior being may have positive effects in the sense of increased intra-group cooperation; to the extent that they outweigh the possible costs of belief, such belief will be favored in cultural selection. However, from an individual's point of view, the best strategy is to be a nonbelieving free-rider and take the benefits of religiously motivated cooperation without paying the costs (Table 1.3.). If neither party believes, the benefits of cooperation are lost. If one believes while others do not, the one who believes ends up paying the costs without any benefits. If one believes and also others believe one gains a reward but also pays a cost (which is less than the benefits). The best strategy might be the so-called tit-for-tat: one is first willing to believe but then does what the other party does (Axelrod 1990, 57–67, 202–05).

	Others believe	**Others do not believe**
Jake believes	5	-10
Jake does not believe	10	-10

Fig. 1.3. Belief in God and sociality

Combining Prisoner's Dilemma and the idea of the benefits of intragroup cooperation, we see that if Jake believes and also others in the group believe both score 5 points for enhanced cooperation. However, the best strategy (10 points) for Jake is to be a free-rider and take the benefits of cooperation but not to give anything himself. If neither party believes, the benefits of cooperation are lost; hence -10. If Jake believes while others do not, Jake scores -10 because he pays costs without getting benefits.

However, to the extent that religious belief does not arise from a rational decision, this modeling should not be understood as a model in the spirit of the rational choice theory. Evolution does not necessarily create optimal functions or strategies; it relies on emotions and motivational systems, and religiosity is rather a question of the unintended effects of intuitive choices (see Grinde 2008; Panksepp 2007). These intuitions are about agents and agency, intentionality, and teleology (Pyysiäinen 2009): we tend to see agency even where there is none (Guthrie 1993), we intuitively use intentional explanations even for mechanical events (Heider and Simmel 1944), and we use teleological explanation as default (Kelemen 2004; Kelemen and DiYanni 2005; Kelemen and Rosset 2009).

Moreover, these types of explanations are not restricted to individual events and individuals as the responsible agents: people rather see the whole world and various forms of life as "intelligently designed" for a purpose (Pyysiäinen 2005b). I am not talking about creationism only; also more liberal believers tend to see evolution and history as following a pre-given plan. Such views are based on an idea of a superior being with full access to strategic knowledge and even to other kinds of knowledge. From the cognitive point of view, there is little difference between gods and other kinds of superior beings in this respect (although gods may be anthropomorphized more than e. g. supercomputers; Barrett and Keil 1996).

This means that representations of different kinds of superior beings trigger the same kinds of intuitions about agency, be it the Christian God or the invisible hand. Thus, there is more than a mere analogy between the concepts of God and the market; it is rather a question of the same cognitive mechanisms operating in both cases. What differentiates between representations like the Christian God and Smith's invisible hand are the second-order beliefs people have about these two superior beings. Religious people believe that their intuitions about God are truth preserving, because they are metarepresented in an unquestionable validating context: the authority of the Church and Bible (Pyysiäinen 2004b). These, in turn, gain their authority in a social process that involves issues of power. In the case of the invisible hand, people may understand that it is only a metaphor when they assume a more reflective stance towards their intuitions. There are, in principle, real mechanisms that instantiate the idea of an invisible hand and that can be identified and explored. This is of course not to deny that on many occasions we give to the market a god-like status, just as authors such as Cox have argued (Kamppinen, this volume).

Thus, human reactions to the ideas of God and of the market are not arbitrary results of two separate developments. Instead, there are cognitive mechanisms that are activated by certain kinds of input and that then produce certain kinds of inferences (Boyer 2001). We are now talking about the mechanisms for reasoning about agents' beliefs and desires and for embedding orders of intentionality within each other, together with mechanisms for "chunking" the intentional attitudes of several persons as in talking about institutions and groups as if they were personal agents. We are also liable to personalize physical and natural phenomena because "hyperactive agent detection" has turned out to be an effective strategy and the false positives it produces are cheaper than its costs (Guthrie 1993; Boyer 1996; Foster and Kokko 2008). The mechanisms for "theory of mind" and social cognition are activated by god concepts as well as by other agent concepts (e.g. McNamara 2001; Schjoedt et al. 2009). To the extent that the market is anthropomorphized its idea triggers these same mechanisms. It is therefore that we feel that somehow the market is like a god.

As this analogy is explained by the same cognitive mechanisms involved, the idea of the market may actually function in much the same ways as god beliefs. First, the financial market necessitates faith because stock prices reflect demand based on stockholders' trust on the enhancement of stockholder value. Any kind of bad news about the company will diminish stockholders' trust in the positive development of the price; they start selling their shares and the price goes further down. Thus, stock price directly reflects the amount of stockholders' belief that the price will go up. Faith creates its own object.

Second, also orders of intentionality are involved in the sense that an individual stockholder's faith and beliefs reflect her or his beliefs about the beliefs of others. In market economy, anticipation of others' thoughts and actions thus is especially important: the value of a given move always depends on whether someone else makes a particular move. Such "coalitional psychology" that evolved in the tribal contexts of our ancestors has been put to new kind of use in the executive and supervisory boards of companies (see Boyer 2001, 125–26, 288–91). It is forms of economic exchange that define the various hierarchical relations in modern societies and create intra-group solidarity.

Third, the belief that the market is completely self-regulatory and always realizes the best possible world can lead to the same kind of fatalism that characterizes some forms of religion. Once an individual has made the foundational choice in favor of market capitalism he or she can no longer backslide as it were. The invisible hand of the market is what determines one's fate. Theologians have reflected on the issue of whether God wants something because it is good or whether something is good because God wants it; the same question can be asked about the market, if it is thought that the market mechanism always produces the maximum of well-being.

Thus, just as the relationship between religion and ethics has been important in theology and philosophy of religion, so also the relationship between economy and ethics has become ever more important (Zak 2008). Companies must take ethical issues seriously if stockholders only want to invest in ethically acceptable business. On the other hand, it is often emphasized that the only responsibility of CEOs and their companies is to make money for the owner's of the company. Thus, talk about company culture and ethics may often be only a smokescreen that hides violent competition. In the history of religions, some gods have demanded extremely bloody sacrifices which have not been regarded as unethical because the gods are above morals; in the same manner, business may sometimes require that extremely selfish actions are taken with the excuse that ethics cannot and should not be part of business.

When a theistic religion dominates society, social life is understood as a striving for a perfection exemplified by the concept of 'God.' But when religion is merely one subsystem among others, the whole of society may become economicized. Within economics there is no ideal of perfection, only endless open-ended growth (Luhmann 1984; 1982, 222). Henrich and Boyd (2008) argue that stratification in the sense of institutionalized economic differences between social groups may take place when there is (1) greater surplus production, (2) more equitable divisions of the surplus among specialists, (3) greater cultural isolation among subpopulations within a society, and (4) more weight is given to economic success through cultural learning. People are predisposed to learn from economically successful people, a bias which leads to the spread of cultural variants that increase individual economic success. People thus acquire economic strategies from others via observational learning, imitation, and teaching. This can give rise to a process of cultural group selection, in which groups that establish certain forms of unequal social exchange may outcompete more egalitarian societies (Henrich and Boyd 2008, 715–16; Boyd and Richerson 2005, 83–97).

Religion is not necessarily an antidote on such open-ended development. Vision of God is not a concrete goal; it can be used to legitimate many kinds of things, goals, and values (see Pyysiäinen 2001, 73–74). Thus, religion has been used both to criticize and legitimate market economy, for example. In Christianity, there is a long tradition in the criticism of avarice (one of the deadly sins), beginning from Matthew's (6:20–24) advice to store up treasures in heaven, "where moth and rust do not destroy, and where thieves do not break in and steal." No one can serve two Masters, both God and Money (see Ray 2006, 141–98; Atherton 2007; North this volume).

On the other hand, especially in the Calvinist tradition, earthly prosperity has been regarded as a sign of being chosen by God, as Max Weber famously argued (see Nelson this volume). The so-called "prosperity theology" within the charismatic and some Pentecostal traditions teaches that God desires the material prosperity of those he favors (see e.g. Hasu 2006). Thus, the relationship between economy and theology can take different forms and ultimately must be decided by some non-religious and non-economical standards.

5. Conclusion

So, why do we give money to beggars and help complete strangers? One way of answering this question is to try to model the population-level consequences of such altruism and to show that groups of behavioral altruists outperform those of nonaltruists (Richerson and Boyd 2005). Thus, it is also in the selfish persons' interest to advance cooperation in the group (which is a resource to him or her). Although this is a population-level argument, the mechanisms by which biological and cultural evolution have produced this state of affairs are part of individual psychology. Our intuitions about good and bad drive our behavior and moral judgment. Adam Smith (1984) spoke of moral sentiments that lead us to appreciate another's well-being and thus contribute to the development of a cooperative community (see Fusfeld 1994, 23–24, 29–30).

Currently, moral psychologists and philosophers argue about the role of emotions in moral decision making (Sinnott-Armstrong 2008). There is, for example, experimental evidence that immorality elicits the same feeling of disgust as diseases and bad tastes (Chapman et al. 2009). Morality is either based on reasoning and judgment that follow from certain emotions (Humean), on an emotional response that follows from reasoning (Kantian), judgment that is based on emotion and reason (hybrid), on emotion and reason that follow from judgment which is based on an action analysis (Rawlsian), or on reason that follows from judgment that is based on an action analysis and emotion (hybrid Rawlsian) (Huebner et al. 2008). Marc Hauser (2006), for example, builds his moral psychology on the view that there is a moral competence based on reasoning that is only emotionally *motivated.* Our moral judgments are mediated by a fast, unconscious process that operates over causal-intentional representations, with emotions motivating action (Huebner et al. 2008, 5; Greene et al. 2008; cf. Haidt 2001, 2007).

Specific individuals may of course have differing motivations for their action and moral reasoning may even be severely compromised in some individuals. To an extent, persons may also be prone to follow the example of immoral individuals, with population-level models showing that groups of cooperators can always sustain a certain number of selfish individuals (see Maynard-Smith 1982). However, if Claidière and Sperber's (2007) modeling is realistic, the natural attractiveness – what Henrich and Henrich (2007, 10–11, 229) call content bias – of moral ideas (as of any ideas) actually trumps the tendency to imitate prestigious and successful individuals (context bias) (cf. Henrich and Henrich 2007, 11–27).

However, many moral philosophers argue that evolutionary considerations only concern customs or practical social arrangements, not morality strictly speaking. Chimpanzees, for example, may have moral feelings in particular situations but they cannot make *generalized* moral judgments, which would require language. Thus, it is not at all clear in what sense human morality is continuous with the moral feelings of other primates (Kitcher 2006). It is also not logically possible to derive "ought from is" and to base normative ethics on moral psychology (see May et al. 1998; Pyysiäinen 2001, 158–73). Frans de Waal (2006) replies that morality only concerns helping or (not) hurting others and that, for example, same-sex marriage thus is not a moral issue. Such morality is continuous with animal feelings in the sense that it cannot exist without the lower levels of feeling; infants thus have the innate capacity to *learn* morality (see Hauser 2006). I will not try to solve this philosophical problem here; I am only concerned with the empirical issue of human behavior.

So, *on the average*, people give money to beggars, feed monks and nuns, and so forth, because they intuitively feel that such things are good and right. An especially effective way of expressing and justifying such intuitions is to say that these behaviors have been prescribed by God, gods, or ancestors who are "interested parties" in our social life (Boyer 2001, 2002). By the same token, religious beliefs set constraints for all economic activity, as the history of religions testifies. Modern "anarcho-capitalism" that knows no limits (Shermer 2008; see Norquist 2008) thus is a novel phenomenon. Two questions now emerge. First, how it has been possible for humans to by-pass evolved intuitions about reciprocity as well as individual responsibility in front of some greater whole represented as supernatural agents, and to assume a complete freedom of choice? Second, what might be the long-term population-level consequences of this development?

My answer to the first question is that free market economy has only been able to overthrow the gods by itself assuming the role of the gods. The metaphor of the invisible hand is a tell-tale sign of this. In the 18th century political economy in Great Britain the large-scale interactions of human beings actually were for the first time explained by empirical observation and reasoning, without the use of theological argument (see Pyysiäinen 2001, 56).

Thus, free pursuit of self-interest has been accepted and justified by the belief that there is a fool-proof mechanism that ensures that the selfish behavior of individuals leads to everybody's good. This answer also sets the second question in perspective: we are not talking about the consequences of the complete abandonment of the idea of gods; we are speaking of what follows from regarding the market as a supernatural agent. The crucial difference is in that, whereas the idea of gods may make individuals more cooperative, the idea of the invisible hand has precisely the opposite effect. However, the rationale of free market economy is that it is more effective than economies based on all kinds of irrational constraints on economic activities; cooperation is somewhat paradoxically supposed to be best realized as the by-product of individual self-interest (e.g. Norquist 2008).

The consequences of belief in gods do not depend on whether gods exist or not, because they are consequences of *belief.* The case of the market is different in the sense that it is not merely belief in the market that has consequences; the invisible hand is supposed to be a real mechanism, although the way it works may be impossible to describe in detail (much as in the Indian case of *karma*). So, how do we know whether it is true that free market economy always brings about the greatest amount of goodness? If we think that something is good *because* the market "wants" it, we are not dealing with an empirical issue but, instead, with an analytical, conceptual truth. Good is whatever the market "wants." If, on the other hand, we think that the market "wants" something because it is good, the issue is empirical and we need some independent criteria to differentiate between good and bad.

The testing of this hypothesis is, nevertheless, difficult because the hypothesis describes an idealized case, not the actual conditions of any society. It is like Newton's first law of motion which says that the natural state of a physical object is motion along a straight line at constant speed. We do not see anything like that in the real world because there are always opposing forces such as friction. The law thus describes an idealized case. The idea of a completely free market is a similar idealization which, however, lacks such systematic connections to testable empirical hypotheses that typify Newton's mechanics. Second, the idea of the market mechanism is not only descriptive; it may also influence the behavior of human agents and it can be used to justify certain political decisions. If it is not true, it may lead to problems; if it is true, it seems to deprive humans of moral responsibility.

If the belief in the invisible hand of the market mechanism is not true, we need some other criteria for making the right political decisions. If it is true, we need somehow to relate the idea of personal moral responsibility to the idea of the inevitable workings of the market mechanism, much as theologians have to explain the nature of human responsibility in the face of God's omnipotence and omniscience (from theodicy to "econodicy"). Let me emphasize that I am not necessarily arguing against secularization and saying that it is dangerous to reject religion. "Religion" and "god beliefs" are categories based on a specific content, while the market problem is a problem of functions in the sense that we need something that performs the function of guiding human action towards common good. It is not a priori necessary that this something is religion or god beliefs. Here I cannot dwell on this issue, however; I have only wanted to explicate the cognitive connection between religion and economy.

In my view, the idea of the market mechanism has been culturally successful, even contagious, because it explains an important dimension of modern societies in a way that is both intuitively appealing and cognitively cheap (that is, easy to process in mind). This is because it makes the market into a quasi-agent and thus provides an intentional and teleological explanation, instead of a mechanical explanation. This also explains why we are so easily led to think that the market is somehow godlike.

References

Alles, Gregory D. (2000). Exchange. In *Guide to the study of religion*, edited by Willi Braun & Russell T. McCutcheon, 110–24. London: Cassell.

Alles, Gregory D. (2005). Economy. *Revista de Estudos da Religião* – REVER 5(4).

Ariew, André. (2003). Ernst Mayr's 'ultimate/proximate' distinction reconsidered and reconstructed. *Biology and Philosophy* 18, 553–65.

Atherton, John. (2007). Exploring the paradox of prosperity: Developing agendas for Christian social ethics and political economy. In *Through the eye of a needle: Theological conversations over political economy*, edited by John Atherton and Hannah Skinner, 82–101. Peterborough, UK: Epworth.

Atran, Scott. (2002). *In gods we trust: The evolutionary landscape of religion*. New York: Oxford University Press.

Axelrod, Robert. (1990/1984). *The evolution of co-operation*. London: Penguin.

Barrett, Justin L. (1998). Cognitive constraints on Hindu concepts of the divine. *Journal for the Scientific Study of Religion* 37, 608–19.

Barrett, Justin L. (2004). *Why would anyone believe in God?* Walnut Creek, CA: AltaMira Press.

Barrett, Justin L., & Frank Keil. (1996). Conceptualizing a nonnatural entity: Anthropomorphism in God concepts. *Cognitive Psychology* 31, 219–47.

Bateson, Melissa, Daniel Nettle, & Gilbert Roberts. (2006). Cues of being watched enhance cooperation in a real-world setting. *Biology Letters* 2, 412–14. doi:10.1098/rsbl.2006.0509

Becker, Gary. (1976). *The economic approach to human behavior*. Chicago: The University of Chicago Press.

Beit-Hallahmi, Benjamin. (In press). Morality and immorality among the irreligious. In *Atheism*, edited by Phil Zuckerman. Westport, CT: Greenwood Publishing Group.

Bering, Jesse M. (2006). The folk psychology of souls. *Behavioral and Brain Sciences* 29(5), 453–62.

Bering, Jesse M., & Dominic D.P. Johnson. (2005). "Oh Lord … you perceive my thoughts from afar": Recursivenes and the evolution of supernatural agency. *Journal of Cognition and Culture* 5(1–2), 118–42.

Bloom, Paul, & Tim P. German. (2000). Two reasons to abandon the false belief task as a test of theory of mind. *Cognition* 77, B25–B31.

Boyd, Robert, Herbert Gintis, Samuel Bowles, and Peter J. Richerson. (2003). The evolution of altruistic punishment. *Proceedings of the National Academy of Sciences USA* 100(6), 3531–35.

Boyd, Robert, & Peter J. Richerson. (2005). *The origin and evolution of cultures.* Oxford: Oxford University Press.
Boyer, Pascal. (1994). *The naturalness of religious ideas: A cognitive theory of religion.* Berkeley: University of California Press.
Boyer, Pascal. (1996). What makes anthropomorphism natural: Intuitive ontology and cultural representations. *The Journal of the Royal Anthropological Institute*, n.s., 2, 83–97.
Boyer, Pascal. (2001). *Religion explained: The evolutionary origins of religious thought.* New York: Basic Books.
Boyer, Pascal. (2002). Why do gods and spirits matter at all? In *Current approaches in the cognitive science of religion*, edited by Ilkka Pyysiäinen & Veikko Anttonen, 68–92. London: Continuum.
Boyer, Pascal. (2004). Religion, evolution, and cognition. A review of Scott Atran: *In gods we trust*, and David Sloan Wilson: *Darwin's Cathedral. Current Anthropology* 45, 430–33.
Boyer, Pascal. (2006). Prosocial aspects of afterlife beliefs: Maybe another by-product. A commentary on Bering. *Behavioral and Brain Sciences* 29(6), 466.
Boyer, Pascal, Brian Bergstrom. (2008). Evolutionary perspectives on religion. *Annual Review of Anthropology* 37, 111–30.
Brams, Steven J. (2007/1983). *Superior beings: If they exist, how would we know?* New York: Springer.
Bronkhorst, Johannes. (2000). *Karma and teleology: A problem and its solution in Indian philosophy.* (*Studia Philologica Buddhica, Monograph Series*, 15.) Tokyo: The International Association of Buddhist Studies.
Bulbulia, Joseph. (2004). The cognitive and evolutionary psychology of religion. *Biology and Philosophy* 19, 655–86.
Bulbulia, Joseph, & Andrew Mahoney. (2008). Religious solidarity: The hand grenade experiment. *Journal of Cognition and Culture* 8(3–4), 295–320.
Cargile, James. (1970). A note on "iterated knowings." *Analysis* 30(5), 151–55.
Cavalli-Sforza, Luigi L., & Marcus W. Feldman. (1981). *Cultural transmission and evolution: A quantitative approach.* Princeton, NJ: Princeton University Press.
Chapman, H. A., D. A. Susskind, A. K. Anderson. (2009). In bad taste: Evidence for the oral origins of moral disgust. *Science* 323, 1222–26.
Claidière, Nicolas, & Dan Sperber. (2007). The role of attraction in cultural evolution: Reply to J. Henrich and R. Boyd, "On modelling cognition and culture." *Journal of Cognition and Culture* 7(1–2), 89–111.
Cowan, Nelson. (2000). The magical number 4 in short-term memory: A reconsideration of mental storage capacity. *Behavioral and Brain Sciences* 24, 87–185.
Cox, Harvey. (1999). The market as God. *Atlantic Monthly* 3/1999, 18–23.
Deacon, Terrence W. (1998/1997). *The symbolic species: The co-evolution of language and the brain.* New York: Norton.
Dennett, Daniel C. (1993/1987). *The intentional stance.* Cambridge, MA: MIT Press.
Dennett, Daniel C. (1991). *Consciousness explained.* Harmondsworth: Penguin.

Dunbar, Robin I. M. (2003). The social brain: Mind, language, and society in evolutionary perspective. *Annual Review of Anthropology* 32, 163–81.

Dunbar, Robin I. M. (2006). Brains, cognition, and the evolution of culture. In *Evolution of culture: A Fyssen Foundation symposium*, edited by Stephen Levinson & Pierre Jaisson, 169–79. Cambridge, MA: MIT Press.

Durkheim, Émile. 1926 (1893). *De la division du travail social*. Paris: Felix Alcan.

Durkheim, Émile. (1968/1895). *Les régles de la méthode sociologique*. Paris: Presses universitaires.

Durkheim, Émile (1930/1897) *Le suicide*. Félix Alcan, Paris.

Durkheim, Émile. (1925/1912). *Les formes élémentaires de la vie religieuse*. Paris: Alcan.

Evans, Jonathan St. B. T. (2008). Dual-processing accounts of reasoning, judgment, and social cognition. *Annual Review of Psychology* 59, 255–78.

Foster, Kevin R., & Hanna Kokko. (2008). The evolution of superstitious and superstition-like behaviour. *Proceedings of the Royal Society*, B. Published online. doi:10.1098/rspb.2008.0981

Fusfeld, Daniel R. (1994). *The age of the economist*. 7th ed. New York: Harper Collins.

Geertz, Clifford. (1960). *The religion of Java*. Glencoe: The Free Press.

Gilovich, Thomas, Dale Griffin, & Daniel Kahneman. (2005/2002). *Heuristics and biases: The psychology of intuitive judgment*. New York: Cambridge University Press.

Goodchild, Philip. (2009). *Theology of money*. Durham, NC: Duke University Press.

Gothóni, René (Ed.). (2005). *How to do comparative religion: Three ways, many goals*. (*Religion and Reason*, 44.) Berlin: De Gruyter.

Greene, Joshua D., Sylvia A. Morelli, Kelly Lowenberg, Leigh E. Nystrom, Jonathan D. Cohen. (2008). Cognitive load selectively interferes with utilitarian moral judgment. *Cognition* 107, 1144–54.

Grinde, Bjørn. (2008). Fitness optimizing theory can be misleading when applied to human behavior. *The Open Behavioral Science Journal* 2, 32–35.

Grüne-Yanoff, Till. (2007). Bounded rationality. *Philosophy Compass* 2(3), 534–63.

Guth, Werner, R. Schmittberger, & B. Schwarz. (1982). An experimental analysis of Ultimatum bargaining. *Journal of Economic Behavior and Organization* 3(4), 367–88.

Guthrie, Stewart. (1993). *Faces in the clouds*. New York: Oxford University Press.

Haidt, Jonathan. (2001). The emotional dog and its rational tail. *Psychological Review* 108, 814–34.

Haidt, Jonathan. (2007). The new synthesis in moral psychology. *Science* 316(5827), 998–1002.

Hamilton, W(illiam) D. (1964). The genetic evolution of social behaviour I, II. *Journal of Theoretical Biology* 7, 1–16, 17–52.

Hari, Riitta, & Miiamaaria Kujala. (2009). Brain basis of human social interaction: From concepts to brain imaging. *Physiological Reviews* 89, 453–79.

Härle, W. (1989). Kirche, dogmatisch. In *Theologische Realenzyklopädie* 18, 277–317. New York: de Gruyter.

Hasu, Päivi. (2006). World Bank and Heavenly Bank in poverty and prosperity – A Case of Tanzanian faith gospel. *Review of African Political Economy* 33(110), 679–92.

Hauser, Marc D. (2006). *Moral minds: How nature designed our universal sense of right and wrong*. New York: Harper Collins.

Heider, Fritz, & Mary-Ann Simmel. (1944). An experimental study of apparent behavior. *American Journal of Psychology* 57, 243–49.

Henrich, Natalie, & Joseph Henrich. (2007). *Why humans cooperate: A cultural and evolutionary explanation*. Oxford: Oxford University Press.

Henrich, Joseph, R. Boyd, S. Bowles, H. Gintis, E. Fehr, C. Camerer, et al. (2005). 'Economic man' in cross-cultural perspective: Ethnography and experiments from 15 small-scale societies. *Behavioral and Brain Sciences* 28, 795–855

Henrich, Joseph, et al. (2006). Costly punishment across human societies. *Science* 312, 1767–70.

Henrich, Joseph, & Robert Boyd. (2008). Division of labor, economic specialization and the evolution of social stratification. *Current Anthropology* 49(4), 715–24.

Hölldobler, Bert, & Edward O. Wilson. (1995). *Journey to the ants: A story of scientific exploration*. Cambridge, MA: Harvard University Press.

Huebner, Bryce. (2008). Do you see what I see? An investigation of an argument against collective representation. *Philosophical Psychology* 21(1), 91–112.

Huebner, Bryce, Susan Dwyer, & Marc Hauser. (2008). The role of emotion in moral psychology. *Trends in Cognitive Sciences* 13(1), 1–6.

Iannaccone, Laurence R. (1994). Why strict churches are strong? *American Journal of Sociology* 99(5), 1180–1211.

Iannaccone, Laurence R. (1995). Voodoo economics? Reviewing the rational choice approach to religion. *Journal for the Scientific Study of Religion* 34(1), 76–89.

Irons, William. (2001). Religion as a hard-to-fake sign of commitment. In *Evolution and the Capacity for Commitment* , edited by Randolp M. Nesse, 292–309. New York: Russell Sage Foundation.

Johnson, Dominic. (2005). God's punishment and public goods: A test of the supernatural punishment hypothesis in 186 world cultures. *Human Nature* 16(4), 410–46.

Johnson, Dominic, & Oliver Krüger. (2004). The good of wrath: Supernatural punishment and the evolution of cooperation. *Political Theology* 5(2), 159–76.

Johnson, Dominic, & Jesse Bering. (2006). Hand of God, mind of man: Punishment and cognition in the evolution of cooperation. *Evolutionary Psychology* 4, 219–33.

Kahneman, Daniel. (2002). Maps of bounded rationality: A perspective on intuitive judgment and choice. Nobel Prize Lecture, December 8, 2002. A pdf-file available at: http://nobelprize.org/economics/laureates/2002/kahnemann-lecture.pdf (accessed in December 14, 2005).

Kahneman, Daniel. (2003a). A psychological perspective on economics. *American Economic Review* 93(2), 162–68.

Kahneman, Daniel. (2003b). A perspective on judgment and choice: Mapping bounded rationality. *American Psychologist* 58(9), 697–720.

Kapogiannis, Dimitrios, Aron K. Barbeya, Michael Sua, Giovanna Zambonia, Frank Kruegera, & Jordan Grafmana. (2009). Cognitive and neural foundations of religious belief. *Proceedings of the National Academy of Sciences* 106(19). Doi:10.1073_pnas.0811717106.

Kelemen, Deborah. (2004). Are children "intuitive theists"? Reasoning about purpose and design in nature. *Psychological Science* 15(5), 295–301.

Kelemen, Deborah, & Cara DiYanni. (2005). Intuitions about origins: Purpose and intelligent design in children's reasoning about nature. *Journal of Cognition and Development* 6(1), 3–31.

Kelemen, Deborah, & Evelyn Rosset. (2009). The human function compunction: Teleological explanation in adults. *Cognition* (in press).

Kitcher, Philip. (2006). Ethics and evolution: How to get here from there. In Frans de Waal, *Primates and philosophers: How morality evolved*, edited by Stephen Macedo and Josiah Ober, 120–39. Princeton: Princeton University Press.

Laidlaw, James. (1995). *Riches and renunciation: Religion, economy, and society among the Jains.* New York: Oxford University Press.

Lawson, E. Thomas, & Robert N. McCauley. (1990). *Rethinking religion: Connecting cognition and culture.* Cambridge: Cambridge University Press.

Leslie, Alan M., Ori Friedman, and Tim German. (2004). Core mechanisms in "theory of mind." *Trends in Cognitive Sciences* 8(12), 528–33.

Leslie, Alan M., Tim P. German, and Pamela Polizzi. (2005). Belief-desire reasoning as a process of selection. *Cognitive Psychology* 50, 45–85.

Lickel, Brian, David L. Hamilton, Grazyna Wieczorkowska, Aamy Lewis, Steven J. Sherman, & A. Neville Uhles. (2000). Varieties of groups and the perception of group entitativity. *Journal of Personality & Social Psychology* 78(2), 223–46.

Luce, R. Duncan, & Howard Raiffa. (1967/1957). *Games and decisions: Introduction and critical survey.* New York: Wiley.

Luhmann, Niklas. (1984/1977). *Religious dogmatics and the evolution of societies.* Tr. by Peter Beyer. New York: The Edwin Mellen Press.

Luhmann, Niklas. (1982). *The differentiation of society.* Tr. by S. Holmes, and C. Larmore. New York: Columbia University Press.

Lukes, Steven. (1977/1973). *Émile Durkheim.* Harmondsworth: Penguin.

Mäki, Uskali (Ed.). (2009). *The methodology of positive economics: Reflections on the Milton Friedman legacy.* Cambridge: Cambridge University Press.

McKay, Ryan T., & Daniel C. Dennett. (2009). The evolution of misbelief. *Behavioral and Brain Sciences* 32(6), 493–510.

McNamara, Patrick. (2001). The frontal lobes and religion. In *Religion in mind: Cognitive perspectives on religious belief, ritual and experience*, edited by Jensine Andresen, 237–56. Cambridge: Cambridge University Press.

Marlowe, Frank W., J. Colette Berbesque, Abigail Barr, Clark Barrett, Alexander Bolyanatz, Juan Camilo Cardenas, et al. (2008). More 'altruistic' punishment in larger societies. *Proceedings of the Royal Society* B 275, 587–90.

May, Larry, Marilyn Friedman, & Andy Clark (Eds). (1998/1996). *Mind and morals: Essays on ethics and cognitive science.* Cambridge & London: MIT Press.

Maynard-Smith, John. (1982). *Evolution and the theory of games.* Cambridge: Cambridge University Press.

Nelson, Robert H. (2003/2001). *Economics as religion: From Samuelson to Chicago and beyond.* University Park, Penn.: The Pennsylvania University Press.

Norenzayan, Ara, & Azim F. Shariff. (2008). The origin and evolution of religious prosociality. *Science* 322 (3. October), 58–62.

Norquist, Grover. (2008). *Leave us alone: Getting the government's hands off our money, our guns, our lives.* New York: William Morrow.

Nowak, Martin A., & Karl Sigmund. (2005). Evolution of indirect reciprocity. *Nature* 437(7063), 1291–98.

Nowak, Martin A., Akira Sasaki, Christine Taylor, & Drew Fudenberg. (2004). Emergence of cooperation and evolutionary stability in finite populations. *Nature* 428(6983), 646–50.

Panksepp, Jaak. (2007). The neuroevolutionary and neuroaffective psychobiology of the prosocial brain. In *The Oxford handbook of evolutionary psychology*, edited by Robin I.M. Dunbar & Louise Barrett, 145–62. New York: Oxford University Press.

Perner, Josef. (1993/1991). *Understanding the representational mind.* Cambridge, MA: MIT Press.

Pinker, Steven. (2002). *The blank slate: the modern denial of human nature.* New York: Penguin.

Politser, Peter. (2008). *Neuroeconomics: A guide to the new science of making choices.* New York: Oxford University Press.

Pyysiäinen, Ilkka. (2001). *How religion works: Towards a new cognitive science of religion.* Leiden: Brill.

Pyysiäinen, Ilkka. (2004a). Intuitive and explicit in religious thought. *Journal of Cognition and Culture* 4(1), 123–50.

Pyysiäinen, Ilkka. (2004b). *Magic, miracles, and religion: A scientist's perspective.* Walnut Creek, CA: AltaMira Press.

Pyysiäinen, Ilkka. (2005a). Religion, *délire* and counterintuitiveness. *Durkheimian Studies/Etudes durkheimiennes* 11, 3–10.

Pyysiäinen, Ilkka. (2005b). God: A brief history with a cognitive explanation of the concept. *Temenos* 41(1), 77–128.

Pyysiäinen, Ilkka. (2006a). Amazing grace: Religion and the evolution of the human mind. In *Where God and science meet: How brain and evolutionary studies alter our understanding of religion*, I–III, edited by Patrick McNamara. Volume I, *Evolution, genes, and the religious brain*, 209–25. (*Praeger Perspectives.*) Westport, CT: Praeger.

Pyysiäinen, Ilkka. (2006b). No evidence of a specific adaptation. A commentary on Bering. *Behavioral and Brain Sciences* 29(5), 483–84.

Pyysiäinen, Ilkka. (2009). *Supernatural agents: Why we believe in souls, gods, and buddhas?* New York: Oxford University Press.

Pyysiäinen, Ilkka. (In press). Mechanical explanation of ritualized behavior. In *Religious ritual, cognition and culture*, edited by Armin Geertz & Jesper Sørensen. London: Equinox.

Pyysiäinen, Ilkka, & Marc Hauser. (2010). The origins of religion: Evolved adaptation or by-product? *Trends in Cognitive Sciences* 14(3), 104–09.

Ray, Darby Kathleen (Ed.). (2006). *Theology that matters: Ecology, economy, and God*. Minneapolis: Fortress Press.

Redfield, Robert. (1956). *Peasant society and culture*. Chicago: University of Chicago Press.

Richerson, Peter, & Robert Boyd. (2005). *Not by genes alone: How culture transformed human evolution*. Chicago: University of Chicago Press.

Ridley, Matt. (1998/1996). *Origins of virtue: Human instincts and the evolution of cooperation*. Harmondsworth: Penguin.

Saxe, R., S. Carey, & N. Kanwisher. (2004). Understanding other minds: Linking developmental psychology and functional neuroimaging. *Annual Review of Psychology* 55, 87–124.

Schjoedt, Uffe, Hans Stødkilde-Jøgensen, Armin W. Geertz, & Andreas Roepstorff. (2009). Highly religious participants recruit areas of social cognition in personal prayer. *Social Cognitive and Affective Neuroscience*. Doi:10.1093/scan/nsn050

Schmaus, Warren. (2004). *Rethinking Durkheim and his tradition*. Cambridge: Cambridge University Press.

Sen, Amartya K. (1977). Rational fools: A critique of the behavioral foundations of economic theory. *Philosophy and Public Affairs* 6(4), 317–44.

Sharot, S. (2001). *A comparative sociology of world religions*. New York: New York University Press.

Shermer, Michael. (2008). *The mind of the market*. New York: Holt.

Simon, Herbert A. (1955). A behavioral model of rational choice. *The Quarterly Journal of Economics* 69(1), 99–118.

Simon, Herbert A. (1959). Theories of decision-making in economics and behavioral science. *The American Economic Review* 49(3), 253–83.

Sinnott-Armstrong, Walter (Ed.). (2008). *Moral psychology 1–3*. Cambridge, MA: MIT Press.

Sinnott-Armstrong, Walter. (2009). *Morality without God*. New York: Oxford University Press.

Smith, Adam. (1984/1759). *Theory of moral sentiments*. Ed. By D.D. Raphael and A. L. Macfie: Indianapolis: Liberty Fund.

Smith, Adam. 1952 (1776). *An inquiry into the nature and causes of the wealth of nations*. (*Great Books of the Western World*, 39.) Chicago: Encyclopædia Britannica, Inc.

Sosis, Richard, & Candace Alcorta. (2003). Signaling, solidarity, and the sacred: The evolution of religious behavior. *Evolutionary Anthropology* 12, 264–74.

Spiro, Melford E. (1970). *Buddhism and society*. New York: Harper & Row.

Stark, Rodney. (1997). *The rise of Christianity*. San Francisco: Harper.

Stark, Rodney, & William Sims Bainbridge. (1987). *A theory of religion.* (*Toronto Studies in Religion*, 2.) New York: Peter Lang.

Tomasello, Michael, & Malinda Carpenter. (2007). Shared intentionality. *Developmental Science* 10(1), 121–25.

Trivers, Robert. (2002). *Natural selection and social theory: Selected papers of Robert Trivers.* New York: Oxford University Press.

de Waal, Frans. (2006). The tower of morality. In Frans de Waal, *Primates and philosophers: How morality evolved*, edited by Stephen Macedo and Josiah Ober, 161–81. Princeton: Princeton University Press.

Weber, B. H., & Depew, D. J. (Eds.). (2003). *Evolution and learning: The Baldwin effect reconsidered.* Cambridge, MA: MIT Press.

Whitehouse, Harvey. (2000). *Arguments and Icons: Divergent Modes of Religiosity*, Oxford: Oxford University Press.

Wiessner, Polly. (2009). Experimental games and games of life among the Ju/'hoan Bushmen. *Current Anthropology* 50(1), 133–38.

Wilkinson, Nick. (2008). *An introduction to behavioral economics.* New York: Palgrave.

Wilson, David Sloan. (2002). *Darwin's cathedral: Evolution, religion and the nature of society.* Chicago: University of Chicago Press.

Wilson, David Sloan. (2008). Evolution and religion: The transformation of the obvious. In *The evolution of religion: Studies, theories, & critiques*, edited by Joseph Bulbulia, Richard Sosis, Erica Harris, Russell Genet, Cheryl Genet, & Karen Wyman, 23–29. Santa Margarita, CA: Collins Family Foundation.

Zak, Paul J. (Ed.). (2008). *Moral markets: The critical role of values in the economy.* Princeton: Princeton University Press.

Religious Culture and Cooperative Prediction under Risk: Perspectives from Social Neuroscience

JOSEPH BULBULIA AND UFFE SCHJOEDT

1. Religion and Cooperation

1.1 Religion as Policing

The 4th Century B.C.E Greek dramatist Critias explains religion's success from its moral effects:

> *Some shrewd man first, a man in judgment wise,*
> *Found for mortals the fear of gods...*
> *So that everything which mortals say is heard*
> *And everything done is visible.*
> *Even if you plan in silence some evil deed*
> *It will not be hidden from the gods: for discernment*
> *Lies in them.* (Critias, s.a.)

Critias's ideas are remarkably prescient of contemporary evolutionary treatments, which replace this 'shrewd man' with 'natural selection' (see for example Bering 2006). Yet while Critias's theory explains the benefits of religion, it does not explain religion's evolutionary conservation. If we suppose that religion polices exchange, this policing would appear to create opportunities for the impious to cheat the religiously restrained. Modernising Critias's theory therefore requires an account for how religious partners reliably recognize each other and interact while avoiding non-cooperative imposters.

1.2 Costly Signalling Theory

Costly signalling explains how religious cooperation is *assured*. It uses the *cost problem* (Atran 2002) to explain the cooperative assurance problem. A cost problem arises because the actions that religion inspires appear to harm religious practitioners. Indeed, the costs of piety – blood rituals, trials by fire, celibacy – seem the sort of practices likely to have been eliminated in nature's thrifty economy (Irons 2001). Signalling theory explains such apparent waste as cooperation's efficiency (Sosis 2003; Bulbulia 2004a).[1] Signalling theorists observe that expressions of religious piety are associated with moral commitments and are also hard to fake. This means that pious expressions provide a medium in which partners may express and evaluate genuine moral commitments. Importantly then, costly signalling holds that both the conservation of religion and its apparent irrationality can be accounted for by a single model, one that combines moral policing with virtue signalling.

⋆**Costly signalling:** where ($\rightleftharpoons$) = mutual signals of cooperative intent

(1) $\textbf{partner}^{\text{Ann}} \rightleftharpoons \textbf{partner}^{\text{Ray}}$

Because classical signalling theory thus solves the *recognition problem* with the *cost problem*, the theory is elegant. Classical signalling theory is also backed by evidence. Indeed a growing number emprical studies reveal that cooperative partners attune to expressions of piety, and that greater productions of religious costs are found as the need for assurance for cooperative interaction action rises (Chen 2007; Soler 2008).

Despite classical signalling theory's virtues, however, we believe that to understand how religion evolves to support cooperative exchange more explanation is required. Specifically, cassical signalling does not explain how individuals are able to predict the future behaviours of unknown partners. The theory does not solve the problem of cooperative recognition in *anonymous societies.*[2]

1.3 The Problem of Anonymous Exchange

Large cooperative societies brings the benefits of specialization, intricate divisions of labor, and the strength of numbers for territorial defense and exploit. However such worlds also increase the scope for anonymous in-

1 As Irons notes, 'costs' need only be apparent for religious signalling to work. (Irons 2008)

2 For a recent attempt to integrate signalling theory with the evolution of learning biases see: (Henrich 2009).

teraction; commitment signalling cannot directly assure anonymous exchange. Among obscure partners, the relevant signals for evaluation are absent. To assure cooperation among anonymous partners, it would therefore seem that something more than sender-receiver signalling is needed.

(2) **partner**^{i} $\rightleftharpoons$ **partner**$^{?}$

⋆note: ($\rightleftharpoons$) cannot obtain for unknown partners: mutual signalling is ruled out for the anonymous.

Costly signalling theorists, then, face two choices respecting large-scale exchange:

1. **to suggest limited cooperative effects:** religious signalling is not relevant to the assurance of anonymous cooperation.
2. t**o suggest persistent benefits from evolutionary constraints:** religious signalling supports anonymous cooperation because our evolved minds are adapted to ancestral contexts, and fail to optimise strategic responses in modern worlds.

Against the first option, the data suggest that religious culture does indeed align the cooperative motivations of members in large anonymous groups (Atran et al. 2007).

Against the second option, even if we suppose that many structural features of cognition are adaptations to ancestral worlds, there is much evidence that humans are nevertheless able to revise their responses to novel strategic circumstances. Indeed, the evidence shows that strategic response is especially sensitive to adjustments to local circumstances so subtle that they escape awareness (Norenzayan and Shariff 2008).

Below we explore a third option for signalling theory, which we call *charismatic signalling*. The option explains how religious practices equip partners to solve a recognition problem for anonymous cohort. Yet to understand this extension of signalling theory, we must first reconsider how defection threatens cooperation in crowds.

2. Cooperation and Confidence

2.1 The Problem of Cheating

Standard evolutionary approaches treat cooperative interaction as threatened by 'a tragedy of a commons'. Cooperation can be decomposed to the investments and labours of individuals. The advantages of cooperation exceed those available to indiviuals taking on the world alone. Accessing larger benefits is cooperation's evolutionary advantage. For cooperative goods are rarely threatened when defection is rare. For the goods are rarely threatened by a single defection. Temptations to cheat arise, then, because the contribution of any single partner to the goods of civilization are typically nominal. Cheating cooperation enables individuals to access civilization's benefits without the costs of investments and labours. Moreover, defection also pays better when others do not cooperate. For if many others fail to contribute, a lone cooperator will invest and labour at a net deficit. Under conditions where cheating can be anticipated it is prudent to defect.

We agree with those who argue this assessment of cooperation's threat presents of a false picture (Skyrms 2004; Bicchieri 2006). Not all defection arises from opportunism. Indeed, perhaps little cooperation is threatened specifically by cheating. By expanding our understanding of cooperation's risks, we will be better able to perceive how religious culture assures large-scale cooperative prediction and response, from the mechanisms of *charismatic signalling*.

2.2 The Problem of Anonymous Exchange Is Not Cheating but Sensitivity to Risk

To begin, it is difficult to imagine how cheating could present stable incentives. While cooperation sometimes poses a tragedy of the commons, there is little evidence that cheating offers cooperation's most general or fundamental problem. To assume so requires that cheating allow a *reliable benefit*. Yet as Calcott observes, cheating requires a stable benefit to take (Calcott 2008). Why should anyone suppose that cheating will be reliable if the problem of cooperation has not first been solved? Similarly, why should anyone predict this motivation in others to cheat if the problem of cooperation has not been solved?

For much human interaction, it would appear that the transparency of cheating's benefit is typically lacking. Instead, uncertainty pervades social prediction. There are simply too many ways the world might turn out for any individual to foresee payoffs in numbers of grandchildren as the consequence of most actions. Indeed, we suggest that outside the extremities of love and warfare, such forecasting is plainly impossible. We believe, rather, that widespread and enduring preferences for cooperation presents a more fundamental evolutionary mystery.

To understand how partners become confident for cooperation's advantages, it is important to reflect on what individuals can confidently predict. While partners cannot generally foresee the consequences of their actions in fitness payoffs (grandchildren), partners are not totally blind in their ability to formulate cooperative preferences. Specifically, partners can know:

1. That in most circumstances, cooperation would be benefiting if many were to participate.
2. That it would be desirable to be a member of such a cooperative group, even if membership were to require my cooperation.
3. That in most circumstances cooperation would not be benefiting if many were to defect.
4. That it would undesirable to be a cooperative member of a non-cooperative group.

The knowledge given in (1–4) can be summarized in a simple conditional preference: to cooperation where many cooperate may be desirable but not otherwise. We believe that cooperation's most evolutionary fundamental problem is not the threat of a cheating benefit, but more basically the widespread availability of doubts for cooperative benefits.

Thus evolutionary designs, genetic and cultural, will tend to be ratified and conserved wherever they express and conserve strong preferences for cooperation, despite the availability of doubts (Bulbulia 2009). *Charismatic signalling* explains how religious cultures afford motivation to anonymous partners sufficient to stabilize cooperation in large societies. Before turning to the model, we explain how distinctively human cognitive capacities potentially hinder the elaboration and conservation of cooperative prediction among anonymous others.

2.3 Theory of Mind Strongly Facilitates the Representation of Risk by Enabling a Common Knowledge of Uncertainty

Theory of mind (ToM) names the human capacities for attributing mental states – such as beliefs, desires, and intentions – to self and others. We suppose there is no single attributional capacity but rather many, and furthermore that there is individual and cultural variation in the expression of specific aptitutes. Sometime acts of projecting to the thought and desires of others is called 'mentalising' (Frith and Frith 2006). With respect to cooperation, we observe, quite generally, that mentalising enables partners to represent strategies and preferences – of self and others – prior to decisions about exchange. Notably, many researchers have credited ToM as a key player in the evolution of large Hominin society (Dunbar 1998). Though the problem of cooperation threatened by uncertainty (instead of cheating) is not widely studied, it might appear that theory of mind will indeed play a strong supporting role here as well. This is because any partner who possesses the capacity for theory of mind, and is aware that her partners have ToM, may easily generate a representation of the fact that everyone desires cooperation as a top preference. Moreover, such a representation will generalise. Every partner will know and that everyone knows this representation of conditional preferences to be common knowledge. Specifically, a 'mindsighted' agent can know that:

1. I prefer cooperation
2. others prefer cooperation
3. everyone is able to act cooperatively
4. everyone wishes to act cooperatively if others do
5. everyone knows (1–4) to be common knowledge.[3]

ToM enables partners to understand the *rationality* of mutually benefiting exchange. It would seem that the power to represent conditional preferences and strategies as common knowledge will strongly accommodate the evolution of cooperative solutions: 'We want to cooperate: let's cooperate.'

However we believe that a closer assessment of the strategic circumstances that ToM reveals a strategic context with substantial new obstacles. These obstacles have trace their roots to the conditional nature of

3 For a discussion of common knowledge see: (Lewis 1969). For a criticism that partners require common knowledge see: (Binmore 2008).

our cooperative preferences. Because preferences to cooperate are conditional on the prediction that cooperation will actually occur, partners equipped with theory of mind must *explicitly* consider whether others (similarly equipped with ToM) will be sufficiently motivated to exchange. We think about ToM's risk elevation in the following way.

For simplicity, let us imagine that the cooperative of some subpopulation of a larger, anonymous group is sufficient for success, and known to be sufficient by common knowledge (i. e. there are no other risks to success that cooperation of a minimal group 'r' in a larger group R: $r \subseteq R$

Let → denote 'represent'.[4]
Let '(. . .)' contain the contents of a representation.

We begin by thinking about how cooperative assessment will take place among those lacking ToM capacities. Among mindblinded partners, the world is evaluated as it is sensed, or as sensations are remembered. Thus for any mindblinded partner:

(3) $\mathbf{partner}^{i} \rightarrow (\mathit{world})$

We assume that mindblind agents will evolve or learn behaviours based on observable outcomes. Given that significant large-scale cooperation appears to be rare among unrelated organisms, we expect that such learning is difficult.

However it is not clear that ToM gives the decisive advantage. Again, for simplicity, let us imagine that mind-sighted partners judge that if the minimal group 'r' acts for cooperation, a greater benefit will certainly come to members of r. Mind-sighted partners also know that if r does not arise, cooperation will be costly. The mind-sighted represent the

4 Later we use → to mean 'sense', without loss of generality, because the representations that ultimately motivate behavior need not be explicit: it is not the representational character of this representation that matters to cooperative solutions, and indeed we suggest that the automation of cooperative affect benefits from the recruitment of non-declarative representations. Cognition is therefore best approached as 'embodied' by which we mean multi-modal, nonlinear, and grounded in situations. From and embodied perspective on cognition, the concept of 'awareness' is not exhausted by the concepts of 'belief' or 'perception' or 'attention'.

contents of minds (self or others) – beliefs, desires, confidence, expectations, strategies . . . – as strategic factors in the world. Thus mind-sighted partners encounter an enlarged world, one in which the representation of mental facts as well as of physical facts matters to strategic decision making.

(4) $\textbf{partner}^{i} \rightarrow (\textit{world} + \textbf{minds})$

Of course, not every representation will be relevant to cooperative prediction. (Whether Alice believes that John prefers white to gray, for example, will be irrelevant). Yet there is one mental fact that will be particularly important to every cooperative partner. Those who think about cooperation carefully will understand that the conditions needed to satisfy cooperative prediction must be strong enough to satisfy *the most doubting member of the minimal group* (r) required for cooperative benefits to be generated. We chall call this most doubting member of the minimal coopertive group: **partner**^{D}. Why is **this** person's confidence so important to cooperative prediction?

In the simplified situation we have imagined, it is the decision of this weakest link – **partner**^{D} – that will make or break cooperation's success. Any partner (**partner**^{i}) who is able to represent the cooperative confidence of others should therefore not wish to set her confidence higher than that of the weakest link in the minimal group. Thus, in thinking about the strategies of others, any given partner (**partner**^{i}) must telescope attention to how the most doubting partner of the minimal group (**partner**^{D}) will assess cooperation's future.

(5) $\textbf{partner}^{i} \rightarrow (\textbf{partner}^{D} \rightarrow (. . .))\ i \neq \mathrm{D}$

Indeed, because the weakest link possesses a Theory of Mind, every partner in the minimal cooperative group will require information that will be *commonly known* to satisfy to this weakest link. Where the identity of this weakest link of the minimal group is unknown, partners will be left to their imaginations in evaluating whether the conditions for satisfying this unknown, most doubting partner have been satisfied. At the limit, partners might imagine an incorrigible skeptic to occupy this role.

(6) **partner**[i] → (**skeptic** →(**How everyone imagines the skeptic**))

Will the confidence of all partners who are able to imagine this scenario inevitably decline? While cooperative confidence may actually increase in situations where mentalising partners imagine their most doubting members will be satisfied, we observe that such confidence is difficult to secure for partners who remain obscure. For anonymous partners must guess at the standards of unknown others, without the ability to verify these guesses. Where the benefit-to-risk ratio warrants cooperating in the face of strong doubts, the inability to dispatch such doubts may not impair cooperative response. However such indifference to doubt is not available to those who mentalize risky exchange. For example, where risky cooperation has recently failed, where unprecedented and seemingly dangerous cooperative circumstances arise, where the differences between cooperative and non-cooperative benefits are slight, or where evidence is vivid that cooperation is failing, the inability to prevent doubt will support predictions for cooperation's failure. For cooperation requires a coordinated response. The representation of doubt as common knowledge will undermine cooperation that partners judge to be hazardous.

2.4 Cooperation's Success Is Possible because Cooperation Does Not Typically Require the Recognition of Partner Virtue

There are numerous means by which cooperation is practically assured among strangers. Indeed, many of these solutions do not have anything to do with religion. For example, David Hume noticed that social partners come to develop cooperative expectations from experience, and from habit:

> … experience assures us still more, that the sense of interest has become common to all our fellows, and gives us confidence of the future regularity of their conduct; and it is only on the expectation of this that our moderation and abstinence are founded. In like manner are languages gradually established by human conventions without any promise. In like manner do gold and silver become the common measures of exchange, and are esteemed sufficient payment for what is of a hundred times their value (Hume 1739).

Familiarity combines with common interest to gradually build expectations that mutually benefitting cooperation will indeed occur and persist. Importantly cooperative prediction that is threatened by uncertainty, rather than by cheating, does not rely on the identification of partner specific virtue. For there is no specific motivation to cheat. The virtuous and vicious alike *predictably* benefit from living in a cooperative world.

Yet while assurances do build over time, it is precisely their persistence and endurance that requires explanation. We agree with those who notice that our conventions are fragile. For once confidence for our conventions is lost, confidence is difficult to restore. The fragility of trust is well-illustrated by societies in which corruption is rife. Cristina Bicchieri notices that in such societies most people would prefer not to bribe the police and politicians (Bicchieri 2006). Indeed, if all the disadvantaged were to resist at once, corruption would surely end. This fact is common knowledge. Yet it is also common knowledge that no single hero can bring an end to such corruption. In corrupt worlds those who act alone go missing in the night. Reform requires a synchronous resistance of many. The question: 'Why do the conventions mediating risky exchange not collapse more regularly?' remains, to our minds, a fundamental, unsolved evolutionary mystery. Given the potential for cooperative decline, the resilience of the prediction that cooperation's benefits will persist would appear to require specific supporting designs. Indeed, the elaborations of such designs presents a more fundamental problem for cooperation than the elimination of cheating. What explains the stable production of this benefit, what Calcott calls 'the other cooperation problem'. Mathematical and experimental results agree that cooperative behaviour responds to social and ecological cues. Moreover cooperation's failure produces evidence for future failure, as current defection presents evidence for future defection (Keizer et. al 2008).

In the remainder of this chapter, our purpose will not be to examine the fragility of human conventions (Bicchieri 2006). Rather, we shall consider how religious culture provides exquisite solutions to the problem of cooperative prediction among strangers. We conjecture that religious cultures evolve to generate cooperative motivations among obscure partners, without doubts. We use this conjecture to explain otherwise puzzling findings in the social neuroscience of religion.

3. Charismatic Culture: Affordance and Alignment

We define 'charismatic signals' loosely according to the classic theory of Max Weber who put emphasis on subjects recognising a person or institution as endowed with special powers, and being moved to act in accordance with the sensibility (Weber 1958; see also Taves 2009). For us (as for Weber) charismatic signalling does not exclusively point to information emitted by persons with extraordinary persuasive abilities. Rather charismatic signalling encompasses objects, institutions, roles, spatial arrays, symbolic productions, ritual theaters, ceremonies, musical projection and other factors harboured within shared environments, whose presentations affect both declarative and non-declarative cognition. It is the relationship of these governing factors to embodied cooperative cognition that shall interest us here.

Charismatic signalling hypothesizes that religious cultures strongly enhance confidence by factors that both:

1. **afford** strong cooperative sensibilities, and
2. **synchronise** these affordances.

Recall that for cooperation to operate at large social scales, such sensibilities must be recruited and aligned among potentially anonymous partners. Because cooperative assurance does not require that partners receive assurances of each others virtues, the factors that recruit and align these cooperations may work in a relatively widespread and automated fashion, without the need for costly signalling.

(7) $\textbf{partner}^{i} \not\to. \textbf{ partner}^{q}$
(8) $\textbf{partner}^{q} \not\to \textbf{partner}^{i}$
(9) $\textbf{partner}^{i} \to \textbf{charismatic signal} \leftarrow \textbf{partner}^{q}$
(10) $\textbf{partner}^{i} \Leftarrow \textbf{charismatic signal} \Rightarrow \textbf{partner}^{q}$

*where ($\not\to$) ≠ reliably sense, and ($\to$) = reliably sense and ($\Rightarrow$ = affect (make confident))

Thus, even where partners are unable to sense each other ((7),(8)), anonymous partners may be motived to cooperate from the effect on motivation of exogenous factors ((10)). Specifically, where partners are reliably exposed to information that (i) generates and (ii) aligns their cooperative sensibilities, mutually benefitting exchange will be assured. We believe that the problem of risky anonymous cooperation largely amounts to the distribution of factors that promote cooperative sensibilities in a relatively automated fashion, at potentially large social scales (as per (7)) – that is by *charismatic signals*. Moreover, we suggest that religious cultures harbour some of the oldest and most powerful recipes for charismatic response. Such assurances do not arrive from the synchronous orchestration of cooperative actions among partners, at potentially anonymous scales. Such an orchestration relies on a relatively automatic production of confidence among partners, in response to common ecological signals.

3.1 Affording Cooperative Cognition

Having expressed the problem of cooperation as a problem relating to the uncertainty of social prediction, we suggest that the affordance of a benefiting cooperation requires factors that either:

1. promote the expectation of rewarding exchange, and/or
2. distract partners from thinking about risks.

Thus:

(11) **charismatic signal** $\not\rightarrow$ **risk**
(12) **charismatic signal** $\rightarrow$ **cooperative motivation**

*Where ($\not\rightarrow$) means 'does not reliably sense' and ($\rightarrow$) means 'reliably sense'

We suggest that religious cultures provide charismatic factors that potentiate confidence by altering the perceived, imagined, remembered, and felt environments that religious persons perceive themselves to inhabit. One might say that religious culture rearranges the mental furniture of those situatied in (potentially) anonymous societies, in ways that provoke cooperative sensibilities.

(13) **partner**^{i} $\Leftarrow$ **charismatic signal** $\Rightarrow$ **partner**^{q}
(14) **partner**^{i} , **partner**^{q} $\rightarrow$ (**sacred world-minds**) $\rightleftharpoons$ (**embodied states**)

Preliminary evidence (reviewed below), suggests that designs that augment confidence and that depress risk-sensitivity come in many varieties. Importantly, charismatic signals generate representations operating at the level both of declarative and embodied representations. Moreover, while charismatic signals suppress risk sensitivity and enhance expectations for future benefits, there appears to be no single type of charismatic effect. Indeed, we shall see that variation in the neural phenotypes of religious practice exists even within the practices of a homogenous religious community.[5]

3.2 Aligning the Cooperative Affordances of Anonymous Partners

Notice that the generation of cooperative affordances by itself remains insufficient to maintain cooperative benefits over time. For evolutionary processes to conserve charismatic signals, it is not enough that partners feel strong motivations to exchange. If cooperation is to indeed occur, partners must feel sufficient motivations in *synchrony*.

Because cooperative (trivially) requires coordination cooperative actions, cooperation among distinct individuals (nontrivially) requires an alignment of the cooperative motivations of these individuals. Where partners remain obscure to each other, we must look for factors capable of producing cooperative alignment outside the cognitive and affective states of individuals. The modulators that facilitate social exchange must rather be embedded in external features of the world. To be coincidentally accessible to members of a minimal cooperative group, such signals must be either:

1. Focally placed: such that anonymous partners simultaneously observe identical charismatic signals

or

5 Again, we notice that it is the interaction of culture and cognition that leads to cooperative modulation. This requires both genetic and epigenetic contributions. The proximate mechanisms underlying both vectors remain poorly understood. Thus, while evolutionary theory helps to guide the investigation of the proximate engines of success, it can offer no substitution for such investigations.

2. Widely distributed: such that anonymous partners are exposed to charismatic signals, distributed across a cooperative setting, at a rate of exposure sufficient to integrate cooperative actions.

For selection to target and amplify cooperative responses to either focally placed or widely distributed signals, the motivational effects from exposure to such signals must endure sufficiently long (in concert with knowledge about how specifically to act) to integrate cooperative actions among sufficiently many partners to generate cooperative benefits.

4. The Neural Correlates of Charismatic Signals

So far we have argued that an important, and much overlooked threat to cooperation among anonymous partners is uncertainty. Such uncertainty brings risk to cooperative decisions. We have noticed that theory of mind (ToM) enhances the risks of anonymous cooperative interaction, by enabling partners to represent uncertainty as common knowledge. More damaging still, ToM enables partners to consider how the most skeptical among an anonymous cooperative group might respond to the representation of uncertainty, as common knowledge. We have seen that such representations steal optimism from cooperative prediction.

There is, nevertheless, a bright side to cooperative problems threatened by predictive uncertainty. We observed that where partners share a common interest in solving the problem of anonymous recognition, any solution to the problem of cooperative prediction will be highly evolvable. If we assume absolute benefits overwhelm relative benefits (i. e. that a partner cannot benefit by spiting cooperation), then all share an interest in cooperative solutions. Moreover virtue and vice need not be specifically assessed. It is not virtuous to cooperate when there is no benefit from defection. Our analysis also revealed that commonly accessible signals, focally placed or widely distributed, which provoke cooperative motivations reliably, will be strongly conserved for their benefits to cooperative prediction. We called such cooperative triggers 'charismatic signals'. We suggested that religious culture harbours charismatic signals of exquisite and durable power, and suggested that such benefits form part of the explanation for religion's astonishing evolutionary conservation. Such functionality explains how Critias's theory of religious policing can be maintained among anonymous populations.

Yet for our religions to promote cooperative responses at anonymous social scales, religious cultures must activate powerful cooperative commitments, in synchrony, among sufficiently many partners to yeild cooperative benefits.

It is time now to consider some evidence from the social cognitive neuroscience of religion. These data were not gathered to test the model we have been developing. Rather we use the model to explain lingering anomalies in the data. Thus, charismatic signalling offers an 'inference to the best explanation'– or an abductive explanation–for otherwise puzzling observations (Harman 1965). Much scientific progress occurs from abductive reasoning. There is the part of science where we gather data to test hypotheses, and the part of science where we use hypotheses to explain the data. The following presents an exercise in the latter type of scientific practice.

4.1 Charismatic Authority and Hypnotic Suggestion: Focal Charismatic Affordance

For many religious practices, subjects participate as passive spectators or as recipients of actions performed by religious authorities. The central feature of commitment within such passive practices lies in the subjects acceptance of the divine powers of a focal practitioner or authority. Indeed, in many instances, it is the participants's representation of the powers entertained by priests, shamans, healers and witches that separate effective rituals from meaningless actions.

Though commonplace, the evolutionary dynamics of such assenting remains poorly understood.[6] On the standard model of social exchange, such granting of control to another must remain perplexing, a type of loss that invites exploitation. However, where the problem of exchange is one of synchronous alignment to coordination points, the mystery of this deliberate granting of control to another more easily resolves. For we have seen that the problem of securing cooperation is better accommodated by factors that express and coordinate confidence among members of a distributed group. Thus, where entrainment coordinates affective states in the right way, a trusting of focal authority can form a stable evolutionary target. We believe that considering charismatic authority from the vantage point of social exchange reveals functionality in

6 Though see Henrich 2009; Johnson and Fowler 2009.

those practices/responses defined by the subjective granting of control over to a charismatic authority. Consider the case.

Recent data suggest that charismatic signals operate on the same cognitive mechanisms used to induce hypnotic responses and placebo effects in patients. In hypnotic practices, the perceived authority of the practitioner strongly predicts facilitation of patient responses. Such findings point to a specific cognitive processing that renders subjects more susceptible to a psycho-physical governance mediated by confidence in focal authorities. Indeed, findings in the hypnotic literature reveal that cognitive inhibition of executive function is a central component in this generation of this assent (Schjoedt et al. 2010). Using functional magnetic resonance imaging (fMRI), Schjoedt et al. (2010) investigated how assumptions about the healing powers of praying speakers changed the evoked BOLD response in secular and Christian participants who received prayers of healing. The researchers found that Christians down-regulated their social cognitive and executive networks when they believed they were listening to speakers known to have healing powers. Indeed, those who down-regulated social-cognitive and executive networks most strongly were subsequently found to express the most positive experience of the healer. Interestingly, none of these effects were observed in the secular group when they listened to the same healer. This absence of an observed down-regulation suggests that secular participants did not experience charismatic governence. These findings suggest that the observed response to charismatic authority is therefore linked to how subjects frame the social relationship to focal authorities. Moreover such framing, combined with exposure, subsequently produces predictable attitudes. These effects correspond to findings in hypnosis research demonstrating that hypnotic susceptibility is associated with frontal inhibition (Jamieson and Sheehan 2004; Gruzelier 2006; Oakley et al. 2007; Raz et al. 2007) and that instructions received during hypnotically induced inhibition influence how subjects subsequently perceive and relate to stimuli (MacLeod and Sheehan 2003). Given the results of these hypnosis studies, it would appear that secular listeners do not respond by inhibiting the relevant networks because they do not manage to believe in the powers of the healer.

Schjoedt et al.'s (2010) study provides early evidence that charismatic factors promote strong affective alignment to focal authorities from (at least) two related mechanisms: 1) from the strong modulation of trust and acceptance to central authorities; 2) from an intriguing interplay of declarative and non-declarative representations – explicit beliefs and the inhibition of explicit awareness. From the vantage point of *charismatic signalling*, this puzzling interaction exhibits impressive functionality. For coupling the states of a potentially large (and anonymous) audience to a central figure enables strong affective alignment, without scale constraints: precisely what cooperation in nameless, faceless society requires. Charismatic influence appears to function at the neuronal level through a subtle orchestration of social cognitive response, involving the recruitment and modulation of both reflective and embodied networks in the brain. It is this interplay that results in an increase in subjective susceptibility to messages and attitudes among committed followers. Finally, the study helps to clarify charismatic signalling, by revealing a potential channel of reinforcement feeding back from experiential outcomes in response to charismatic influence to beliefs consistent with the maintenance of traditional perspectives. Thus, the data reveal how charismatic experience may lead to greater confidence in religious authority, thus supporting the propagation the charismatic traditions in which such authority is maintained.

4.2 Distributed Charismatic Affordance from Personal and Repetitive Prayer

There is, of course, much more to religion than the trusting of charismatic authorities. Perhaps the most fascinating and salient feature of our religions is the experience many have of divinities. We next focus to the social neuroscience of private prayer. In thinking about the relationship of prayer to cooperative prediction, two facts stand out. Prayer plays a central role in religious traditions with diffuse networks of exchange. However, while ostentatious prayer may help to facilitate exchange by costly signalling (see: Irons 2001) much prayer appears to be performed in private. Among anonymous cohort it is difficult to understand how such costly private prayer could be conserved (though for a costly signalling explanation for private prayer, see: Sosis 2003). However if prayer is a practice whose benefits arise to suppress risk-sensitivity, and to generate confidence, then private prayer, when common, may be strongly conserved as a charismatic trigger point for social mobilization. Findings from recent social neuroscience reveal that prayer generates the types of representations that may lead to the expression of confident feeling and reward expectations. Because the data suggest that such representations will be common among those that frequently prayer, it would appear that prayer may align cooperative behaviours among potentially anonymous cohort. These data thus shed light on three puzzling observations:

1. religious cultures potentiate strong affective responses, even in anonymous populations.
2. religious cultures remain strongly conserved over historical timescales.
3. religious psychology remains strongly conserved over evolutionary timescales

In a recent study investigating the neural basis of private prayer, Schjoedt et al. (2009) found that social cognitive regions were strongly active in highly religious Christian participants while they engaged in personal prayer, with weaker effects among those who prayed less frequently (Schjoedt et al. 2009). These data suggest that Christians who pray frequently represent God as a real person who responds to communication with reciprocity. While personal prayer typically occurs in private, and thus does not afford cooperative signalling – nevertheless, cortical activations observed in this study are strongly consistent with the functions of a system designed to support cooperative response among potentially anonymous partners. Consider how the experience of Divinity may support cooperative motivation among relative strangers who synchronise their expectations and responses through experiences of Divinity.

First, Schjoedt et. al.'s (2009) studies reveal that personal prayer provides the prayerful with a remarkable experience of God's personal involvement. Thus, prayer does not merely produce abstract expectations (in a manner that might be discounted – 'if you do your homework, one day you will be rich . . .') personal prayer provides an immediate and moving experience of God's personal reality, and interest.[7] Some evolutionary researchers suggest that religion relies on a 'belief in belief' (Dennett 2006). Others doubt any religious belief whatsoever (e.g. Palmer and Steadman 2004). Schjoedt et. al.'s (2009) findings demon-

7 The question brings no disrespect to religious persons. The best religious minds agree that Gods reality is not that of an ordinary person, but rather is a Reality that vastly exceeds any such limitation. We believe that this puzzle of experiencing God as a person therefore can be raised by religious persons too. Indeed, if the unbounded God the theologians, mystics, and saints describe is real, this evolutionary puzzle might be felt acutely among those who believe.

strate something more than belief, namely the generation of evidence from encounter. When such experience of a personal God is paired with cooperative norms, and made widely available to partners, prayer will both anchor and orchestrate cooperative responses, even for partners who remain anonymous.

Second, reward expectations from interaction with divinities need not be given as purely instrumental goods – payments or punishments, say, in the afterlife. Rather, those who pray receive motivation to follow God's ways directly from an empathetic sharing of God's desires and expectations, from responses to God's suffering, or from intrinsic desires to please a God who is experienced as personally significant. Thus, an embodied relationship to Divinity allows for emotional recruitment, motor responses, affective mirroring, modifications to sensation, and other multi-modal representations, to express and orchestrate normative motivations, with fascinating complexity. While much remains to be discovered about the social/affective effects of prayer, preliminary evidence for the expression among those who pray of theories of God's mind (ToGM) exhibits an impressive tool for the synchronous expression of solidarity.

Third, personal prayer offers a means for meeting life's inevitable challenges. These are the recurring problems of illnesses, loss, suffering, and insecurity about the future. Given that resolution of such concerns often remains outside the scope of individual control, worry cannot be remedied from individual responses. However, by locating the control of future events in the actions of an all-loving, all-powerful Deity (or with the help of less perfect spirits), new possibilities for security and comfort become available to those who discover committed gods in prayer. Specifically, reductions to anxiety may enhance cooperative performance, given that too much anxiety destroys performance. Moreover, the future really is brighter for cooperative groups. Praying groups who use their religion to access cooperative goods find evidence to support religious experience, which in turn ratifies cooperative confidence. Moreover when cooperation fails, the perspective of eternity enables partners to discount losses, thus retain a confidence not available to those who adopt purely natural evaluative frames.

Fourth, by allocating theory of mind processing to God's mind, inferences about the risks of other partner's minds become less available. For God is believed to ultimately determine whether partners cooperate. Here we find the suppression of risk judgments from practices that locate confidence in a strategic landscape whose supernatural furniture finds no seat for cooperative risk-aversion. Partners distracted by God's mind, are less easily distracted by doubts about each other's doubts.

Further evidence for the manufacture of cooperative confidence comes from a study on formulaic prayer which observed strong activations from repetitive prayer in the striatal reward system (Schjoedt et al. 2008). (Repetitive prayer differs from personal prayer because it involves the repetition of standard phrases). This finding is interesting, in the first instance, because reward processing in the dorsal striatum has been demonstrated to depend on trust in social exchange studies.[8] Thus greater trusting in God and his sanctioned practices may correspond to the observed involvement of reward processing. It is noteworthy, moreover, that the generation of implicit reward signals occurs in somewhat automated fashion among those who pray regularly. From an evolutionary stance, the conservation of reward representations in response to such ostensibly non-utilitarian behaviour remains mysterious. For while reward circuits can be co-opted by novel agents (drugs, unhealthy foods, marketing) the long-enduring survival of religious practices hints at potential benefits. Yet the automation of reward-affect fits the design specifications of an intervention designed to robustly support the alignment of confidence among potentially unknown partners. Here again, Schjoedt et. al.'s (2008) study reveals the expression of charismatic affordances through yet another intricate orchestration of declarative and embodied states. Focusing specifically on the activation of embodied representations – here motor habits, automated speech, and (outside the scanner) body postures – *charismatic signalling* enables researchers to examine how these activations possess strong social utilities. While it remains to be seen whether other religious practices suppress anxiety and express the expectation for reward, these preliminary studies reveal how personal and repetitive prayer may contribute to produce confidence, even among strangers.

8 For example, King-Casas et. al. (2005) have demonstrated that learning to trust partners in economic exchange games are predicted and mirrored by activation of this structure.

5. Conclusion

Charismatic signalling extends costly signalling theories of religion by explaining how religious culture equips partners for anonymous exchange in situations where signals of virtue cannot be assured. We observed that where the problem of cooperation comes from an uncertainty over cooperation's benefit, rather than from a certainty for defection's benefit, cooperation fails not from defection but from uncertainty and risk. We found that theory of mind (ToM) has the potential to strongly impair cooperative prediction. For in thinking about the likelihood that others will adopt cooperative strategies, partners require information that will satisfy the most skeptical among them. Such a requirement would appear to render cooperation especially fragile.

It is well known that selection does not always optimise, and for this reason, many have preferred by-product explanations for religious culture and cognition. If the persistence of costly religion can be explained without attributing design, such an by-product explanation may appear preferable for their apparent simplicity. Yet while the endurance of certain facets of specific religions may be partially explained as a by-product, and while our religions do bring harms, we do not share enthusiasm for by-product perspectives when explaining long enduring trends. For religion has experienced a conservation that is unrivaled.

Here we have considered how the problem of cooperative prediction under uncertainty is managed by charismatic signals. We noticed that where information can be elaborated to reliably express and align strong cooperative sensibilities among potentially anonymous others, such information will be targeted by cultural and perhaps natural selection.

Charismatic signalling explains how our religions facilitate cooperative confidence and trust for anonymous populations. They do so through factors that suppress sensitivity to risk, and that evoked heightened states of confidence, in *synchrony*. In reviewing recent work in the social neuroscience of religion from the stance of *charismatic signalling* we resolved anomalies presented in these data.

Specifically, the data show that charismatic authority relies on a subtle orchestration in both declarative and non-declarative representations, that is, from the modulation of embodied cognition. Surprisingly, it seems this orchestration relies on an executive inhibition of error monitoring in response to charismatic authority. We noticed that while the effects of this interaction appear to rely on initial confidence, charismatic interaction also produces experiences consistent with this initial confidence – a track record which supports further success downstream. More fundamental, we noticed that because such confidence is shared, charismatic authority enables a coupling of the internal states of potentially anonymous and large audiences to the signals produced by focal figures. This coupling of many-to-one enables a powerful alignment in the thoughts, moods, and motivations of those who fall under charisma's spell. While such large-scale hypnotic effects appear to invite opportunism (occasionally realised, no doubt) we suggested that the conservation of hypnotic effects arrives from the benefits of large-scale cooperative interactions whose motivations hypnotic cultures support.

In our review of the neuroscience of personal prayer, we found that different patterns of explicit and implicit are activated in the neuronal populations that support prayerful cognition. However we noticed that activations, though substantially different to interactive prayer, nevertheless revealed a similar capacity for alignment of the thoughts and expectations of widely distributed partners. In personal prayer we found a strong recruitment of the social cognitive network, pointing to experiences of God as a real person, whose benefits can be expected. Prayer appears to elaborate ToM in a manner that belies extraordinary functionality, both by reducing anxiety and by increasing the expectation of future rewards in social exchange.

In considering the data on repetitive prayer, we noticed how an automated activation of a reward signal was observed among those who prayer regularly. Charismatic signalling observes specific benefits from automation in the production of this signal. Such automation in the potentiation of reward expectation displaces the suppression of risk from declarative awareness while expressing strong emotion. Such displacement grounds the expectation of reward in feelings, which cannot be readily doubted, explicitly. *Charismatic* signalling predicts the generation of such benefits through embodied states. Presently, however, we do not know how far these affects generalise to other religious practices.

It is worth closing with a remark about variation, and its relationship to evolutionary theory. We have seen that even within a relatively homogenous religious community, the scope for variation in religious cognition from distinct practices is rather large. Thus, we might expect that as cognitive scientists explore religious practices among distinct and heterogeneous religious populations, further variation will likely be disclosed. Yet our discussion already illustrates how evolutionary theory is able to help researchers to find such adaptive functionality amid strong variation in cognitive effects, by focussing attention to how various practices occupy our bodies and minds with tasks that deliver strikingly similar social-cognitive benefits. Do the strong conservation of these effects tell a functional story? More studies are needed before researchers can be certain. Specifically needed are studies that show direct evidence of cooperative outcomes from charismatic interventions.[9]

While *charismatic signalling* focuses attention to cooperative benefits, it must be remembered that there may be non-cooperative benefits arising from cooperative practices too, such as the benefits to individuals of increased health or the benefits of retaining time-tested wisdom. We must therefore allow the prospect that non-cooperative benefits play a role in the impressive durability of our ancient religions. Indeed, such benefits are not incommensurable with the advantages religion brings to social exchange. Though the proximate effects of religion can be costly, or inert, we do not share enthusiasm for the hypothothesis that religion has been conserved accidentally. For it has occupied centre stage in the Hominin lifeway for too long, we think, for the accident hypothesis to be probable.

We have motivated an approach to our sacred traditions as impressive technologies for human flourishing. Cognitive and evolutionary science is only beginning to understand how these long-enduring technologies work. Many discoveries lie ahead.

References

Atran, S. (2002). *In gods we trust: the evolutionary landscape of religion*. New York: Oxford University Press.

Atran, S., R. Axelrod., & R. Davis. (2007). Sacred barriers to conflict resolution. *Science* 317, 1039–140.

Bering, J.M. (2006). The folk psychology of souls. *Behavioral and Brain Sciences* 29, 453–98.

Bicchieri, C. (2006). *The grammar of society: The nature and dynamics of social norms*. Cambridge, MA: Cambridge University Press.

Binmore, K. (2008). Do conventions need to be common knowledge? *Topoi* 27(1–2), 17–27.

Bulbulia, J. (2004a). Religious costs as adaptations that signal altruistic intention. *Evolution and Cognition* 10(1), 19–38.

Bulbulia, J. (2009). Charismatic signalling. *Journal for the Study of Religion, Nature, Culture* 3(4), 518–51.

9 For a review of recent studies suggesting such effects see Bulbulia (2009).

Calcott, B (2008). "The other cooperation problem: generating benefit." *Biology and Philosophy*, 23(2), 179–203.

Chen, D. (2007). Islamic resurgence and social violence during the indonesian financial crisis. In *Institutions and norms in economic development*, edited by M. Gradstein & K. Konrad., 179–234. Cambridge, MA: MIT Press.

Cosmides, L., & J. Tooby. (2000). Consider the source: The evolution of adaptations for decoupling and metarepresentation. In *Metarepresentations*, edited by D. Sperber, 53–116. New York: Oxford University Press.

Critias (s.a.). The Critias fragment, from Sextus Empiricus, Adversus Mathematicos. http://people.wku.edu/jan.garrett/302/critias.htm.

Darwin, F. (1958/1892). *The autobiography of Charles Darwin and selected letters.* New York: Dover.

Dennett, D. (2006). *Breaking the spell: Religion as a natural phenomenon.* New York: Viking.

Dunbar, R. (1998). The social brain hypothesis. *Evolutionary Anthropology* 6, 178–190.

Frith, C., U. Frith. (2006). How we predict what other people are going to do. *Brain Research* 1079, 36–46.

Gruzelier. J. H. (2006). Frontal functions, connectivity and neural efficiency underpinning hypnosis and hypnotic susceptibility. Contemporary Hypnosis 23 (1), 15–32.

Harman, G.H. (1965). The inference to the best explanation. *The Philosophical Review* 74, 88–95.

Henrich, J. (2009). The evolution of costly displays, cooperation, and religion:-credibility enhancing displays and their implications for cultural evolution. *Evolution and Human Behaviour* 30, 244–60.

Hume, D. (1739). *A treatise of human nature.* London: John Noon.

Irons, W. (2001). Religion as hard-to-fake sign of commitment. In *Evolution and the capacity for commitment*, edited by R. Nesse, 292–309. New York: Russell Sage Foundation.

Irons, W. (2008). Why people believe (what other people see as) crazy ideas. In *The evolution of religion: Studies, theories, and critiques*, edited by J. Bulbulia, R. Sosis, R. Genet, E. Harris, C. Genet, & K. Wyman, 51–60. Santa Margarita, CA: Collins Foundation Press.

Jamieson, G., & P. Sheehan. (2004). An empirical test of woody and bowers's dissociated-control theory of hypnosis. *International journal of clinical and experimental hypnosis* 52(3), 232–49.

Johnson, D.D.P., & J.H. Fowler. (2009). The evolution of overconfidence. *Quantitative Biology: http://www.citebase.org/abstract?id=oai:arXiv.org:0909.4043*

Keizer, K., S. Lindenberg., & L. Steg. (2008). The spreading of disorder. *Science* 322, 1681–85.

King-Casas, B., Tomlin, D., Anen, C., Camerer, C. F., Quartz, S. R., Montague, P. R. (2005). Getting to Know You: Reputation and Trust in a Two-Person Economic Exchange. *Science* 308, 78–83.

Lewis, D. (1969). *Convention.* Cambridge, MA: Harvard University Press.

MacLeod, C., & P. Sheehan. (2003). Hypnotic control of attention in the stroop task: A historical footnote. *Consciousness and Cognition* 12 (3), 201–203.

Norenzayan, A., A. Shariff. (2008). The origin and evolution of religious prosociality. *Science* 322(58), 58–62.

Oakley, D.A., Q. Deeley., & P.W. Halligan. (2007). Hypnotic depth and response to suggestion under standardized conditions and during fmri scanning. *International Journal of Clinical and Experimental Hypnosis* 55(1), 32–58.

Palmer, C.T., & L.B. Steadman. (2004). With or without belief: A new approach to the definition and explanation of religion. *Evolution and Cognition* 10(1), 138–147.

Raz, A. (2004). Atypical Attention: Hypnosis and Conflict Reduction. In M. I. Posner (ed.) Cognitive Neuroscience of Attention 420–429. The Guilford Press, New York.

Egner, T., Raz, A. (2007). Cognitive control processes and hypnosis. In Hypnosis and Conscious states: The cognitive neuroscience perspective, G. A. Jamieson ed. (New York: Oxford University Press), pp. 29–50.

Schjoedt, U., Stødkilde-Jørgensen, H., Geertz, A. W., Lund, T. E., Roepstorff, A. (2010). The power of charisma – perceived charisma inhibits the frontal executive network of believers in intercessory prayer. *SCAN* (doi: 10.1093/scan/nsq023).

Schjoedt, U., Stødkilde-Jørgensen, H., Geertz, A. W., Roepstorff, A. (2008). Rewarding prayers. *Neuroscience Letters* 443(3), 165–168. doi: DOI: 10.1016/j.neulet.2008.07.068.

Schjoedt, U., A. Geertz, H. Stødkild-Jørgensen, & A. Roepstorff, A. (2009). Highly religious participants recruit areas of social cognition in personal prayer. *Social Cognitive and Affective Neuroscience* 4(2), 199–207.

Skyrms, B. (2004). *The stag hunt and the evolution of social structure*. Cambridge, MA: Cambridge University Press.

Soler, M. (2008). Commitment costs and cooperation: Evidence from candomble, and afro-brazilian religion. In *The evolution of religion: Studies, theories, and critiques*, edited by J. Bulbulia, R. Sosis, E. Harris, R. Genet, C. Genet, & K. Wyman, 167–74. Santa Margarita: Collins Foundation Press.

Sosis, R. (2003). Why aren't we all hutterites? *Human Nature* 14(2), 91–127.

Sterelny, K. (2003). *Thought in a hostile world: The evolution of human cognition*. Oxford: Blackwell.

Taves, A. (2009). *Religious experience reconsidered: A building block approach to the study of religion and other special things*. Princeton, NY: Princeton University Press.

Weber, M. (1958). *The Protestant ethic and the spirit of capitalism*. New York: Scribner.

Wilson, D. (2007). Evolution and religion: The transformation of the obvious. In *The evolution of religion: Studies, Theories and critiques*, edited by J. Bulbulia, R. Sosis, E. Harris, R. Genet, C. Genet, & K. Wyman, 23–29. Santa Margarita, CA: Collins Foundation Press.

Rational Choice Theory and Bounded Rationality[1]

TILL GRÜNE-YANOFF

1. Introduction

Rational Choice Theory (RCT) has dominated economics for more than 50 years, and it is becoming increasingly important in other social-science disciplines. At the same time, the critical voices against it are increasing in volume. One particularly successful research effort in this direction is the modelling of 'bounded rationality'. The idea is that it offers psychologically more plausible models of human decision-making without giving up on the notion of rationality altogether. In many cases, the research is supported by experimental findings that document deviations from standard RCT. However, rational-choice theorists are often not convinced, and most economists have not yet exchanged their mainstream models for a more 'boundedly rational' behavioural economics. This article gives some reasons why this may be so, and more generally why bounded rationality, although an important research programme in its own right, is not likely to replace RCT altogether.

Section 2 of the article briefly sketches the main features of the formal RCT framework, and discusses various normative and positive interpretations. Section 3 gives a taste of the empirical results that seem to contradict RCT, and considers how these results could be interpreted. Section 4 introduces a few of the bounded-rationality models offered in response to the empirical evidence discussed in the previous section. A categorisation of such models is offered, and their interpretation and usefulness in each of these categories are discussed. Section 5 concludes the paper.

---

1 Thanks to Aki Lehtinen for his helpful comments and to Mette Ranta for bibliographic assistance.

2. Rational Choice Theory and Economic Behaviour

RCT is the dominant theoretical approach in microeconomics.[2] It is also widely used in other social-science disciplines, in particular political science. In these disciplines the term rational choice theory is often used in association with the notion of economic 'imperialism', implying that the use of RCT is an extension of economic methodology into their fields.

Explicit theories of rational economic choice were first developed in the late 19th century. These theories commonly linked choice of an object to the increase in happiness an additional increment of this object would bring. Early neoclassical economists (e.g., William Stanley Jevons) held that agents make consumption choices so as to maximise their own happiness. In contrast to them, 20th-century economists dis-associated RCT and the notion of happiness: instead of explicating rationality of choice as a happiness-maximising effort they presented rationality as maintaining a consistent ranking of alternatives. Such a ranking is commonly interpreted as agents' desires or values.

Without a foundation in an ultimate end the notion of rationality is reduced to the consistent ranking of choice alternatives, the consistent derivation of this ranking from evaluations of the possible outcomes, and the consistency of beliefs employed in this derivation. Thus, 'rationality' explicated in rational choice theory is considerably narrower and possibly sometimes at odds with colloquial or philosophical notions of rationality. In such contexts 'rationality' often includes judgments about ends, the prudent weighting of long-term versus short-term results, and insights into purportedly fundamental moral principles. Nothing of this sort is invoked in rational choice theory. It simply claims that a rational person chooses actions in a manner consistent with her beliefs and evaluations. Accordingly, a person considered 'rational' in this sense may believe that the moon is made of green cheese, may desire to waste her life, or may intend to bring widespread destruction.

2 The term 'rational choice theory' is rarely used in economics, but became the term of choice in other disciplines, signifying the core theoretical assumptions of microeconomics.

2.1. Formal Framework

At the core of RCT is a formal framework that (i) makes the notion of preference consistency precise and (ii) offers formal proof that 'maximising one's utility' is identical to 'choosing according to a consistent preference ranking'. A brief sketch of this framework follows.[3]

Let $A = \{X_1, \ldots, X_n\}$ be a set of alternatives. Prospects are either pure prospects or lotteries. A pure prospect is a future event or state of the world that occurs with certainty. For example, when purchasing a hamburger from a well-known international restaurant chain I may expect with near certainty the pure prospect of certain taste experiences. Lotteries, also called prospects under risk, are probability distributions over events or states. For example, when consuming 'pick-your-own' mushrooms an agent faces the lottery $(X_1, p; X_2, 1\text{-}p)$, where X_1 denotes the compound outcome (which has probability p) of falling ill due to poisoning and X_2 (with probability $1\text{-}p$) the compound outcome of not doing so. More generally, a lottery X consists of a set of prospects $X_1, \ldots, X_n$ and assigned probabilities $p_1, \ldots, p_n$, such that $X = (X_1, p_1; \ldots X_n, p_n)$, where $p_1 + \ldots + p_n = 1$. Obviously, the prospects $X_1, \ldots, X_n$ can be lotteries themselves.

RCT takes preferences over actions to be evaluations of lotteries over action outcomes. Its main contribution is to specify the relationship between preferences over actions, and preferences as well as beliefs over the compound outcomes of the respective lottery. It does so by proving *representation theorems*. Such theorems show that under certain conditions, all of an agent's preferences can be represented by a numerical function, the so-called utility function. Furthermore, the theory shows that the utility numbers of an action (i. e. lottery) $X = (X_1, p_1; \ldots X_n, p_n)$ and its compound outcomes $X_1, \ldots, X_n$ are related to each other through the following principle:

$$u(X) = \Sigma_i \, p_i \times u(X_i) \qquad (1)$$

In other words, the utility of a lottery is equal to the sum of the utilities of its compound outcomes, weighted by the probability with which each outcome comes about. This is an important result that significantly constrains the kind of preferences an agent can have. Of course, because

3 The framework presented here is based on von Neumann and Morgenstern (1947). Alternative formal frameworks are to be found in Savage (1954) and Jeffrey (1990).

the representation result is a formal proof, all the constraining information must already be present in the theorem's assumptions. I will sketch the main features of these assumptions here.[4]

RCT assumes that at any time, there is a fixed set of prospects $A = \{X_1, \ldots, X_n\}$ for any agent. With respect to the agent's evaluation of these prospects, it assumes that agents can always say that they prefer one prospect to another or are indifferent between them. More specifically, it assumes that the agent has a preference ordering $\geq$ over A, which satisfies the following conditions. First, the ordering is assumed to be *complete*, i. e.

$$\text{either } X_i \geq X_j \text{ or } X_j \geq X_i \text{ for all } X_i, X_j \in \mathrm{A}. \tag{2}$$

Second, the ordering is assumed to be *transitive*, i. e.

$$\text{if } X_i \geq X_j \text{ and } X_j \geq X_k, \text{ then also } X_i \geq X_k \text{ for all } X_i, X_j, X_k \in \mathrm{A}. \tag{3}$$

Completeness and transitivity together ensure that the agent has a so-called weak ordering over all prospects.

The second domain in which RCT makes consistency assumptions concerns beliefs. In particular, it assumes that each rational agent has a *coherent set of probabilistic beliefs*. Coherence here means that beliefs can be represented as probability distributions, which satisfy certain properties. In particular, it is assumed that there is a probability function p over all elements of A, and that this function satisfies the following assumptions: first, for any X, $1 \geq p(X) \geq 0$; second, if X is certain, then $p(X) = 1$; third, if two alternatives X and Y are mutually exclusive, then $p(X \text{ or } Y) = p(X) + p(Y)$; finally, for any two alternatives X and Y, $p(X \text{ and } Y) = p(X) \times p(Y|X)$ – in other words the probability of the alternative 'X and Y' is identical to the probability of X multiplied by the probability of Y *given* that X is true.

The third domain in which rational choice theory makes consistency assumptions concerns preferences over lotteries. In particular, it assumes the *independence condition*. If a prospect X is preferred to a prospect Y, then a prospect that has X as one compound outcome with a probability p is preferred to a prospect that has Y as one compound with a

4 For a detailed discussion, see the references in footnote 3. For more in-depth overviews, see textbooks such as Luce and Raiffa (1957); Mas-Collel et al. (1995, chs. 1&6) and Resnik (1987). Hargreaves Heap et al. (1992, 3–26) give an introductory treatment.

probability p and is identical otherwise: i.e. for all X, Y, Z: if $X \geq Y$ then $(X,p;Z,1\text{-}p) \geq (Y,p;Z,1\text{-}p)$.

These assumptions (together with a few others that are not relevant here), imply that preferences over lottery prospects $X = (X_1,p_1;\ldots X_n,p_n)$ are represented by a utility function such that for all X, Y:

$$X \geq Y \Leftrightarrow \Sigma_i [p_i \times u(X_i)] \geq \Sigma_i [p_i \times u(Y_i)] \quad (4)$$

This formal result has been given different interpretations, which are discussed in the next two subsections.

2.2. Normative Interpretations

RCT is often interpreted as a theory of how people *ought* to form their preferences (and by extension how they ought to choose). Accordingly, people who violate RCT in their actual deliberations or behaviour might still be subject to a normative standard of preference consistency spelled out in RCT.

Such a normative standard has been justified in various ways. The most prominent justifications are pragmatic: they seek to show that agents who fail to retain consistency in the way RCT prescribes incur certain losses. Two well-known examples are the *money pump* and the *Dutch book* arguments.

The money pump (Davidson et al. 1955) can be illustrated as follows. A stamp collector has preferences with respect to three stamps, denoted *A*, *B*, and *C*. She prefers *A* to *B*, *B* to *C*, and *C* to *A*, hence violating the transitivity assumption of RCT. She is willing to pay 10 cents for a prospect that she prefers to the status quo. She goes into a stamp shop with stamp *A*. The dealer offers to trade *A* for *C* if she pays 10 cents. She accepts the deal. The dealer then offers to trade *C* for *B*, which she again accepts, paying another 10 cents. The dealer then offers to trade *B* for *A*. Again, given her preferences, she will accept the deal and pay 10 cents. Thus her preferences leave her open to being 'pumped': she leaves the shop with the same stamp she had when she entered it, but 30 cents poorer. It seems that violations of transitivity yield a certain loss for the violating agent.

The Dutch book argument (Ramsey 1931) can be illustrated as follows. An agent *A*'s degrees of belief in S and $\neg S$ (written $p(S)$ and $p(\sim S)$) are each .51. Their sum is 1.02, and hence *A* violates the axioms of

RCT. According to RCT a person with degree of belief p in sentence S is assumed to be willing to pay up to and including $\$p$ a bet on the truth of S, and is willing to sell it for any price equal to or greater than $\$p$. Now a bookmaker sells a bet on S to A – A being willing to pay $\$p(S)$ – and also sells a bet on $\neg S$ –A being willing to pay $p(\neg S)$). A's beliefs make her pay \$1.02 on a combination of wagers guaranteed to pay exactly \$1. She would thus have a guaranteed net loss of \$.02. It seems that violations of probability laws yield a certain loss for the violating agent.

Interpreted literally, neither the money pump nor the Dutch book is very convincing. An agent could simply refuse to accept money-pumping trade or Dutch-booking bets. Rationality does not literally require that one is willing to wager in accordance with the RCT assumptions described above. It is more plausible to interpret these arguments hypothetically. Both could be conceived of as a heuristic in determining when one's preferences or degrees of belief have the potential to be *pragmatically self-defeating*. Given any reasonable way of translating one's mental states into action, preferences or degrees of belief that violate RCT motivate one to act in ways that make things worse than they might have been when, as a matter of mere logic, alternative actions would have made things better.[5]

2.3. Positive Interpretations

RCT is often conceived of as a formalisation of folk psychology (e. g., Ferejohn 2002; Cox 1999; Coleman 1990). 'Folk psychology' here refers to pre-theoretical psychology based on intentional states of belief and desire. People who use this term commonly believe that our everyday or 'folk' understanding of mental states constitutes a theory of mind, which could also be used to explain purposeful action. According to this interpretation, RCT models the folk notion of belief as probabilities and the folk notion of desire as preferences, and becomes a formally exact basis for explaining intentional action.

Many economists would disagree with such an interpretation. In 1938, Paul Samuelson showed that all RCT assumptions could be reinterpreted as constraints on choices, and that the whole theory of con-

5 For more on this and other normative justifications, see Hansson and Grüne-Yanoff 2009, sec 1.

sumer behaviour could thus be 'freed from any vestigial traces of the [hedonistic] utility concept' (Samuelson 1938, 71). Choices reveal preferences, and choices over lotteries reveal subjective probabilities. Without attributing any mental states to the subject, RCT merely uses the consistency of choice as an explanatory device.[6]

Consistency, in both its psychological and its behavioural interpretation, offers only relatively weak constraints on actual preferences or choices. The problem is that without definite descriptions of preference content or choice options it is easily possible to provide *ad hoc* explanations of seemingly anomalous behaviour. For example, players who cooperate in a one-shot Prisoners' Dilemma (behaviour that violates standard utility maximisation) could be said to be acting from altruistic motives, or to believe in playing an indefinitely repeated game. People who mount such a defence commonly see RCT as a mere conceptual scheme that needs to be filled with content for specific tasks. In their view, the framework is not open to empirical refutation.[7]

Mainstream economists have mostly taken a different route. They conceive of RCT not as a mere conceptual frame, but as a substantial theory of rational self-interest. In their theories of consumer choice they supplement its consistency requirements with the assumptions of self-interest (all agents' preferences are independent of each other), non-satiation (more is always preferred to less) and the marginal rate of substitution (for all goods *X*, *Y*, all individuals are willing to exchange more of *Y* for a unit of *X* as the amount of *Y* is increasing relative to *X*) (Hausman 1992, 30). Most microeconomic models are based on these assumptions, and they are used to explain a wide range of phenomena, from consumer demand, goods prices and bargaining behaviour to social conventions and legal institutions.

It is important to understand (i) that these additional assumptions are not strictly part of RCT, and (ii) that they have an explanatory or predictive purpose, but not a normative one. Indeed, as Sen (1987) points out, it would be absurd to assume self-interest or non-satiation as a normative rationality requirement. Nevertheless, these two dimensions are often confused in the debate about RCT.

6 See Wong 1978 for a critical analysis of the revealed preference approach.

7 For an argument to that end, see Gintis (2009, ch. 12).

3. Anomalies

According to Thomas Kuhn's account of scientific revolutions, anomalies are worrying puzzles for a scientific discipline that could lead to a loss of confidence in the discipline's paradigm. 'Anomalies' also was the heading of a regular column written by economist Richard Thaler in the *Journal of Economic Perspectives* (from 1987 to 1990), in which he documented instances of individual behaviour that seemed to violate RCT. These cases helped to raise economists' doubts about the theory, although many similar anomalies were documented before and have been since. This section discusses a few cases of this kind.[8]

A prominent example of an RCT anomaly is the so-called Allais' Paradox. Allais' (1953) idea was to find two pair-wise choices such that RCT would predict a specific choice pattern, and then check the prediction in the laboratory. This choice experiment is described in Figure 1.

Choice problem 1 – choose between:

A:	\$2500	with probability 0.33	*B*:	\$2400	with certainty
	\$2400	with probability 0.66			
	\$0	with probability 0.01			

Choice problem 2 – choose between:

C:	\$2500	with probability 0.33	D:	\$2400	with probability 0.34
	\$0	with probability 0.67		\$0	with probability 0.66

Fig. 1

RCT prescribes and predicts that agents choose *C* if they have chosen *A* (and vice versa), and that they choose *D* if they have chosen *B* (and vice versa). To see this, simply re-partition the prizes of the two problems as follows. Instead of '2400 with certainty' in *B*, partition the outcome such that it reads '2400 with probability 0.66' and '2400 with probability 0.34'. Instead of '0 with probability 0.67' in *C*, partition the outcome such that it reads '0 with probability 0.66' and '0 with probability

8 For more detail, see e.g., Kahneman et al. 1982; Thaler 1992; Gigerenzer et al. 1999.

0.01'. Of course, these are just re-descriptions that do not change the nature of the choice problem. They are shown in Figure 2.

Choice problem 1★ – choose between:

A:	$2500 with probability 0.33		*B★:*		
	$2400 with probability 0.66			$2400 with probability 0.66	
	$0 with probability 0.01			$2400 with probability 0.34	

Choice problem 2★ – choose between:

C★:	$2500 with probability 0.33		D:		
	$0 with probability 0.66			$0 with probability 0.66	
	$0 with probability 0.01			$2400 with probability 0.34	

Fig. 2

Through this re-description we now have an outcome '2400 with probability 0.66' both in *A* and in *B★*, and an outcome '0 with probability 0.66' both in *C★* and in *D*. According to the RCT independence condition, these identical outcomes can be disregarded in the deliberation. But once they are disregarded it becomes clear that option *A* is identical to option *C★* and option *B★* is identical to option *D*. Hence, anyone choosing *A* should also choose *C* and anyone choosing *B* should also choose *D*. However, in sharp contrast to this claim, in an experiment involving 72 people, 82 per cent of the sample chose *B*, and 83 per cent chose *C* (Kahneman and Tversky 1979).

Other major anomalies include Ellsberg's paradox (cf. Resnik 1987, 105–107), according to which a perception of ambiguity distorts rational belief formation. The framing effect (Tversky and Kahneman 1981) shows how background conditions and descriptions of alternatives influence choice, sometimes to the extent that it violates RCT. Status quo bias is the tendency for people to like things to stay relatively the same. It has been detected in various contexts, such as 'loss aversion', where the disutility of giving up an object is greater than the utility associated with acquiring it, and the 'endowment effect', where people often demand much more to give up an object than they would be willing to pay to acquire it (Kahneman et al. 1991).

3.1. Interpreting Anomalies

A valid anomaly is an observation of systematic behaviour (under appropriate laboratory conditions) that contradicts one of the deductive implications of RCT. According to superficial versions of falsificationism, any anomaly poses a serious threat to RCT.

However, section 2 identified various uses and interpretations of RCT. Depending on the envisaged use and the intended interpretation the theorist may be justified in continuing to use it in the face of certain valid anomalies.

The first case concerns the distinction between positive and normative use. Framing effects or status quo biases, for instance, may challenge explanatory or predictive uses of RCT. Yet there is little reason to believe that they pose problems for its normative use. If someone holds that RCT has normative force, the fact that many or even most people violate these principles is irrelevant. On the contrary, it is because these principles are often violated that the importance of their normative content increases.

The issue is more complicated with anomalies such as Ellsberg's and Allais' paradoxes. Not only do they constitute an apparent threat to positive uses of RCT, they are often thought also to affect its normative standing. According to Savage:

> If, after thorough deliberation, anyone maintains a pair of distinct preferences that are in conflict with the sure-thing principle [his version of the independence condition], he must abandon, or modify, the principle; for that kind of discrepancy seems intolerable in a normative theory (Savage 1954, 101).

According to anecdotal evidence, Savage himself was unsure about the normative validity of RCT after being confronted with Allais' paradox. Although there are no clear methodological guidelines for assessing fundamental normative claims, such evidence at least opens up the possibility of a normative rejection of RCT (on the methodological issues involved, see Guala 2000).

The second case concerns the distinction between RCT as a (positive) theory of cognition versus RCT as a (positive) theory of behaviour. The theory may be behaviourally realistic in the sense that it correctly describes human behaviour, and it may be psychologically realistic in the sense that the mental states and processes it evokes can be correctly attributed to decision makers. Thus it could be employed in conjunction with three different kinds of true claims about the world: (i) as both behaviourally and psychologically realistic, (ii) as behaviourally realistic but psychologically unrealistic, and (iii) as psychologically realistic but behaviourally unrealistic. As discussed in section 2, RCT in the social sciences is often interpreted in accordance with both the first and the second claim.

This complicates the question of how relevant observed anomalies are to the positive interpretation of RCT. Clearly, if the findings are valid and systematic they challenge claim (i), but it is more difficult to show that they also challenge claim (ii) concerning behavioural realism. Caution is particularly in order when specific assumptions of RCT are singled out and shown to be 'unrealistic'. Although such claims may be correct, they may not have any relevance for users of RCT who insist on its behavioural realism.[9] Friedman (1953) insisted on this possibility in his highly influential article, arguing that the unrealisticness of its assumptions is no reason for complaint or worry about a theory. This is often interpreted as an argument based on predictive instrumentalism: underlying assumptions, especially psychological ones, need not be realistic as long as the model results succeed in predicting behaviour well. Mäki (2009a), however, notes that Friedman often leaves predictive purposes aside when considering the benefits of unrealistic assumptions, suggesting instead that he conceived of theory construction as a matter of theoretical isolation whereby economists abstract essential features of complex reality.

This brings me to the third kind of claim, that RCT may be psychologically realistic but behaviourally unrealistic. Although it attracts less attention in the scientific literature, it offers a plausible interpretation, which in turn challenges the relevance of many of the anomalies. It is a long-standing tradition, going back at least to Mill and Marshall, to argue that successful theory isolates the workings of certain factors in the world. To take an example, wealth maximisation is an important causal factor of choices made in the economic domain, but it is not the only one. Rather, its influence on choice is compounded by other causal factors. Thus, in the real world we should not expect to observe the unobstructed operation of wealth maximisation: what one could hope for at best is to observe its unobstructed operation in con-

9 The examples mentioned in this section do challenge even this interpretation, however, as they show that people systematically *choose* in a way that is inconsistent with RCT.

trolled experiments. Nevertheless, if causal factors such as wealth maximisation could be neatly separated from other factors, our theories may strive to represent the operation of these factors in their purity (Mäki 1994, 2009b). If RCT is interpreted in this fashion, the above anomalies may not challenge it. We should expect observed behaviour to deviate from the conclusions of an isolating theory: it may well also be influenced by other factors. What matters is whether the theory successfully isolates the actual operation of one of the contributing factors. Most behavioural experiments give no answers to such questions about the underlying cognitive mechanisms.

4. Bounded Rationality

The development of models of bounded rationality was largely triggered by dissatisfaction with the dominant RCT theories. According to Herbert Simon, who is commonly seen as its main pioneer, the point of bounded rationality is to

> designate rational choice that takes into account the cognitive limitations of the decision maker – limitations of both knowledge and computational capacity (Simon 1987, 266).

Simon's efforts were largely directed at finding an adequate formal characterisation of rationality. Today, the term 'bounded rationality' has acquired a more general meaning that includes all efforts at modelling choices with more cognitive and informational limitations than RCT assumes.[10] As I aimed to show in the last section, the way in which RCT is considered unsatisfactory depends on the interpretation and the kind of anomalies considered. Accordingly, at least three strands of bounded-rationality models can be distinguished, as shown in Fig. 3.

	Positive	**Normative**
Behaviourally realistic	Positive behavioural models	
Psychologically realistic	Positive procedural models	Normative procedural models

Fig. 3

10 On the history of the concept of bounded rationality, see Klaes and Sent (2005).

Models of bounded rationality have been developed for the positive purposes of explanation and prediction as well as for the normative purpose of explicating what it is to be rational. On the positive side some models claim only to capture behavioural deviations from RCT, whereas others claim to capture them by modelling the underlying psychological mechanisms. On the normative side, in turn, the aim is to propose deliberation procedures that rational agents should follow. It is noteworthy that no normative behavioural models of bounded rationality have been put forward. This may be a contingent matter of fact, but one could speculate that it seems conceptually difficult to challenge RCT as a normative standard for choice results.

4.1. Positive Models

An influential family of positive behavioural models focuses on agents' probability misperception.[11] Rank-dependent expected utility theory (RDU, Quiggin 1982) has become the most popular member of this family. If the outcomes of a lottery are ordered so that $X_1 > X_2 > \ldots > X_n$, RDU is calculated as the weighted utility of the outcomes:

$$RDU(p_1, X_1; \ldots p_n, X_n) = \Sigma\, \pi_j \times u(X_j) \tag{5}$$

where the probability weight π_j of an outcome X_j depends on its probability *and* the ranking position of the outcome:

$$\pi_j = w(p_1 + \ldots + p_j) - w(p_1 + \ldots + p_{j-1}) \tag{6}$$

The intuition behind the theory is that the degree of attention agents give to an outcome depends not only on its probability, but also on its favourability in comparison to other possible outcomes (Diecidue and Wakker 2001). Pessimists, for example, tend to overemphasise 'bad' outcomes of a lottery, believing (irrationally) that unfavourable events tend to happen more often. Their attitude is characterised by the convex weighting function *w*. Optimists, on the other hand, tend to overemphasise favourable outcomes, hence their attitude is character-

11 For a wider 'sampler' of bounded rationality in economic models, see Conlisk (1996) or Starmer (2000); for an in-depth presentation of a selection of models, see Rubinstein (1998).

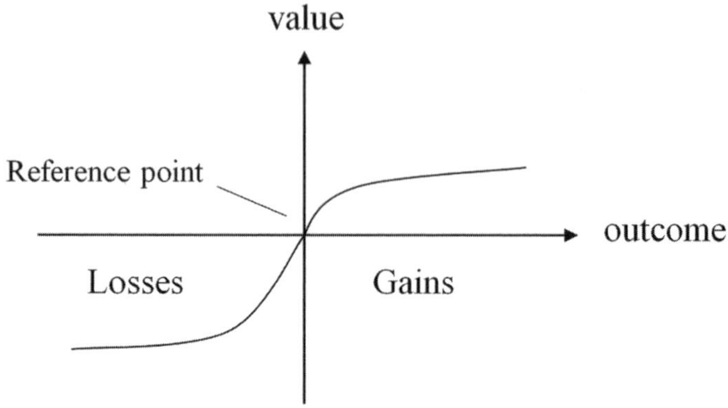

Fig. 4

ised by a concave w. Rank-dependent utility satisfies basic intuitions about rationality.[12] Nevertheless, it accounts for the agents' behaviour in the Allais' paradox: a lot of people are pessimistic, and pessimists choose B because they overemphasise the possibility in A of not winning, whereas this does not make a big difference in comparison between C and D.

In contrast to such positive behavioural models, positive procedural models often attempt to spell out how agents *actually* reason and deliberate. One of the most prominent of these is Kahneman and Tversky's (1979) prospect theory. According to this theory the deliberation process is divided into two stages: editing and evaluation. In the editing stage the different choices are ordered following a variety of heuristics, and a reference point is determined. In particular, people decide which outcomes they see as basically identical. Then they set one such equivalence class as their reference point. In the evaluation stage prospects below the reference point are interpreted as losses, and prospects above it as gains. The value function (sketched in Figure 4) passing through this reference

12 In particular, it satisfies stochastic dominance, according to which within a given lottery, shifting positive probability mass from an outcome to a strictly higher outcome leads to a strictly higher evaluation of the transformed lottery.

point is s-shaped. It is concave for gains and convex for losses, and it is steeper below the reference point.

Kahneman and Tversky (1979) interpret these two properties as *diminishing sensitivity* and *loss aversion*. Diminishing sensitivity implies that the psychological evaluation of an incremental increase of gain or loss will decrease as one moves further away from the reference point, hence the s-shape of the value function. Loss aversion holds that losses loom larger than corresponding gains, hence the increased steepness of the value functions below the reference point. The original version of prospect theory violates stochastic dominance. The editing phase may overcome this problem, but not necessarily so. A revised version, called cumulative prospect theory, uses probability weighting in a similar way to rank-dependent expected utility theory. Although this shows the closeness of prospect theory to positive behavioural models, the editing phase distinguishes it as a procedural theory.

These positive theories are subject to a number of criticisms. First, it is clear that none of the models capture human behaviour perfectly. Moving away from RCT at best gives us models that are a little less false. Thus the question arises whether the purported increased predictive and explanatory potential of bounded-rationality theories is enough to offset the undeniable decrease in parsimony of the new theories when compared to RCT. Such decreased parsimony has negative effects on explanation and prediction. Less parsimonious models are more difficult to grasp, and hence less likely to enhance understanding. They are also more likely to 'overfit' the data: the increased degrees of freedom produce a better fit to existing data, but they are more likely to pick up on irregularities in the sample that do not reflect the true trend. Formalising these trade-offs in order to facilitate proper theory choice is an important task that requires more attention (for a good example, see Harless and Camerer 1994).

Secondly, positive procedural models are open to instrumentalist critique. As Friedman (1953) argued, economic theories should not be judged by their assumptions but by their predictive implications. Yet procedural models focus precisely on the underlying cognitive mechanisms, possibly to the detriment of a more predictively powerful theory (in the sense argued in the preceding paragraph). Of course, this applies only to procedural models employed for predictive purposes, which arguably are rather rare.

Thirdly, it is a widespread misconception that the main goal of RCT is the explanation of individual behaviour. Most rational-choice theorists and, in particular economists, rather argue that the theory was designed mainly to explain aggregate-level phenomena. Specific psychological assumptions in RCT models may not be relevant for such explanatory purposes, even if the same assumptions are explanatorily relevant to individual behaviour. What is relevant, however, is whether or not the aggregate-level model result (e.g., an equilibrium allocation or a dependency of variables derived from comparative statics) is an artefact of particular RCT modelling assumptions. In order to investigate this question modellers employ robustness analysis (Lehtinen and Kuorikoski 2007). They examine how hypothetical changes in the values of model variables or parameters would change the analytical results, and what they would leave intact. From this perspective bounded-rationality models have a role in that they suggest ways in which to vary model parameters in robustness analysis. At the same time it shows the limits of such models: although they identify deviations from RCT models in individual psychological or behavioural features, these deviations may turn out to be irrelevant in the analysis.

Fourthly, not all economic models are built with a view to prediction or explanation, and some rather serve as tools for conceptual exploration (Hausman 1992), or the investigation of possible explanations (Grüne-Yanoff 2009). Such models are often interpreted as counterfactual worlds in which assumptions and hypotheses can be tested in the same way as a thought experiment, and neither predictive success nor explanatory realism is an objective. If the aim is conceptual exploration or possible explanation the introduction of a bounded-rationality assumption must somehow enhance understanding of the modelled counterfactual world. It is not always obvious that models such as the ones discussed above do indeed further understanding in these ways.

Finally, with the rapidly increasing number of competing bounded-rationality models, the danger of arbitrariness arises. Many disciplines and sub-disciplines that make use of such models only adopt the assumptions that suit their needs, and disregard others. This has aroused suspicion that bounded-rationality assumptions are employed as *ad hoc* remedies for deficient models, without any underlying theory providing clear guidance. Simon, in a letter to Rubinstein (1998), raised such a concern: "At the moment we don't need more models; we need evidence that will tell us what models are worth building and testing" (Simon, in Rubinstein 1998, 190).

Instead of constructing models from the armchair we need to develop a more general theory explaining why bounded-rationality assumptions are relevant in certain contexts and not in others, which is testable and tested. Only on the basis of such a theory can a more principled model involving such assumptions be constructed.

4.2. Normative Procedural Models

The positive models discussed thus far focus largely on human cognitive limitations. Yet Simon's original account proposes two kinds of limitation on agent rationality, which operate together like a pair of scissors whose two blades are "the structure of task environments *and* the computational capacities of the actor" (Simon 1990, 7, emphasis added). Research on the first of these, the structure of the environment, focuses on establishing the dependence of computational or mental factors on environmental pressures, and on how environmental forces have selected simple heuristics for making decisions. The resulting concept of rationality differs substantially from any optimisation effort. Instead, the decision maker adapts the use of his choice rule to the environment in which he lives. On a wider scale this idea takes on an evolutionary perspective: biological evolution endowed humans with a multitude of special-purpose psychological modules for reasoning and decision-making.

This approach has contributed to both positive and normative procedural models. Its proponents argue that biological evolution has equipped humans with heuristics that make them *ecologically rational.* Ecological rationality is seen as conflicting with the demands of a normatively understood RCT, with its emphasis on maximising choices based on all available information.

> A computationally simple strategy that uses only some of the available information can be more robust, making more accurate predictions for new data, than a computationally complex, information-guzzling strategy that overfits (Gigerenzer et al. 1999, 20).

In stressing the procedural view on rationality defenders of ecological rationality argue that it may be disadvantageous to follow a procedurally understood RCT instead of employing intuitive heuristics that arose in the form of adaptation to specific environments. Thus, the approach assumes that agents have an *adaptive toolbox* at their disposal:

> …the collection of specialised cognitive mechanisms that evolution has built into the human mind for specific domains of inference and reasoning, including fast and frugal heuristics (Todd and Gigerenzer 2000, 740).

In the long ancestral history of humanity, the assumption goes, the selected features of the toolbox have been those that prove to be most useful for survival *in a specific environment*. In terms of normative rational assessment it is a question of how well these heuristics work in the experimental environments in which RCT anomalies are observed. Forcing people into environments that are irrelevant to them (say, expressing a relation to the world in terms of probability correlations in an experimental set-up) is not pertinent to normative assessment. This, defenders of ecological rationality claim, is exactly what the experiments devised by Kahneman and Tversky and others do: Subjects are placed in artificially created environments to which they are not adapted (Gigerenzer 1996). Against this, proponents of ABC insist that deliberation rules must only be tested in relevant environments, and that they work well in environments for which they have been adapted.

This adaptive argument faces two challenges, however. First, evolutionary arguments point to a disposition, not an actuality. Traits selected for fitness tend to be optimal, but there are various lacunae that provide causes why they are not. For example, suboptimal traits may be 'bundled' with traits that ensure survival, the environment may provide resources in such abundance that selective pressure is low, or competing traits may not be challenging. The fact that certain mechanisms are evolutionarily selected thus does not guarantee their optimality even for the environments for which they have been adapted. If this was the case, RCT could help humans improve on their adapted heuristics.

Secondly, competences adapted to pre-historic circumstances may be of no help in the modern world. The above claims imply that deliberation procedures are adapted to ancestral circumstances. To be normatively relevant, however, these procedures must also be adapted to current circumstances. Otherwise they may face the same fate as the Dodo when confronted with human settlers and their domesticated animals. Defenders of ecological rationality tend to suggest that adaptation to current circumstances follows from adaptation to ancestral circumstances, but no clear arguments are given to support this claim.

5. Conclusion

Without doubt, bounded rationality has proven to be a very fruitful and multifaceted research program. It has increased social scientists' sensitivity to the cognitive mechanisms underlying choice, and to systematic behavioural deviations from the standard view. In many cases it has led to the development of innovative models that take account of these features. It has also cast some doubt on the normative adequacy of RCT, and motivated the search for alternative accounts of rationality.

Nevertheless, I hope to have shown in this article that the significance of these experimental results and modelling efforts are sometimes overemphasised. There is no reason for the social sciences to adopt bounded-rationality models across the board. Indeed, true appreciation of the multitude of different purposes for which RCT is employed makes it clear that it is better suited to some purposes than models of bounded rationality. At the very least, the question of which approach is better must be decided case by case, taking into account the available data, the scientific purpose, the results of robustness analysis, and general considerations of understandability.

References

Allais, Maurice (1953). Le comportement de l'homme rationnel devant le risque: critique des postulats et axiomes de l'école Américaine. *Econometrica* 21, 503–46.

Coleman, James S. (1990). *Foundations of social theory.* Cambridge: Harvard University Press.

Conlisk, John (1996). Why bounded rationality? *Journal of Economic Literature* 34, 669–700.

Cox, Gary W. (1999). The empirical content of rational choice theory: A reply to Green and Shapiro. *Journal of Theoretical Politics* 11(2), 147–69.

Davidson, Donald, John McKinsey, & Patrick Suppes. (1955). Outlines of a formal theory of value, I. *Philosophy of Science* 22, 140–60.

Diecidue, Enrico, & Wakker, Peter P (2001). On the intuition of rank-dependent utility. *Journal of Risk and Uncertainty* 23(3), 281–98.

Ferejohn, John A. (2002). Symposium on explanations and social ontology 1: Rational choice theory and social explanation. *Economics and Philosophy* 18(2), 211–34.

Friedman, Milton (1953). The methodology of positive economics. In *Essays in positive economics*, 3–43. Chicago: University of Chicago Press.

Gigerenzer, Gerd (1996). On narrow norms and vague heuristics: A reply to Kahneman and Tversky. *Psychological Review* 103(3), 592–96.

Gigerenzer, Gerd, Todd, Peter M. & the ABC Group. (1999). *Simple heuristics that make us smart.* Oxford: Oxford University Press.

Gintis, Herbert. (2009). *The bounds of reason: Game theory and the unification of the behavioral sciences.* Princeton, NJ: Princeton University Press.

Grüne-Yanoff, Till. (2009). Learning from minimal economic models. *Erkenntnis* 70(1), 81–99.

Guala, Francesco. (2000). The logic of normative falsification: rationality and experiments in decision theory. *Journal of Economic Methodology* 7(1), 59–93.

Hansson, Sven Ove, & Till Grüne-Yanoff. (2009). Preferences. In *The Stanford encyclopedia of philosophy (Spring 2009 Edition)*, edited by Edward N. Zalta. <http://plato.stanford.edu/archives/spr2009/entries/preferences/>

Hargreaves-Heap, Shaun, Martin Hollis, Bruce Lyons, Robert Sugden, & Albert Weale. (1992). *The theory of choice: A critical guide.* Oxford: Blackwell.

Harless, David W., & Colin F. Camerer. (1994). The predictive utility of generalized expected utility theories. *Econometrica* 62, 1251–89.

Hausman, Daniel M. (1992). *The inexact and separate science of economics.* Cambridge: Cambridge University Press.

Jeffrey, Richard (1990). *The logic of decision.* 2nd ed. Chicago: University of Chicago Press.

Kahneman, Daniel, & Amos Tversky. (1979). Prospect theory: An analysis of decision under risk. *Econometrica* 47, 263–291.

Kahneman, Daniel, Paul Slovic, & Amos Tversky (Eds.). (1982). *Judgment under uncertainty: Heuristics and biases.* New York: Cambridge University Press.

Kahneman, Daniel, Jack L. Knetsch, & Richard H. Thaler. (1991). Anomalies: The endowment effect, loss aversion, and status quo bias. *The Journal of Economic Perspectives* (American Economic Association) 5(1), 193–206.

Klaes, Matthias, & Esther-Mirjam Sent. (2005). A conceptual history of the emergence of bounded rationality. *History of Political Economy* 37(1), 27–59.

Lehtinen, Aki, & Jaakko Kuorikoski. (2007). Unrealistic assumptions in rational choice theory. *Philosophy of the Social Sciences* 37, 115–38.

Luce, R. Duncan, & Howard Raiffa. (1957). *Games and decisions: Introduction and critical survey.* New York: Wiley.

Mäki, Uskali. (1994). Isolation, idealization and truth in economics. In *Idealization VI: Idealization in economics*, edited by Bert Hamminga & Neil De Marchi. (*Poznan Studies in the Philosophy of the Sciences And the Humanities* 38, 7–68).

Mäki, Uskali. (2009a). Unrealistic assumptions and unnecessary confusions: Rereading and rewriting F53 as a realist statement. In *The methodology of positive economics: Reflections on the Milton Friedman legacy*, edited by Uskali Mäki, 90–116. Cambridge: Cambridge University Press.

Mäki, Uskali. (2009b). Realistic realism about unrealistic models. In *Oxford handbook of the philosophy of economics*, edited by H. Kincaid, & D. Ross, 68–98. New York: Oxford University Press.

Mas-Colell, Andreu, Michael D. Whinston, & Jerry R. Green. (1995). *Microeconomic theory*. New York: Oxford University Press.

von Neumann, John, & Oskar Morgenstern. (1947). *The theory of games and economic behavior*. 2nd ed. Princeton, NJ: Princeton University Press.

Quiggin, John (1982). A theory of anticipated utility. *Journal of Economic Behavior and Organization*. 3(4), 323–43.

Ramsey, Frank P. (1931). Truth and probability. In *The foundations of mathematics and other logical essays*, edited by Richard B. Braithwaite, 156–98. London: Routledge and Kegan Paul.

Resnik, Michael D. (1987). *Choices: An introduction to decision theory*. Minneapolis: University of Minnesota Press.

Rubinstein, Ariel. (1998). *Modeling bounded rationality*. Cambridge, MA: MIT Press.

Samuelson, Paul. (1938). A note on the pure theory of consumer behavior. *Economica* 5(17), 61–71.

Savage, Leonard. J. (1954). *The foundations of statistics*. New York: Wiley.

Sen, Amartya K. (1987). *On ethics and economics*. Oxford, Blackwell.

Simon, Herbert A. (1987). Bounded Rationality. In *The New Palgrave Dictionary of Economics*, edited by John Eatwell, Murray Milgate, and Peter Newman. London: Macmillan.

Simon, Herbert A. (1990). Invariants of human behavior. *Annual Review of Psychology* 41, 1–19.

Starmer, Chris (2000). Developments in non-expected utility theory: The hunt for a descriptive theory of choice under risk. *Journal of Economic Literature*, 38, 332–82.

Todd, Peter M., & Gerd Gigerenzer. (2000). Simple heuristics that make us smart. *Behavioral and Brain Sciences 23*(5), 727–41.

Thaler, Richard H. (1992). *The winner's curse: Paradoxes and anomalies of economic life*. Princeton, NJ: Princeton University Press.

Tversky, Amos, & Daniel Kahneman (1981). The framing of decisions and the psychology of choice. *Science* 211, 453–58.

Wong, Stanley. (1978). *Foundations of Paul Samuelson's revealed preference theory: A study by the method of rational reconstruction*. London: Routledge.

Playing against Superior Beings in Religion, Technology and Economy

MATTI KAMPPINEN

1. Navigating in the World of Uncertainty

The universe as we know it contains possible courses of events in the sense that things could have gone otherwise. As events unfold, it may happen that we are lucky in trying to affect them, or some other time, it may turn out that we run out of luck, despite of our efforts to change the course of events (Rescher 2001).

Courses of events are causally dependent upon various things: upon ourselves and our capabilities, our fellow human beings, laws of nature, economics, complex hybrid situations of natural laws and social commitments and so on. Some causal factors in our lives are more predictable than others, some are even known to scientific research, whereas some are just assumed to exist and have causal power. Some of these assumed causal factors are interpreted as superior beings, anthropomorphic agents whose causal powers are mightier than ours. In certain cultural settings, these superior beings are elements of religions, they are revered and ritually manipulated, whereas in certain other cultural settings the superior beings are feared and taken into account as necessary features of technological progress. What is common to the superior beings of religions and the risks of modern societies is that they provide challenging antagonists for games of life, for different projects of navigating in the world of uncertainty.

We experience ourselves as beings situated in the network of possible worlds. Some possible worlds are behind us, some lie in the future; some of them are accessible to us, and some are beyond our reach for one reason or another. We ethnographers believe all this. In addition, we believe that the people we study are very much like us. They, the study objects, are cognitively competent, culturally groomed actors finding their way in the networks of possible worlds.

Mental models are tools for navigating in world of uncertainty. Mental models portray simplified worlds, in which relationships bind entities together into systemic networks (Senge 1990). Mental models concern, not only physical world and its material aspects, but also abstract entities like social relationships, moral obligations, and deities (D'Andrade 1990; Shweder 1991). Models of risk provide maps with which to navigate in the world of uncertainty (Saarinen and Kamppinen 2009; Vihervaara and Kamppinen 2009).

Risks are culturally manipulated not only in the sense that their existence and properties are conceptually specified, but also in the sense that material culture or technology is utilised in the processes of risk management and containment. Technological structures, together with other cultural systems, not only help to manage risks, but they create risks as well.

Mental models of risk provide tools for navigating in the world of uncertainty in the sense that they provide us with information concerning relevant features of the situation. These features include, for example, the causal structure of the world, its ontological furniture, and most important, information on the other agents to be taken into account. Mental models of risk thus specify the game in which we find ourselves.

In what follows I will first look at the system of folk religion in Peruvian Amazon and discuss how mental models specify the game against culturally postulated superhuman agent, *yashingo*. After that I will look at how mental models function in the perception of risks of technology and of environmental risks, and will provide a case study to illustrate the point. After that, I will move on to the field of market forces and economic risks, and finally look at the differences between games against superior beings.

2. Playing against *Yashingo* and other Culturally Postulated Superhuman Agents

As argued in the above section, mental models of risk provide tools for navigating in the world of uncertainty. Folk religion in the Peruvian Amazon contains various tools for dealing with uncertainty. It postulates multiple superhuman agents that provide cultural information on how to conduct oneself in the world of uncertainty (Taussig 1980, Kamppinen 1989a, Kamppinen 1989b, Saarinen and Kamppinen 2009). Rivers, for example, are occupied by the river people, *aguaruna*, who oversee the aquatic realm and interact with human beings. Rainforest hosts the forest people, *sacharuna*, and multiple other superhuman agents. One of these is *yashingo*, or *chullachaqui*, who is the guardian of animals and also the gardener of forests.

Yashingo is an anthropomorphic agent, who is able to appear in the disguise of an old man, or he can assume the form of a game animal, by means of which he wants to lure the hunters to follow him. When conducting interviews on *yashingo*, I asked several times, what does *yashingo* want. It became evident that the desires and beliefs of the *yashingo* are difficult to know, and consequently its behaviour is difficult to predict. For example, *yashingo* wishes to lead his life in solitude, and not to be bothered by human beings. In fact, the ever more intensive human presence in the rainforest has forced *yashingos* to move farther away from noise, light and the smell of gasoline. On the other hand, they will approach humans and punish, for example, for too intensive use of natural resources. Further, they are attracted to humans and will kidnap human beings for the purpose of copulating with them. *Yashingos* use kidnapped human beings for procreation, even though they can also breed within themselves.

Yashingo is a complex superhuman agent–there is no straightforward winning strategy when playing with it–*yashingo* challenges rational strategies (Kamppinen 2009). It has human-like interests (food, shelter and procreation), but its interests are not expressed as clearly as with humans. Furthermore, it has superhuman powers: it can transform itself to a game animal, and it can bewitch its victim. It can also shoot invisible shots to its victim, and these, in turn, can be removed only by the local healer. The *yashingo* is not omnipotent, though. It must obey some of the spatiotemporal constraints that concern us humans, too. It cannot, for example, move from one spot to another in an instant, but requires time just as we do. It can be expelled by means of tobacco smoke, or by means of magic song. It also avoids more brute antidotes like gasoline, noise and light.

An Amazonian hunter preparing himself for the risk of encountering a *yashingo* should, therefore, have some tobacco with him, learn magic songs and avoid known *yashingo* territories. Tobacco involves a risk, since *yashingo* is attracted to unsmoked tocacco leaves–hence tobacco must be smoked or shared with *yashingo*. A hunter may choose between defence, attack or cooperation. Defence means using the traditional combination of tobacco and magic songs. Attack would involve gasoline and light, and cooperation would mean giving *yashingo* its share of natural resources and items it wants like tobacco leaves.

Due to modernisation of the Amazonia, games against *yashingos* are not played as frequently as before. They are not taken into account in the utilisation of natural resources except in remote areas. In more urbanised settings, *yashingos* appear as characters in folklore, for example n children's stories or in commercialised tradition for tourists. They still carry the information of how to play against them, but these games are for purposes of fun, tourism or child rearing.

Playing against *yashingo* and functionally equivalent superhuman agents is like playing against fellow human beings who possess weird interests and capabilities. Still, *yashingo* is bound by approximately the same constraints as humans. The omnipontent creator gods of Judaism, Christianity and Islam are different. As they have been subject to theological cultivation, they have lost most of their human qualities and have gained new superhuman qualities instead. The god of Christianity is perhaps the most superhuman of the three. On the basis of biblical and theological writing, the Christian god sees, oversees, feels anger and love, expects, forgives, punishes and so on. But most distinctively, it can do anything, it knows all knowable things, and it is not subject to spatial or temporal constraints. It dwells in an everlasting moment where all moments of time are equally accessible. Also, its benevolence is unbounded. Playing against the Christian god is notoriously paradoxical: Christians are encouraged to talk to god (to pray) even though god knows beforehand what one is about to say; Christians are encouraged to make decisions about their moral conduct even though their future is foreseen by and causally dependent on the god; and the causally omnipotent and loving god allows bad things to happen although it could have cancelled them.

Steven Brams (2007) has explicated the game-theoretical patterns in Judaism and Christianity. One of his examples is what he calls the Revelation Game. The god of the Old Testament prefers not to reveal himself, but rather have humans to believe in him without evidence. The message is the same in Lutheran Christianity: our valuable intuition (shaped by evolution) that we should have grounds for our beliefs is cast aside and we are required just to believe, without any hint of evidence. In the Revelation Game the god prefers to hide himself and the believer (quite naturally) prefers to believe if he has evidence. Hence people end up in a situation where the god does not reveal himself and the believer does not believe, even though they could end up in a situation where the god would reveal himself and the believer could believe on the basis of evidence. The Revelation Game ends up in a less than optimal outcome since the god has the original steadfast dominant strategy not to reveal himself.

The millions of Christians (and Jews and Muslims) interpreting the tradition do not play the revelation game against the mute god, but rather they play against anthropomorphic god, who has human-like qualities and whose theologically correct properties are discarded (Guthrie 1993, Slone 2004). For example in Pentecostalism, the god figure is very human: he is addressed to as powerful human being, he is expected to intervene in causal processes, for example in sickness and health, and the attributed signals of his actions are eagerly identified and gathered into a pool of evidence, on the basis of which the believer has grounds for his or her beliefs and actions. The theologically incorrect Christian god is not very different from the *yashingo* creature we encountered above, except that the Christian god is supposed to be benevolent and interested in the wellbeing of humans. What is even more interesting is that among Pentecostals, for example, the figure of Jesus Christ enters the game as an independent player, who can be used for purposes for taking the message to God or who can be asked to help in minor matters that do not require that much causal powers.

A Finnish charismatic movement, the Nokia Mission, has a homepage where members and other believers can post their requests for collective prayers. The things that are asked for range from dental bill and next month's rent to happier marriage and fitting shoes. Superhuman agent that understands and sympathises these prayers is very human indeed.

What is common to religious games is that they are played against superior beings. Some culturally postulated superhuman agents like *yashingos* are not so much superior as they are weird and equipped with some superhuman qualities. Theologically correct creator gods of Judaism, Christianity and Islam are truly superior beings and playing against these agents is bound to lead into paradoxical outcomes. That must be one of the reasons why religious people in these traditions rather play against anthropomorphic, more concrete and theologically incorrect agents. It leaves more room for rational prediction and assessment of other players and allows one to gather evidence and form beliefs on the basis cumulative evidence. Religious actor purports to be a rational actor (Kamppinen 1988, 2009).

Navigating in the world of uncertainty has always been a risky business. Anthropomorphic forces of nature or anthropomorphic cosmos have provided worthy opponents. They have been the superior beings against whom the games of life have been played. As we have come to know more about nature, supernatural superior beings have been transformed into known and partly manageable lawful forces of nature. Life has become safer in many respects. For an average citizen of Western world, there are no capricious superior beings who should be taken into account in conducting one's daily life.

Life is safer, but technology, environment and market forces host risks and also superior beings. It can be argued that the dominant superior beings to be played against can be found in these three areas. Citizens in the secular Western world are less worried about the burning flames of hellfire and more worried about environment, technology and economy. Let us look at these areas of life and at how superior beings enter the games.

3. Playing against Technological Risks

Modern technology as well as environmental risks host superior beings. Lay people are exposed to technological innovations and environmental risks, the possible harmful impacts are difficult to perceive, and we lay people feel as if we are left at the mercy of fate and experts.

Attitudes towards technology–or the perception of risks of technology–are dependent upon their roles in the worldviews of the informants. The nature of conceived technology is affected by its cognitive and cultural context. Risk perceptions are embedded in general models of reality; attitudes towards technology depend upon basic beliefs, which concern (i) the material world, its structure and dynamics, especially the probabilities and the furniture of the world, and (ii) the social world, especially the structures of power, trust, and knowledge.

When, for example, the laypeople's and the experts' views on technology collide, this usually stems from the fact that the respective parties live in different realities which are furnished with different kinds of things (Kamppinen et al., 1995). As Mary Douglas and Aaron Wildavsky (1982) have said, the magnitude of any risk is proportional to what bits of information are connected to it (see also Tonn et al. 1990; Kates et al. 1985).

Psychological studies on risk and technology assessment suggest as well that risks are cognised as parts of larger networks of things (see Cvetkovich and Earle, 1985; Johnson and Tversky 1984; Brehmer 1987; Sampson 1981).

This line of research sees risks (or risk representations) as mental models that are constructed, maintained and modified by social processes. The papers in Johnson and Covello (1987) and Brown (1989) criticize the psychological work on risk for ignoring the social and cultural reality of human beings, whose cognitions they have proposed to study. Four specific points of criticism have been presented in the literature:

(1) Risk models are generated in cultural contexts – they are negotiated in and by social groups, and they are subject to change. The individual risk models are products of social processes, and the psychologist's overall individualism is unwarranted. That is, the ontological status of risk is not the one suggested by psychologists. Risks are constituted by negotiated mental models, whose presence or absence in the individual minds depends on social dynamics.

(2) As the psychological studies have shown, media and the salience of a risky item affect its reception. Yet social networks are of primary importance in the formation and propagation of risk models.

(3) The concepts of probability and negative utility that constitute the common-sense conception of risk, are themselves culture-relative. The fixing of either of them is a process of negotiation that is affected by ideological and religious factors, the cognised plausibility of institutions, economy, and so on (cf. Cashdan 1990).

(4) The gestalt of risk – on which dimensions it is assessed – is also affected by institutions, and by the interaction that takes place in the workplace, among friends and family members.

The classical work on the cultural construction of risk is *Risk and Culture* (1982) by Mary Douglas and Aaron Wildavsky. Its main tenet is largely based on the earlier work by Douglas (1966) and it can be summarised as follows: The classifications of risks are not based on the actual (for example physical) hazardousness of the items, but rather on their moral qualities and connections; the classification of risks, and by the same token their identification, perception and management, all serve social purposes–the maintenance of group identity, group survival, the concomitant reduction of cognitive dissonance, and the expression of moral values. These basic forms of social dynamics govern other cultural activities as well.

Our case study concerning the social and cultural aspects of a construction process of coal power plant in Western Finland supports and illuminates the position outlined (Raivola and Kamppinen 1994).

The aim of the study was to describe the diverse views of the impacts of a new power plant, situated in Meri-Pori in Western Finland. The plant was built during years 1990 to 1993, and the study was commissioned by the Finnish Ministry of Trade and Affairs.

The primary methods of data collection were interviews, documentary analysis, and participant observation. The analysis of official documents revealed that the construction process was unique in the sense that it had its specific historical background. (All real world processes are of course unique in this sense, and their general aspects must be abstracted in order to have material for comparative research.) The construction process was also a process of gradual decision-making: acts of decision under uncertainty followed one another.

The local perspective was reconstructed from the interview and observation material. It was characterised by two themes: acceptability of emissions and trust.

The physical impacts of emissions were framed in widely different ways, depending on how the emissions were contextualized. The locals (and experts) had a shared view of the numbers, but the significance of these numbers was interpreted in various ways. More to the point, the acceptability of emissions depended upon the views concerning for example employment effects and the identity of the community. Those who expected beneficial employment effects were more willing to accept the project. The conceptions of local identity were nicely geared into acceptability. The local community of Reposaari has a long and well-known history as an industrial community, and there were informants who saw the power plant as a natural and acceptable continuation of this tradition. Other half of the informants perceived the community as a potential marina, a tourist attraction for boaters. This future prospect could not tolerate power plants or other heavy industry.

The theme of trust recurred again and again in the interviews, conversations and day-to-day life. The questions pondered by the locals were: Are experts and politicians worth trusting? Are there some players in this game who are systematically untrustworthy, misguiding or even outright evil? The notion of trust was linked with other moral and political qualities, and embedded in general models of reality which depicted the landscape of political actors, flow of knowledge and so on.

The mental model of acceptable emissions thus linked emissions with the perceived history and the future prospects of the area, and with the other players. The trustworthiness and other moral qualities of other players were in particular focus, since these properties determine the nature of the game. The decision-makers, politicians, owners, companies and other superhuman agents (superhuman in the sense that they have more capabilities than lay people) were assessed on the basis of their moral qualities: do they care about the common good, or are they implementing their own good only? Are they fair in the treatment of citizens or do they favour some groups at the expense of others? To communicate with the superior being in the matters of environmental and technological risks required special occasions, like organised hearings, where laypeople were advised to address the representatives of superior beings. The experts present in hearings were not identical with the superior beings, but were representing companies, organisations and other superior beings.

Our study also documented a prevalent rhetoric of irrationality, how the laypeople were accused of NIMBY (not in my backyard) and LULU (locally unwanted land uses) syndromes. We proposed that the laypeople's reactions were in fact rational, if assessed against the background of their mental models. Take, for example, the norm "think globally, act locally." Reacting against construction process within one's living environment is in accord with this norm. It is rational to act in a familiar locality, which embodies personal and social values and which is well known for the actors. Moreover, when playing against superior beings whose moral qualities are not known, it is rational to try to minimise the risk and choose a strategy where your contacts with the superior being are as few as possible. It is safer to act in local conditions and avoid contexts where unknown and probably evil agents are active.

Our finding that the laypeople are rational accords well with the basic assumption in ethnographic and anthropological research: if the subjects appear irrational, then the mental models affecting the situation should be studied more thoroughly. In other words, there is a principle of charity at work: the people we are studying should be interpreted as rational as possible. This principle does not water down the culturally interesting differences between experts and laypeople; neither does it exclude the potential criticism of mental models. To begin with, it points out the shared features of laypeople and experts (both are rational) and explains the differences in behaviour (they operate with different mental models). Next, the rationality and acceptability of lay mental models can be questioned (Kamppinen 2009). For example, laypeople have very vague idea about emissions: imperceptible things that come from somewhere and have cumulative impact on health. The dynamics of emissions and the mechanics that generate emissions are not conceptualised in lay mental models, but they remain superior beings with very little human characteristics or moral qualities. Nature, on the other hand, was conceptualised in lay mental models as something that knows its course and aims at morally optimal result. The "justified revenge of nature" was evoked several times when lay people explained the confrontation between society and nature. Nature was seen as the container of everything that is good and just. In addition, nature was conceptualised as mysterious and partly unfathomable.

4. Playing against Market Forces

Economy rests on shared beliefs. If a company stock is believed to gain value, its price will go up. If the Euro is believed to be a strong currency, it will be so. Things come into existence as they are believed to be so and so. Mutual beliefs are mutually supporting, since it is safe to believe what the others are believed to believe.

At times mutual beliefs generate catastrophes, when, for example, a pyramid scheme is constructed. People enter pyramid financing on the basis of little evidence: they have heard, for example, that someone they know has benefited from the system, or they get the recommendation from someone they trust, a relative or a business partner (Ariely 2008). For the keepers of the pyramid it is essential to give some evidence of wealth, a small amount of money as a signal of forthcoming revenues. The keepers of the pyramid also usually give the appearance that they have privileged knowledge of the behaviour of market forces, and they are willing to share this knowledge for mutual benefit. Only the chosen ones are invited to participate in the system, and they will gain special access to market forces. Success stories in the world of stock exchange further strengthen the belief that by means of specialised knowledge one could become really rich.

The constructors of pyramid schemes claim to provide unique access to market forces. Market forces do not reveal their intricate nature for a common onlooker, but require specialists.

There are also specialists who play fair. A common client planning to make investments in his bank is advised to negotiate with an investment counsellor, who, in turn, utilises special knowledge of market forces in giving recommendations. The counsellor's information is not perfect, and he has to navigate in the world of uncertainty as well. He does not foresee the movements of market forces and can only give his best, educated guess. The client must have a strong belief in the capabilities of the counsellor. The model of market forces that is constructed is based on the information given by the counsellor and according to it the market forces are partly unfathomable, have a will of their own, and are heading towards some optimal state of balance that may or may not be known for human players. The client planning an investment takes the risk, closes his eyes and puts the eggs in the baskets that look most secure. The common client is playing against market forces with the help of a specialist.

If one should point out one entity in secular society whose behaviour is functionally equivalent to superhuman agents of religions, market forces would by the one.

Market forces have assumed the role of fate in various discussions. In this role the market forces can act for good or for bad end result.

For example, the bailout of General Motors by US government was seen by some (e. g. Alabama Sen. Richard Selby) as a harmful intervention in the process that would be better done by market forces. The government intervention was seen as giving birth to a company that will not survive on the market. Market forces, if let operate by themselves, would have produced a better outcome.

According to empirical studies, market forces do produce better results now and then. Unproductive East German energy sector was cleaned (dismantled) after the German unification due to market forces (Boehmer-Christiansen 1992). It left jobless people in East Germany, but was good for the environment.

Iceland had to downsize whaling because the demand for whale meat had sunken – the laws of supply and demand worked for the good of the whales (*New Scientist* September 2007). The same mechanisms of market forces that benefit whales increase misery for human players. In India and China, the emerging markets for new consumers drive poor urban dwellers to live in slums, as their traditional living areas are reoccupied for shopping malls, for which "the market forces want prime land." (*Down to Earth* 13/2004).

In European Union, where labour unions traditionally have had strong positions, market forces are conceptualised as forces that must be controlled for the common good. Market forces unleashed, without any societal control, tend to generate human losses. Market forces are seen as blind forces that do not foresee the social good, but only optimise the revenues for stockowners. Therefore labour unions call for governments to act on their behalf and control the market forces by means of appropriate legislation.

5. Playing against Superior Beings in Archaic and Modern Societies

Most of us modern people think in terms of risks rather than in terms of gods. Peter Bernstein (1996) argues that the notion of risk is the watershed line between archaic and modern societies:

> The distant past was studded with brilliant scientists, mathematicians, inventors, technologists, and political philosophers. Hundreds of years before the birth of Christ, the skies had been mapped, the great library of Alexandria built, and Euclid's geometry taught. Demand for technological innovation in warfare was as insatiable then as it is today. Coal, oil, iron and copper have been at the service of human beings for millennia, and travel and communication mark the very beginnings of recorded civilization.
>
> The revolutionary idea that defines the boundary between modern times and the past is the mastery of risk: the notion that the future is more than a whim of the gods and that men and women are not passive before nature. Until human beings discovered a way across that boundary, the future was a mirror of the past or the murky domains of oracles and soothsayers who held a monopoly over knowledge of anticipated events (Bernstein 1996, 1).

Yet the complex systems of risks and insurance, scientific knowledge and complicated technology have created a milieu for a common citizen that shares many features with the archaic society.

A citizen living in the late modern world and facing the risks of technology, environment and economy, lives in the risk society, where the ultimate boundary conditions of his life are known and controlled only by a small group of specialists.

The importance of moral qualities and the prevalence of ultimate questions in risk assessment have been interpreted as a central characteristic of our era of late modernity. The situation in our late modernity resembles the situation of archaic societies, as Ulrich Beck (1986) has noted. In both types of societies, the games of social life are played with and against superior beings: gods, evil spirits, and destiny in archaic societies, and supra-individual collective entities like transnational companies in post-modern societies. Both players are difficult to understand, to cope with, and to manipulate. Our age of late modernity has been characterised as religious age: for example, the rituals by means of which we maintain our body and health against invisible toxicants are comparable to the rituals of archaic societies.

I am willing to concur with Bernstein rather that with Beck. There is one major difference between the real archaic society and archaic appearance of the risk society. In modern society, the citizens can in principle find out how things are, and can have reasonable, testable answers for their questions. Even though the world of uncertainty known only for experts may appear unfathomable for the common citizen, experts and lay people share the view that it can be systematically investigated, its properties can be reasonable argued about, and participants can come into rational agreement on what the world is composed of and what it is like. The mental models of risk in the modern risk society can be assessed on rational grounds, they can be questioned and cultivated. The mental models of archaic contexts are more immune and less open to critical assessment. Therefore the apparent shared properties of archaic and modern societies are only apparent.

6. Transferring the Features of Religions into Other Cultural Systems

Superior beings in archaic and modern contexts are analogous, that is, they share some functional properties that can be explicated by means of game-theoretical analysis. Even though the archaic context is that of religion, it does not follow that the superior beings of modern contexts are in any sense religious. The causal factors in technological and environmental risks as well as the factors pertaining to market forces are not believed to be supernatural agents, even though they surely are superhuman (or at least supraindividual). In the context of modern worldview, the risks of technology and environment as well as the market forces are in principle analysable in naturalistic terms. What we have is the generic human phenomenon, playing against superior beings. It can actualise in different contexts, and religion is one of them.

The same holds for other features that are deemed religion-like. Joining together under shared symbolism and participating in rituals is one of the hallmarks of religion. It is a generic feature of social human behaviour and can be found in numerous other contexts, too. The celebration of the national independence, or the interaction in a company get-together has these features as well. It would be a poor argument to claim that these human celebrations are religious. Some gatherings take place in contexts of religion, and in those occasions the symbolism and the rituals articulate religious beliefs. Again, what we have here is a generic human phenomenon that can be actualised in various contexts. Inferring that all human symbolisations or rituals are religious is like claiming that since humans are primates, all primates are humans.

Tracing the features of religions in other cultural systems can be framed as reasonable scientific project if one takes it as heuristic tool of research. Namely: if playing against superior beings is one of the hallmarks of religions, how is it in other cultural systems? When, for example, we are studying the games in the areas of technology, environment or economy, are there rituals for the purpose of interacting with the superior beings? Is the expert knowledge such that it can be studied by laypeople? And how is knowledge formed–what are the roles of open, democratic assessment, of participation, of critique and questioning in the formation of knowledge? Utilised as a heuristic tool of research, the shared properties of religion and other cultural systems will be investigated, not assumed.

References

Ariely, Dan. (2008). *Predictably irrational: The hidden forces that shape our decisions.* New York: Harper.

Beck, Ulrich. (1986). *Risikogesellschaft. Auf dem Weg in eine andere Moderne.* Frankfurt am Main: Suhrkamp.

Bernstein, Peter. (1996). *Against the gods: The remarkable story of risk.* New York: John Wiley & Sons.

Boehmer-Christiansen, S.A. (1992). Taken to the cleaners: The fate of the East German energy sector since 1990. *Environmental Politics* 1(2), 196–228.

Brams, Steven. (2007). *Superior beings: If they exist, how would we know?* Second edition. New York: Springer.

Brehmer, Berndt. (1987). The psychology of risk. In *Risk and decisions*, edited by W.T. Singleton & J. Hovden. New York: John Wiley.

Brown, Jennifer. (Ed.) (1989). *Environmental threats: Perception, analysis, and management.* London: Belhaven Press.

Cashdan, Elizabeth. (Ed.) (1990). *Risk and uncertainty in tribal and peasant economies.* Boulder: Westview Press.

Covello, V.T., J. Menkes, & J. Mumpower (Eds.). (1986). *Risk evaluation and management.* New York: Plenum.

Cvetkovich, G., & Earle, T. (1985). Classifying hazardous events. *Journal of Environmental Psychology* 5, 5–35.

D'Andrade, Roy. (1990). Some propositions about the relations between culture and human cognition. In *Cultural psychology: Essays on comparative human development*, edited by J.W. Stigler et al. Cambridge: Cambridge University Press.

Douglas, Mary. (1966). *Purity and danger.* London: Routledge & Kegan Paul.

Douglas, Mary, & Aron Wildavsky. (1982). *Risk and culture.* Berkeley: California University Press.

Guthrie, Stewart. (1993). *Faces in the clouds: A new theory of religion.* New York: Oxford University Press.

Johnson, B.B., & V.T. Covello. (Eds.) (1987). *The social and cultural construction of risk: Essays on risk selection and perception.* Boston: Reidel.

Johnson, E.J., & A. Tversky. (1984). Representations of perceptions of risk. *Journal of Experimental Psychology: General* 113, 55–70.

Kamppinen, Matti (1988). Homo religious intelligens: Outline for a cognitivist theory of religious behaviour. *Temenos* 24, 29–38.

Kamppinen, Matti. (1989a). *Cognitive systems and cultural models of illness: A study of two Mestizo peasant villages of the Peruvian Amazon.* (Folklore Fellows' Communications, 244). Helsinki: Academia Scientiarum Fennica.

Kamppinen, Matti. (1989b). Dialectics of evil: Politics and religion in an Amazon Mestizo community. *Dialectical Anthropology* 13, 143–55.

Kamppinen, Matti. (2009). Rationality, religion and intentional system systems theory: From objective ethnography to the critical study of religious beliefs. *Method and Theory in the Study of Religion* 21, 274–84.

Kamppinen, Matti. et al. (1995). *Riskit yhteiskunnassa: Maallikot ja asiantuntijat päätösten tekijöinä* (Risks in the society: Laypeople and experts as decision-makers). Helsinki: Gaudeamus.

Kates, R.W., C. Hohenemser, & J.X. Kasperson. (Eds.) (1985). *Perilous progress: Managing the hazards of technology.* Boulder: Westview.

Raivola, Petri, & Matti Kamppinen. (1994). *Kannattiko vauhkoontua: hiilivoimalan sijoituksen sosiokulttuurisia vaikutuksia* (Was it worth raving: The sociocultural impacts of the siting of a coalpower plant). Reports from the Satakunta Environmental Research Centre A5, Pori.

Rescher, Nicholas. (2001). *Luck: The brilliant randomness of everyday life.* Pittsburgh: University of Pittsburgh Press.

Saarinen, Sanni, & Matti Kamppinen. (2009). The models of nature and the politics of sustainable development in the Peruvian Amazon. *International Journal of Sustainable Society* 1(4), 311–24.

Sampson, E. (1981). Cognitive psychology as ideology. *American Psychologist* 36, 7, 730–43.

Senge, Peter. (1990). *The fifth discipline.* New York: Doubleday.

Shweder, Roy. (1991). *Thinking through cultures: Expeditions in cultural psychology.* Cambridge: Harvard University Press.

Slone, D. Jason. (2004). *Theological incorrectness: Why religious people believe what they shouldn't.* Oxford: Oxford University Press.

Taussig, Michael. (1980). *The devil and commodity fetishism in South America.* Chapel Hill: The University of North Carolina Press.

Tonn, B.E., C.B. Travis, R.T. Goeltz, & R.H. Phillippi. (1990). Knowledge-based representations of risk beliefs. *Risk Analysis* 1, 169–84.

Vihervaara, Petteri, & Matti Kamppinen. (2009). The ecosystem approach in corporate environmental management – expert mental models and environmental drivers in the Finnish forest industry. *Corporate Social Responsibility and Environmental Management* 16, 79–93.

Durkheim and Psychology

WARREN SCHMAUS

Durkheim is well-known for having denied any explanatory role for individual psychology in sociology. He is considered one of the founders of methodological collectivism or holism, which opposes the methodological individualist position that explanations of social facts should be reduced to facts about individuals. Methodological collectivism is sometimes thought to entail the very opposite point of view, in which social facts are explanatorily prior to individual facts. Thus, some have believed that Durkheim was a sociological determinist who held that individuals were completely shaped by their social environment, leaving psychology with a very diminished role in explaining human thought and behavior. However, this was not Durkheim's position. For Durkheim, the full story concerning the relationship between the individual and society depended on psychology as well as sociology. Implicit in his work are suggestions for cooperative research between these disciplines.

To make my case, I will re-examine Durkheim's arguments concerning the separation between sociology and psychology to see just what they do and do not entail. These arguments need to be evaluated in their historical context. What "psychology" meant for Durkheim is not necessarily what it means for us today. We need to consider just what sort of psychology he would deny. We will see that he rejected attempts to explain human social phenomena in terms of various individual needs, desires, and tendencies ascribed to human nature by a philosophical psychology. He also refused to allow philosophical psychologies that relied on the method of introspection. There is no evidence that he was as negative about experimental, empirical, or scientific psychology as he was about philosophical psychology.

To be sure, in *The Rules of Sociological Method* he said that "Every time a social phenomenon is directly explained in terms of a psychological phenomenon, one may be assured that the explanation is false" (1895a, 128; 1982a, 129).[1] His rejection of explanations that appeal to

1 All translations from the French are my own. I also cite the page numbers in the most recent English translations for the convenience of my readers. Following

psychological *phenomena* appears to be independent of the scientific, epistemic, or methodological status of the psychological theory in which these phenomena are characterized. Nevertheless, his targets in the chapter from which this quotation is taken are philosophical theories of human nature. Furthermore, even if this injunction against psychological explanations in sociology is understood to include scientific psychology, it amounts to no more than a stand against reductionism. It does not imply that Durkheim had no interest in psychology or that he thought that sociology and psychology had nothing to learn from each other. I will show that other passages that have been cited in support of the sociological determinist reading of Durkheim also entail nothing more than a stand against reductionism. Similarly, careful attention to Durkheim's arguments in *The Elementary Forms of Religious Life* (1912a) will reveal that his sociological theory of the categories does not imply that society determines the forms of thought of its individual members. This conclusion would follow only if one did not distinguish causal from functional explanations and the categories from their collective representations. Durkheim himself was not always careful with these distinctions, making possible the determinist reading of his sociology of knowledge.

Key explanatory concepts in Durkheim's works are concepts of things that depend on psychological capacities and processes. The formation of social solidarity not only depends at least in part on psychological processes, but answers psychological needs. Collective representations, which make social life possible, are initially formed from individual representations and depend upon the same psychological capacities that individual representations depend upon. Durkheim's account in *The Elementary Forms of Religious Life* of the episodes of collective effervescence in which collective representations are formed suggests areas for cooperative research among sociologists and psychologists. However, Durkheim's concept of a mental representation was still tied to the centuries-old way of ideas tradition in philosophy. The cognitive sciences have come a long way in the century since Durkheim wrote. It is

---

the standard practice among Durkheim scholars, I refer to Durkheim's writings using the numbering system originally invented by Steven Lukes (1973), which has been updated by Durkheim scholars as new Durkheim texts are discovered and new collections are published. The most recent bibliography of Durkheim's works that uses this system of numbering can be found on the world wide web: http://Durkheim.uchicago.edu/Bibliography/Bib01.html

time to re-think the individual mental processes that accompany the formation of group solidarity.

Durkheim's Injunction against Psychological Explanation in *The Rules of Sociological Method*

As we have seen, Durkheim said that any time a sociological phenomenon is *directly* explained in terms of a psychological phenomenon, the explanation is false. However, he did not define what he meant by "directly." Instead, we are left to figure out what he meant from the context.

For Durkheim, sociology explains social phenomena in terms of their social causes and functions. Social functions are to be distinguished from the conscious goals of individuals. The function of a social fact has to do with its usefulness to society, although it may also produce effects useful to individuals (1895a, 135; 1982a, 134). Sometimes a social institution can even come to serve a new purpose different than the one originally intended. For example, oaths no longer serve as a method of proof but only to solemnize an occasion. Similarly, the causes of social phenomena cannot be found in individual desires, needs, and tendencies. The need that we have for something or our feelings regarding its utility cannot create it out of nothing, he said (1895a, 111–13; 1982a, 120–21). In the essay "Two Laws of Penal Evolution," he added that the fact that something is desirable does not even show that it is possible (1901a(i) [1969c, 260]; 1978a, 167–68). Nor can causes of social phenomena consist in "mental anticipations of the function that they are called upon to fulfill" (1895a, 119; 1982a, 124). Thus, for instance, the cause of the division of labor cannot be an "anticipated representation of its effects" (1902b, 211; 1984a, 179). For Durkheim, to explain a new social institution as created through an act of the will of an individual legislator would be akin to explaining the creation of the universe out of nothingness by appealing to a divine miracle (1912a, 37; 1995, 25). A new social institution can arise only from social causes (ibid.; cf. 1997, 18–19).

The argument that social phenomena cannot be explained in terms of a "mental anticipation" or "anticipated representation" of their effects or functions sounds like an argument against explaining the present in terms of some future state of affairs. Following Donald Davidson

(1963), one might wish to argue that an explanation of some action in terms of someone's intended goal is not an explanation of the present in terms of the future, but an appeal to an agent's present mental state, which contains her goals for the future. However, the problem with the appeal to individual intentions for Durkheim was not just a question of the temporal order of cause and effect. Davidson was interested in explaining individual human action, while Durkheim was writing about the explanation of social phenomena.

For Durkheim, sociological explanations could not be reduced to psychological explanations. Individual psychology cannot explain the power of social constraint that comes from outside the individual (1895a, 125; 1982a, 127). There is the same break in continuity between sociology and psychology that there is between biology on the one hand and physics and chemistry on the other (1895a, 128; 1982a, 129). In the preface to the second edition of *The Rules,* Durkheim added that psychology and sociology have completely separate subject matters, with individual and collective representations forming distinct natural kinds (1901c, xvi; 1982a, 40). As he had explained in *Suicide*, although social life consists in representations, these collective representations are of a totally different nature than individual representations. He had no objection to one regarding sociology as a kind of psychology, as long as one kept in mind that social psychology has its own laws distinct from those of individual psychology (1897a, 352; 1951a, 312).[2] In a letter to the editor of the *Revue néo-scolastique*, defending himself against the charge of having introduced German ideas into French thought, Durkheim replied that the idea that each science explains by its own principles actually went back to Aristotle, and that Auguste Comte, too, had argued that sociology does not reduce to psychology and biology and that biology does not reduce to physics and chemistry (1907b, 613; 1982a, 259). In his article "Individual and Collective Representations," Durkheim asserted that collective representations are distinct from individual representations in the same way that individual representations are from neural states (1898b [1924a, 37–43; 1953b, 23–28]), and in "Sociology in France in the Nineteenth Century," he added that the social realm is as distinct from the psychological as the psychological is from the biological and the biological from the mineral

2 Durkheim made similar remarks in a letter to the editor of the *Revue philosophique*, replying to Gabriel Tarde's charge that Durkheim was moving towards a more psychological conception of sociology (1901d, 704; 1982a, 253).

(1900b [1970a, 128]). Collective representations for Durkheim thus appear to be functionally defined in the same way that individual mental states are for functionalists in psychology and the philosophy of mind. That is, the meanings of collective representations are to be understood in terms of their relations to other collective states in the same way that the meanings of individual mental states are understood in terms of their relations to one another and not to brain states.

Contemporary philosophers such as Margaret Gilbert, Raimo Tuomela, Abraham Roth, Frederick Schmitt, and Philip Pettit have reached conclusions similar to Durkheim's about the relationship between social and psychological facts. They have argued that joint actions cannot be explained simply as the summing up of the outcomes of individual intentional actions. However, they reach their conclusions through an analysis of ordinary language, investigating whether in the explanation of joint action, plural subject concepts such as "we" and "us" can be reduced to or eliminated in favor of terms referring to individuals (see their papers in Schmitt, ed. 2003). Their method can only reveal our common-sense assumptions underlying ordinary usage. In the philosophy of mind, the use of this method may show that our ordinary use of terms for mental states and brain states assumes a kind of dualism, without thereby establishing that dualism must be true. Whether mental states reduce to brain states can be answered only through investigating whether there are any theories in neurophysiology that can explain all the phenomena that our most successful psychological theories can explain. If there are, the translations of our terms for mental states into terms for brain states will then result from this investigation, rather than precede it. Similarly, an analysis of our ordinary terms for plural subject concepts alone cannot tell us whether sociology will reduce to psychology. This question must be answered by investigating whether there are any psychological theories that can account for all of the social facts that our most successful explanatory theories in sociology can explain. In *Suicide* (1897a), Durkheim used this procedure in reverse, arguing that sociology could not reduce to individual psychology because there were no psychological theories that could account for all of the facts that his sociological theory of suicide could explain.

Even if we grant Durkheim's argument that sociology does not reduce to psychology, it does not follow that these two disciplines have nothing to say to each other. An analogy with biology may help to clarify the situation. There are biological concepts such as function that have no correlates at the physical or chemical level. A biological fact such as "the function of the heart is to pump blood" or "the function of the genes is to carry hereditary traits" cannot be explained by physical and chemical laws, even if these laws can explain the mechanics of the pumping action or the chemistry of nucleic acids. However, the fact that these laws can explain *something* that seems relevant shows that it does not follow from the fact that biology does not reduce to the physical sciences that these sciences have nothing to say to biology. Similarly, from the claim that such statements as "the function of religious gatherings is to strengthen social solidarity" cannot be reduced to individual psychology, it does not follow that sociologists may totally ignore research in psychology.

Nevertheless, Durkheim has been read as advocating just such an attitude towards psychology. Evolutionary psychologists such as Leda Cosmides and John Tooby regard Durkheim as a sociological determinist who held that individuals are completely shaped by their cultural and social environments, leaving little for psychology to explain. They quote a passage from *The Rules* where Durkheim spoke of individual human natures as

> merely the indeterminate material that the social factor molds and transforms. Their contribution consists exclusively in very general attitudes, in vague and consequently plastic predispositions which, by themselves, if other agents did not intervene, could not take on the definite and complex forms which characterize social phenomena (Tooby and Cosmides 1992, 24–25, quoting from Durkheim 1938b, 106; cf. 1895a, 130; 1982a, 131).

In *The Moral Animal,* a popular account of evolutionary psychology, Robert Wright (1994, 5–6) quotes part of this passage in support of his interpretation that Durkheim held that the human mind is nothing more than a passive recipient of its society's culture. But there is another way to read this passage, as simply saying that human nature by itself is not sufficient to explain social phenomena. Indeed, this passage occurs just two pages after the one where Durkheim said that social phenomena cannot be directly explained in terms of psychological phenomena.

Also, Durkheim's attacks on appeals to human nature must be considered in historical context. In Chapter V of *The Rules,* where this quoted passage occurs, his targets are the philosophers Comte and Herbert Spencer, who in Durkheim's mind attempted to ground sociology in theories of human nature. He claimed that Comte had tried to explain social progress in terms of a human tendency for progress and that Spencer related it to the need for happiness (1895a, 111; 1982a, 119). Ironically, it was Comte, not Durkheim, who saw no future for psychology. Psychology has no place in Comte's six-fold hierarchy of the sciences, which included only mathematics, astronomy, physics, chemistry, biology, and sociology. Comte thought that whatever human beings are by nature was to be totally explained by biology and that everything else about them was to be explained by sociology. Durkheim never held such an extreme view. For Durkheim, to explain social phenomena in terms of innate tendencies or needs as Comte and Spencer had done was to give them empty verbal explanations, akin to explaining fire in terms of phlogiston or the effects of opium in terms of its dormitive virtue (1895a, 133–34; 1982a, 133). Durkheim's argument is similar to the criticism that philosophers since at least the eighteenth century had been raising against faculty psychology, which attempted to explain our mental abilities by postulating certain faculties that were supposed to be responsible for them, and that philosophers more recently are raising against evolutionary psychology, which postulates mental modules for this purpose. Durkheim made this sort of criticism of Edward Westermarck as well, comparing his appeal to instincts to explain the origin of the institution of marriage and incest prohibitions once again to an appeal to opium's dormitive virtue (1895d, 609). Thus at least some of Durkheim's attacks on the sociological appeal to psychological phenomena amount to attacks on what he considered unscientific, purely verbal explanations in the social sciences. These attacks leave open the possibility of cooperative research with psychologists who employ more rigorous methods.

In *The Rules,* Durkheim recognized that psychology had become more scientific in the last thirty years, just to the extent it had come to consider psychological facts as things in nature. However, he criticized it for continuing to rely on the unscientific introspective methods of philosophers such as Locke and Condillac. According to Durkheim, the facts that introspection reveals are "too rare, too fleeting, too malleable" to serve as controls or counterweights to the ideas that habit has fixed in us (1895a, 38; 1982a, 71). Durkheim's readers at the time would have recognized his reference to Locke and Condillac as an implied criticism of the inheritors of this empiricist tradition in philosophy, the nineteenth-century French spiritualist tradition that derives from the work of François-Pierre-Gonthier Maine de Biran and Victor Cousin. The leading representative of this school in late nineteenth-century France was Paul Janet, a philosopher who had served on Durkheim's dissertation committee and had formerly been Cousin's amanuensis. However, even Janet had come to recognize the need for experimental and physiological psychology, encouraging his nephew Pierre Janet, a former classmate of Durkheim's at the *École normale supérieure*, to go to medical school so he could take up research in this area. Pierre Janet was promoting experimental psychology in France at about the same time that Durkheim was trying to establish sociology as an empirical social science discipline (Brooks 1998, ch. 5). Durkheim appears to have had great respect for what he called the "revolution" that was taking place in psychology (1895a, 38; 1982a, 71). This would have included the experimental work of Wilhelm Wundt, whose laboratory Durkheim had visited during his fellowship visit to Germany as a young man in the years 1885–1886. In *The Elementary Forms,* Durkheim regarded experimental and comparative psychology as taking over the domain traditionally explained by Christian accounts of the soul, much as Christianity had already ceded explanations of physical phenomena to the sciences: "Experimental and comparative psychology has been constituted and today must be counted among the sciences" (1912a, 614; 1995, 431).

Durkheim in fact had so much respect for the emerging traditions in experimental psychology that he held them up as a model for sociology, arguing that it, too, must abandon subjective methods in favor of more objective ones (1895a, 38; 1982a, 71). In the preface to the second edition of *The Rules,* Durkheim said that social facts cannot be studied through mental analysis and that the mind must go outside itself and employ experiment and observation (1901c, xi; 1982a, 36). Earlier, in the introduction to the first edition of *The Division of Labor in Society,* he had argued that introspective methods cannot be used to study moral rules in contemporary society because of individual differences (1893b, 24–25; 1933b, 425). Thus Durkheim saw the need to study a society's collective consciousness through its observable effects or signs, such as its codes of law (1902b, 28; 1984a, 24). In *Suicide,* he had attacked Gabriel Tarde for relying on introspection (1897a, 350–351; 1951a, 311). The collective tendencies responsible for the social suicide rates are known only through their effects (1897a, 348; 1951a, 309). In a letter to Célestin Bouglé, dated 6 July 1897, Durkheim argued that society does not exist in any individual but in individuals organized in a certain way, and concluded that one thus cannot do sociology through the analysis of individual consciousnesses (1975a, 2: 400). He felt that introspection was an unreliable method even for psychology, let alone sociology. At a meeting of the *Société française de philosophie,* Durkheim argued that in psychology, introspection can reveal only psychological effects and not their underlying causes, and that the situation is even more dire in sociology, where the underlying causes are even more hidden from consciousness (1908a(3), 230; 1982a, 212).[3]

However, Durkheim equivocated on this last point in *The Elementary Forms*, in which he argued that we can perceive not only the effects of social forces, but the very operation of these causes, since they take place entirely inside of us (1912a, 522; 1995, 369). We will take up this problem below in our discussion of Durkheim's sociology of knowledge in *The Elementary Forms*.

Suicide and Psychology

Suicide at first appears to be a frontal assault on psychology, since the lonely suicide is central to the explanatory domain of individual psychology, and Durkheim was proposing to replace psychological explanations of suicide with social causes. However, the goal of this work was to provide social causes only for social suicide rates and not for individual suicides. Durkheim provided evidence that these rates could not be accounted for in terms of the distribution of such "extra-social factors" as mental illness, race, and heredity. He did not think that individual suicides could be explained simply by narrowing down the classes to which these individuals belonged. For instance, he held that Protestants committed suicide more often than Catholics and bachelors more often than married men with children. Of course, not all Protestant bachelors commit suicide. However, Durkheim did not think that one could explain the suicide of an individual Protestant bachelor just by finding additional social factors that applied to this individual.

In fact, one of the ways in which Durkheim distinguished his sociology from Tarde's was precisely through his postulation of individual psychological processes that mediate social facts and individual actions and are distinct from Tarde's imitation. According to Durkheim, to act out of respect for tradition or fear of public opinion is not to act by imitation. Even when we revolt against custom, although our motives may be different,

3 In a review of a work by Antonio Labriola, Durkheim said that he shared with the historical materialists the idea that social life is to be explained by hidden causes that escape our consciousness (1897e [1970a, 250]; 1978a, 127; 1982a, 171).

> the psychological mechanism is identically the same. Either way, between the representation of the act and its execution, an intellectual operation that consists in an apprehension, clear or confused, rapid or slow, of the determining character, whatever it is, inserts itself. (1897a, 113; 1951a, 127.)

The same would be true for the social forces of integration and regulation that preserve individuals from suicide. That is, there would also be an intellectual operation that mediates the operation of these social forces on individuals. For instance, *Suicide* provides evidence that the suicide rate is inversely correlated with number of children a man has. But as Alexander Rosenberg has argued, surely Durkheim must have meant the number of *known* children. Unknown illegitimate children could not preserve one from suicide (Rosenberg 1980, 33–34). Nor, one could add, would children that had been put up for adoption.

Durkheim's explanatory concepts in *Suicide* reveal that he did not think that humans were infinitely plastic beings who could be molded by their societies in an indefinite number of ways. Suicide rates are to be explained in terms the levels of social integration and regulation, with integration having to do with interpersonal, interdependent relationships of mutual aid and support, and regulation having to do with legal and moral rules that set limits to acting on economic or sexual desires. Egoistic suicide results from too little integration and altruistic suicide or self-sacrifice results from too much, while anomic and fatalistic result from either too little or too much regulation, respectively. The very ideas of anomic and egoistic suicide imply that people have a basic need to be integrated into and regulated by society. As Massimo Rosati (2008, 56) points out, why would individuals suppress their individual desires and suffer constraint as members of society, unless this kind of suffering were less severe than that which results from unregulated desires and a lack of social integration? Mark Cladis (2008) and Giovanni Paoletti (2008) have similarly argued that for Durkheim, society completes us and makes us whole. Durkheim would have no doubt rejected the suggestion that there could be a society or a culture that shapes people in such a way that they would feel happy or well-adjusted living with only minimal human contact and few rules.

The Division of Labor in Society and the Need for Human Contact

We can find similar assumptions about a basic psychological need for human society in *The Division of Labor in Society*. This work rejects purely economic explanations of specialization. According to Durkheim, human beings did not specialize simply to produce more. Increased production is merely a side-effect of a phenomenon that depends on other kinds of social factors (1902b, 259; 1984a, 217). He also argued that individual desires to increase human happiness could not bring about the division of labor, just as he subsequently proscribed individual psychological explanations from sociology in *The Rules* (1902b, 211–12; 1984a, 179–80). In both of these works, Durkheim made it clear that the division of labor could not be explained in terms of an anticipation of the advantages it would bring. Its good effects could not even be perceived until it had already begun to exist (1895a, 115; 1982a, 122). Nevertheless, even though it could not be explained in terms of individual intentions, the division of labor depended at least in part on the psychological make-up of human beings for Durkheim.

In providing a causal explanation for the division of labor, Durkheim appealed to a Darwinian struggle for existence among human beings, in which the key to survival is to avoid having to compete with others through specialization. He quoted passages from *On the Origin of Species* and a work by Ernst Haeckel regarding how the more diversified the forms of life are in any given area, the more living things that could be supported there. This same explanation, he said, applies to specialization among human beings (1902b, 249; 1984a, 209). According to Durkheim, Darwin called this the "law of the divergence of characteristics" (1902b, 259; 1984a, 217).[4] Although Durkheim drew his examples from economic life, he said that the same explanation applies to all social functions, scientific, artistic, etc. (1902b, 253; 1984a, 212).

However, Durkheim should not be understood as having offered a purely biological explanation of a human social phenomenon. As he said in a review of a work by Westermarck, "to make sociology rest on Darwinism, is to set the science upon an hypothesis, which is contrary to all good method" (1895d, 608). The division of labor in human society depends on social conditions. If individuals who are unknown to one an-

4 Darwin actually called this a principle, not a law.

other come into competition, they will simply disperse. If they reach the limits of the land and are unable to disperse any further, competition will give rise to hostility, which cannot bring people together. For competition to give rise to the division of labor, connections among people must already exist: "it is necessary that the individuals who are engaged in the struggle are already united (*solidaire*) and sense it, that is to say belong to the same society" (1902b, 260; 1984a, 217). If on the other hand "the sentiment of solidarity is too weak to resist the dispersive influence of competition," it will produce completely different effects. Instead of specializing, the inhabitants of a densely populated area will emigrate to other regions (ibid.). In *The Rules*, other possible solutions to the struggle for existence include emigration, suicide, and crime (1895a, 115; 1982a, 122). However, Durkheim also said that for specialization to occur, at the same time the collective consciousness must weaken. That is, the pressure to conform must diminish and the expression of individual differences must become possible (1902b, 268; 1984a, 226–27). The collective consciousness grows weaker as the society increases and spreads over a larger area and people have different experiences and form different ideas; the ideas they have in common become more abstract (1902b, 272; 1984a, 230).[5] In sum, for the division of labor to occur, there must be a waning of shared ideas while at the same time there remains enough social solidarity to make people want to stick together in spite of population pressures. In short, social conditions have to be just right.

Assuredly, many have interpreted Durkheim as having explained the division of labor as due to causes in the physical environment such as population density.[6] However, in both *Division* and *The Rules*, Durkheim distinguished population density from what he called the social or moral density, which is a function not simply of the number of individuals in a society but of the number and strength of the relationships

5 According to Durkheim, the collective consciousness never entirely disappears. It only becomes more general and indeterminate (1902b, 146–147; 1984, 122).

6 The list of people who have read *The Division of Labor in Society* this way would include Jeffrey Alexander (1982, 1986), Charles Andler (1896, 255 n. 1), Paul Barth (1897, 296), Léon Brunschvicg and Élie Halévy (1894), Paul Bureau (1924, 113), R. A. Jones (1986, 41 f), Joseph Llobera (1980, 398), Steven Lukes (1973, 167 f), Talcott Parsons (1937), Dietrich Rueschemeyer (1982), Georges Sorel (1895, 148), Göran Therborn (1976, 254), Kenneth Thompson (1982, 67, 83; 1985, 15, 17), and Jonathan Turner (1990, 1094). I investigate the reasons for this interpretation in Schmaus 1995.

among them. He tried to make it clear that only the social density, which for him is a social fact, and not the mere population density, could be causally responsible for a social phenomenon such as labor specialization. If anything, population density is an effect, not a cause, of social phenomena for Durkheim. For instance, in explaining the rise of towns, he said "But towns always result from the need that pushes individuals constantly to keep in the closest possible contact with one another" (1902b, 239; 1984a, 202). He then went on to explain that towns are like points where the social mass is contracting more strongly than elsewhere and thus that towns multiply and spread as the result of the increase in moral density (1902b, 239–40; 1984a, 202).

While the rise of towns for Durkheim may be due to the increase in moral density, moral density in turn appears to be linked to psychological causes, that is, to this "need" that people have to remain in constant contact with one another. One might then object that I have rescued Durkheim's sociology from economic materialist or biological reductionist interpretations only by saddling him with the very sort of appeal to psychology and human nature that he subsequently rejected in *The Rules*. To raise this objection, however, would be to misunderstand Durkheim's account of specialization and the rise of towns. As we have seen, in *The Rules* Durkheim said that social phenomena are not to be *directly* explained in terms of psychological phenomena. But in *Division*, neither specialization nor the rise of towns is *directly* explained in terms of human nature. Rather, they are explained in terms of such social phenomena as social or moral density and what he called "secondary factors," including the weakening of the collective consciousness. Nor could one argue that social density is directly explained in terms of psychological causes. Durkheim allowed for the possibility of feelings of social solidarity being too weak and the population dispersing. Social density thus appears to depend on social as well as psychological causes. How social solidarity may be formed and strengthened is a question he returned to in *The Elementary Forms of Religious Life*.

Durkheim's Sociology of Knowledge and Religion in *The Elementary Forms of Religious Life*

Durkheim had two goals in *The Elementary Forms of Religious Life*. One was to explain the origins of religion by examining its earliest forms. But the work also contained his sociology of knowledge, which aimed to provide a sociological explanation of the most basic categories of human thought. Some have taken his sociological theory of the categories to support sociological determinism. This would include the social anthropologist Max Gluckman (1949–50), who held that collective representations determine how people perceive even shapes and colors, and Mary Douglas (1970, 20), who has seen an affinity between Durkheim's sociology of knowledge and the Sapir-Whorf hypothesis of linguistic determinism. Drawing also on the paper on primitive classification that Durkheim wrote with his nephew Marcel Mauss (1903a(i); 1963b), Max Horkheimer and Theodor Adorno (1997, 21) interpret his sociology of knowledge as entailing that even logic is socially constructed, with the deductive structure of science reflecting social hierarchy and coercion.

The sociological determinist interpretation of Durkheim's theory of knowledge rests on his identification of the categories with their collective representations, which are social-cultural products. A culture's system of classification and other collective representations are thought to shape perception just as the Kantian categories are supposed to do. However, Durkheim's categories are not the same as Kant's. Durkheim had an open-ended list that included time, space, genus, number, cause, substance, and personality (1912a, 12–13; 1995, 8–9). Kant, on the other hand, had a closed, systematic list of twelve categories, which were distinct from space and time, which he considered forms of intuition. In fact, the only categories on both lists are substance and cause. In a version of the introduction to *The Elementary Forms* that Durkheim had published three years previously, he explained that for "the recent disciples of Kant . . . the categories preform the real, whereas for us, they recapitulate it. According to them, they are the natural law of thought; for us, they are a product of human art." (1909d, 757 and n. 1; t. 1982a, 239–40 and n. 1). Contemporary Kant scholars might insist that Kant had said that the categories are only the logically necessary conditions of experience and not the temporal antecedents. But the "recent disciples of Kant" to whom Durkheim referred in this passage understood the categories as psychological preconditions of experience (Schmaus 2004). However, Durkheim identified his categories with neither the logical nor psychological conditions of experience, but with culturally variable systems of representing directions, times, causal relations, and kinds of things in nature. Contrary to an oft-repeated criticism, Durkheim was not begging the question by trying to derive the Kantian categories from the experience of the forms and patterns of social life.[7] Durkheim's critics rightly object that the categories could not be causally derived from experience if they made this experience possible in the first place. In his *lycée* philosophy course in 1884, Durkheim had in fact raised this very same objection against Spencer's attempt to derive the Kantian categories and forms of intuition from experience (1884a, 135–36; 2004, 102). It seems highly unlikely that Durkheim could have begged the question in the same way that Spencer had, especially given his published statement that the categories for him were not preconditions of experience.

Indeed, without the distinction between something like Kant's sense of a category and Durkheim's, the latter's argument that his sociological theory of the categories can explain their cultural variability as well as their necessity and universality simply makes no sense at all (1912a, 19–21; 1995, 13–14). What he meant was that different cultures have different collective or cultural representations of the same basic set of categories, which are necessary because of the important social functions they serve. The collective representations of the categories make interpersonal communication and thus social life possible. All cultures have concepts of space and time, although cultural systems for measuring distance and time will vary. Collective representations of the category of time provide a system for fixing dates and times so that people can be gathered for hunts, battles, celebrations, and religious rituals. Collective representations of causal relationships make it possible for people to cooperate with the same end in view and to hold one another responsible for their actions. Similarly, all cultures have some concept of genus or kind, although their systems of classification are variable. Society also needs a way of classifying individuals into groups that are then classified in relation to each other, for instance to preserve exogamy. Collective representations of space allow society to divide territory among these groups according to a system of directions recog-

7 Dennes 1924, 39; cf. also Schaub 1920, 336–37. More recently, this objection has been raised by Godlove (1986, 392–93; 1989, 32) and Lukes (1973, 447).

nized by everyone and thus to avoid conflict (1912a, 16; 1995, 11). The function of the categories, for Durkheim, is not to organize experience, but to organize social life.

Durkheim never denied that there were psychological capacities that corresponded to the categories and did not depend upon them. According to Durkheim, "the relations that the categories express exist, in an implicit manner, in individual consciousnesses" (1912a, 628; 1995, 441). Thus, an individual human being has no more need than an animal does of the category of space in order to orient herself. Nor does an individual human being need the category of time in order to satisfy her needs. Similarly, a human being does not need the category of a genus to recognize that one thing resembles another or the category of causality in order to seek her prey and avoid her enemies (1912a, 632; 1995, 444). For Durkheim, the categories depend upon these individual psychological abilities. For instance, he said that even the most primitive systems of classification presuppose the psychological capacity to recognize resemblances among the particular things the mind perceives (1912a, 206; 1995, 146).

In fact, Durkheim held that collective representations are initially formed from individual mental representations. In *The Division*, in which he was still referring to collective representations as states of the collective consciousness, he described a process by which they are formed through the "fusion" of mental representations in individual minds. Somebody expresses an idea in front of us that is the same as one we already have. These ideas then fuse, resulting in a new idea with greater vitality or liveliness than either of the originals (1902b, 67; 1984a, 55). This is clearly a psychological process. One could try to reconcile this passage with his injunction in *The Rules* against psychological explanation by interpreting him as intending that only the *results* of the process of fusion and not the process itself can directly explain social phenomena. One could also say that this process is going on in the mind of each individual concomitantly or contemporaneously with a social process, without this social process thereby reducing to the psychological process. In other words, social facts for Durkheim may supervene on psychological facts in the same way that some contemporary philosophers say that mental processes supervene on brain processes. In "Individual and Collective Representations," Durkheim tried to reconcile the psychological process of fusion with the injunction against psychological explanation another way. He said that once formed, collective representations take on a life of their own, interacting with one another and giving rise to additional collective representations (1898b [1924a, 46; 1953b, 31]). In *The Elementary Forms*, he went a step further and said that the fusion of similar images in an individual mind is *not* sufficient to produce the categories. Here he distinguished the category of a genus from its contents. The contents are formed by the superposition and fusion of images, but are vague and fluctuating, while the category is like a framework with definite borders or limits (1912a, 209, 629; 1995, 147–48, 441–42).

In *The Elementary Forms*, Durkheim's account of the formation of collective representations is linked to his sociology of religion. Here he provided an account of effervescent assemblies during which collective representations, social solidarity, and totemism, the earliest religion, are all formed together. This occurs when the members of a society assemble together and their emotions react upon one another to give rise to a sort of heightened enthusiasm that Durkheim called "collective effervescence," which the members of the society attribute to the presence of religious forces. What happens in these effervescent assemblies brings to mind his account of the formation of states of the collective consciousness in his earlier work, *The Division of Labor in Society*. According to Durkheim, individual consciousnesses are initially closed to one another. For the "fusion" of sentiments to occur, these sentiments must all be expressed by the same cry, the same word, or a gesture directed toward the same object, which then becomes a sacred totemic emblem. The collective sentiment has to focus on some object in order to become conscious of itself. But the emblem is also necessary to keep these feelings alive in the minds of individuals after the gathering is over (1912a, 329–31; 1995, 231–33). There are some interesting differences between this account and that in *The Division*. In the earlier work, he spoke of the psychological fusion of similar images. But in the later work, it was the fusion of ideas that would otherwise appear distinct. That is, the ideas of the clan and the religious force or power become fused with the idea of the totemic emblem. Furthermore, this fusion appears to depend at least in part on social causes, as it occurs as the result of effervescent assemblies (1912a, 339; 1995, 238). Finally, in the earlier work, Durkheim spoke only of the formation of collectively held mental states, while in *The Elementary Forms* he was also explaining the way in which items in the physical environment become public representations.

The totemic emblem becomes the symbol of both the clan and the totemic principle or power because this religious power and the society are one and the same (1912a, 294–95; 1995, 208). According to Durkheim, the primitives who attribute the experience of collective excitement to the presence of religious forces are not deluded. Their experiences are genuine. It is just that they are due to the social forces that are generated in these effervescent assemblies. When the primitives attribute what they have experienced to the powers residing in the sacred emblem, they are simply wrong about the name of the cause (1912a, 322–24; 1995, 226–28). According to Durkheim, religion is not founded on illusion. He in fact rejected the alternative hypotheses that religion originated either with animism or naturism precisely because they attribute religion to illusion and illogic. According to the first hypothesis, religion began with a belief in souls or spirits, while according to the second, it began with the worship of natural phenomena such as the sky or fire. It is true that Durkheim did speak of "that species of delirium that indeed every religion in some sense is" (1912a, 124; 1995, 85). However, Durkheim added that the sort of delirium that he put at the basis of religion is a "well-founded" delirium, unlike the illusory images at the basis of animistic and naturistic religions (1912a, 324; 1995, 228). He argued that it is better described as a kind of idealism rather than a delusion, comparing the religious delusion to the way in which odors, tastes, and colors are not in bodies in the way that we perceive them, or to the way in which the value of a philatelist's prized possession is not in the piece of paper on which the stamp is printed. For Durkheim, the philosophy of idealism is more true in the social realm than anywhere else, for here the idea creates the reality (1912a, 325–27; 1995, 229–30).[8]

Durkheim did not think that identifying god with society would result in undermining religion. In a speech given in 1914 at a meeting of the *Union des Libres Penseurs et de Libres Croyants pour la Culture Morale*, he asked believers for their toleration, suggested that they consider their confessional formulations as merely provisional expressions, and asked them to join him in investigating their underlying reality. He added that those who have characterized his way of interpreting religion as irreligious are simply mistaken. A sociology of religion could not deny the existence of the very thing it is trying to explain (1919b [1970a, 310]). Nor did he think that religion would ever disappear. The source of religion will never run dry:

8 See also Ilkka Pyysiäinen's (2005) discussion of the problem of delirium in Durkheim's sociology of religion.

> Over and above all the dogmas and all the confessions, there exists a source of religious life as old as humanity and that will never dry up: it is that which results from the fusion of consciousnesses, from their communion in the same thought, from their cooperation in the same work, from the morally invigorating and stimulating action that every community of men exercises on its members. (1919b [1970a, 311]).

As Durkheim had explained in *The Elementary Forms*, collective rituals have a kind of restorative force for individuals. People return to their profane lives with more energy and enthusiasm, having lived for a few moments a life that is "less tense, more at ease, and more free" (1912a, 547; 1995, 386). For Durkheim, human beings seem to have a psychological need for these assemblies in the same way that in his earlier works he thought they have a need for social solidarity.

There is no reason to fear that the heavens will ever empty out, Durkheim told those at the meeting of free thinkers and believers, since it is we ourselves who people it with gods. The only reason it appears that religion is on the decline is that we live in a transitional period, when old ideals and divinities are dying out and the new ones have not yet been born. Beneath the "moral chill" that reigns over our collective life, there are "sources of heat" where new religious forces are in the process of formation, particularly within the working classes (1919b [1970a, 311–13]). Of course, not all those in attendance accepted Durkheim's explanation. Gustav Belot insisted that Durkheim was implying that all religions are false to the extent they did not accept Durkheim's account of religion. Also, there are other social institutions that could fulfill what Durkheim regarded as the essential function of religion, which is to provide a basis for social cohesion (Lukes 1973, 518).

Another objection that was brought up by some of Durkheim's earliest critics, including Henri Delacroix, Daniel Essertier, and Alexander A. Goldenweiser, was that his account of collective effervescence derived from Gustave Le Bon's work on crowd psychology. Thus it violated Durkheim's own methodological precepts against the appeal to psychological explanations in sociology (Pickering 1984, 396; 2008, 77). Steven Lukes (1973, 462 n. 45), however, finds no evidence that Durkheim drew on Le Bon's work and suggests that Durkheim would not have regarded Le Bon as a serious social scientist. Nevertheless, Pickering reports that similar objections have been raised more recently by Edward Evans-Pritchard and Mary Douglas. To be sure, one could argue that in effervescent assemblies, people's emotions run free, and thus lacking any apparent form of social constraint, such events do not appear to fit Durkheim's definition of a social phenomenon. However, it is not clear that an effervescent assembly is a psychological phenomenon, either, at least not one of individual psychology. An effervescent assembly cannot be defined simply as the sum of individual emotional behaviors. One individual acting alone, or even two or more complete strangers in the same room displaying emotion, would not illustrate what Durkheim meant by effervescence. Pickering writes about glossolalia in Pentecostalist churches as a contemporary example of what Durkheim had in mind. One person speaking in tongues in private prayer would not count. Even for a collection of individuals speaking in tongues to count as an effervescent assembly, there would also have to be some form of interaction and organization. Pickering argues that Durkheim, in writing about effervescent assemblies, did not use the word *foule* or crowd. Rather, he spoke of *rassemblement,* or sometimes *effervescence des assemblées,* which carry a much stronger sense of *we.* An assembly, unlike a crowd or mob, is organized in some way; it is a group of people with some notion of common purpose and identity (Pickering 1984, 393–98). In *Moral Education*, Durkheim defined a society as a "permanent and organized crowd" (1925a, 71; 1961a, 62).

A more serious problem with Durkheim's account of effervescent assemblies has to do with what he said about the experience of social or religious forces. As I mentioned above, in *The Elementary Forms*, Durkheim appeared to equivocate on the question whether we are able to perceive the operation of social forces or only their effects. In his earlier works, he had said that we can perceive only their effects. This was one of the reasons he gave for rejecting introspective methods in sociology. But in arguing for the social and religious origins of the categories in *The Elementary Forms*, he said that the origin of our idea of a causal force or power was in our experience of social or religious forces. As I mentioned above, Durkheim maintained that social forces are unlike physical forces in that we can perceive social forces in operation and not just their effects, since social forces take place entirely inside us (1912a, 522; 1995, 369). But for the purpose of arguing that the origin of religion is in the collective effervescence experienced during totemic rites, all Durkheim needed to say was that the primitives experience the *effects* of these social forces, which are the feelings of well-being with which they can return to their profane lives. Perhaps then his purpose here was simply to argue for the social origins of the category of causality. His polemic appears to have been directed against the spiritualist tradition of Maine de Biran and Cousin, according to which the source of our idea of force or power and thus of the category of causation was our introspective experience of willed effort (Schmaus 2004). However, it would have been unnecessary for Durkheim to change his philosophical position in order to undermine the spiritualist point of view. His original claim that one could experience only the effects of causal powers would in fact have made for a stronger argument against this tradition, since Durkheim's position in *The Elementary Forms* only begs the question whether we can introspect psychological as well as social causes.

There is another reason that it was unnecessary for Durkheim to have tried to argue that we can experience social forces in action. In his sociological theory of the categories, he had distinguished two parts to the idea of cause: the idea of force or power, and the idea of a necessary connection. He then said that the idea of a necessary connection had a social origin in the obligation of the members of a society to participate in religious rites (1912a, 524–25; 1995, 370–71). It is not entirely clear whether this is supposed to be a causal or a functional explanation, or both. Nevertheless, Durkheim's insight was that the notion of an obligation presupposes that of a necessary connection, and thus that the idea of a necessary connection makes moral rules and thus society possible. The idea of force or power plays no role here. On the contrary, as Rousseau had argued, one is not obligated to do what one is forced to do.

Many of the ambiguities and other difficulties in Durkheim's sociology of knowledge can be traced to the fact that he was still working within the philosophical way of ideas tradition. Like Descartes, Locke, and many of his philosophical predecessors, Durkheim had no other way of talking about concepts except as some sort of mental entity. Even collective representations are a type of mental entity for him. Thus it was difficult for him to make a distinction between a concept and the way in which it is represented, or to express what two different representations of the same concept share in common. When he wrote about members of a society having or expressing similar ideas, he was thinking about mental images that resembled one another. With this rather limited notion of the way in which people may have similar ideas, Durkheim thought that only in primitive societies where everyone shared the same experiences could there be a collective consciousness of shared ideas. Other problems stem from his not always having been careful to distinguish causal from functional explanations, in spite of his warnings in *The Rules* about keeping these separate. If we are not careful to make these distinctions ourselves, it would appear that Durkheim had shown that certain concepts or categories have social causes. What in fact he has shown is that these concepts or categories have social functions and that the ways in which cultures represent them have social causes. This is not to deny that concepts can have social causes; it is only to argue that Durkheim did not succeed in showing that they do.

Conclusion

We have seen that although Durkheim held that social phenomena cannot be explained in terms of psychological phenomena, that he had the greatest respect for some recent developments in psychology. He may have dismissed philosophical psychologies that offered empty verbal explanations or relied on introspection. But what he called "experimental and comparative psychology" was here to stay and could claim its rightful place among the sciences. I think it would be safe to say that he would have recognized what are currently called the cognitive sciences as part of the latter. Furthermore, in spite of the weaknesses I have pointed out in Durkheim's sociology of knowledge, *The Elementary Forms* has nevertheless identified several related areas for possible cooperative research among disciplines such as the sociology of knowledge, cultural anthropology, anthropological linguistics, and cognitive psychology.

One such topic would be the relationship between individual mental capacities and a culture's ways of representing concepts such as space, time, and causality. The cognitive sciences may investigate the basic underlying capacities that make it possible for people to perceive spatial, temporal, causal, and resemblance relations, while the social sciences may study the culturally variable representations through which people communicate about these relations and that thus help to make social life possible. In fact, such research is already underway. Scott Atran (1995, 218) has argued that cultural representations can amplify human conceptual abilities, by for instance clarifying our concepts and drawing further distinctions among them. Over time the sciences continue to refine our concepts of space, time, kind, and causality. The law, too, has been gradually distinguishing different senses of responsibility and thus refining our concept of causality. Durkheim himself compared the collective representations of the categories to tools, regarding them as works of human art that are depositories of human intellectual capital that over time come to represent real relations in nature ever more perfectly (1912a, 25–28; 1995, 17–18; and footnotes). But of course for us to accept Atran's thesis about cultural representations, we must first know what our psychological capacities are. I do not mean to suggest that social scientists have to wait until the psychologists are done with their investigations. Rather, it is only through cooperation that scientists can sort out what is cultural and what is part of our natural endowment. For instance, psychology cannot assume that a concept universally found in all human societies is therefore innate, if the social sciences can explain this fact in terms of convergent cultural development (see Schmaus 2003).

Another possible subject for cooperative investigation concerns Durkheim's claim about the relationship between effervescent assemblies and the formation of collective representations. It appears unlikely, to say the least, that concepts are formed in this manner, given the examples of the refinement of our categorical concepts in the sciences and the law. But if Durkheim is wrong, this only raises such questions as just what are the social conditions that will lead the courts to refine the law of torts so as to hold a defendant causally responsible for damages in such a way that has not been done before, and just what are the social ramifications of this reform? Similarly, what social processes accompany a major change in a system of scientific classification? And so on. Durkheim held that systems for representing categorical concepts are necessary for social life. This raises the question how the development of our concepts may reflect the changing requirements of social life.

But even if effervescent assemblies play no role in the formation or refinement of our concepts, there are other aspects of these social phenomena that can be investigated. Pickering (1984, 399) argues that Durkheim was interested only in the social outcome and not in the psychological phenomenon of individuals losing their self-control in an assembly. Nevertheless, the psychologist would welcome help from the sociologist in identifying the social conditions that are conducive to the individual losing self-control, while the psychologist could help the sociologist in identifying situations in which individuals have genuinely lost such control. It is necessary to identify such situations in order to test whether effervescent assemblies do in fact give rise to feelings of well-being and social solidarity, and to investigate the role that emblems, dances, chants, and other public representations play in these situations. As we have seen, Durkheim thought that people have a psychological need for these experiences of collective effervescence and derive a psychological benefit from participating in them. Testing these claims could be a further area for cooperative research between social sciences and psychology.

For instance, suppose social scientists and psychologists were to identify those conditions under which individuals genuinely lose their self-control at sporting events, rock concerts, or political demonstrations. They could then investigate whether people do in fact come away from such events feeling invigorated. If Durkheim were right about the role of public representations in effervescent assemblies, it would help to explain how it is that people will invest so much emotional energy and wealth on sports teams, buying pennants, items of clothing with team logos, and so on. These are things that economics alone would have trouble explaining: why buy clothing with team logos when unadorned items would cost less? Similarly for rock concerts: Why do people go to them when the tickets are so expensive and they could probably see the band members more clearly on a rock video played at home?

Critics will say that this is not religion. But if Durkheim were right about the benefits of effervescent assemblies, and if some people found that religion did not provide these benefits for them, they may seek out other venues to take its place. Furthermore, these critics could be begging the question by assuming that religion is defined in terms of beliefs in deities or the supernatural, rather than Durkheim's way, in terms of an institution organized around a set of beliefs concerning the distinction between sacred and profane. Certainly sports memorabilia can take on a sacred character among members of a fan club. So can election memorabilia for political junkies. And how is it that rock stars have recently come to be called "rock gods"?

References

Alexander, Jeffrey. (1982). *Theoretical logic in sociology*. Berkeley, CA: University of California Press.

Alexander, Jeffrey. (1986). Rethinking Durkheim's intellectual development I: On 'Marxism' and the anxiety of being misunderstood. *International Sociology* 1, 91–107.

Andler, Charles. (1896). Sociologie et démocratie. *Revue de métaphysique et de morale* 4, 243–56.

Atran, Scott. (1995). Causal constraints on categories and categorical constraints on biological reasoning across cultures. In *Causal cognition: A multidisciplinary debate*, edited by Dan Sperber, David Premack, & Ann Premack. Oxford: Clarendon Press.

Barth, Paul. (1897). *Die Philosophie der Geschichte als Soziologie*. Leipzig, Germany: O.R. Reisland.

Brooks, John I., III. (1998). *The eclectic legacy: Academic philosophy and the human sciences in nineteenth-century France*. Newark, DE: University of Delaware Press.

Brunschvicg, Léon, & Élie Halévy. (1894). L'Année philosophique 1893. *Revue de métaphysique et de morale* 2, 564–90.

Bureau, Paul. (1924). *Introduction à la méthode sociologique*. Paris, France: Librairie Bloud & Gay.

Cladis, Mark S. (2008). Suffering to Become Human: A Durkheimian Perspective. In *Suffering and evil: The Durkheimian legacy*, edited by W. S. F. Pickering & Massimo Rosati. New York: Durkheim Press/Berghahn Books.

Davidson, Donald. (1963). Actions, reasons, and causes. *Journal of Philosophy* 60, 685–700.

Dennes, William Ray. (1924). *The methods and presuppositions of group psychology*. (University of California Publications in Philosophy 6(1), 1–182.) Berkeley, CA: University of California Press.

Douglas, Mary. (1970). *Natural symbols: Explorations in cosmology*. New York: Pantheon Books.

Durkheim, Émile. (1884a). "Cours de philosophie fait au Lycée de Sens." Bibliothèque de la Sorbonne, manuscript number 2351. Also available from the University of Wisconsin – Madison, Microforms Center, film number 9307, and on the world wide web: http://Durkheim.uchicago.edu/Texts/1884a/00.html (Translated in Durkheim 2004).

Durkheim, Émile. (1893b). *De la division du travail social: étude sur l'organisation des sociétés supérieures*. Paris: Alcan. Translated 1933b, 1984a. The pages from the introduction to the first edition that were removed in subsequent editions have been reprinted in 1975a, vol. 2, 257–88 and translated in 1933b, 411–35.

Durkheim, Émile. (1895a). *Les Règles de la méthode sociologique*. Paris: Alcan. (Translated 1938b, 1982a.)

Durkheim, Émile. (1895d). L'Origine du mariage dans l'espèce humaine d'après Westermarck. *Revue philosophique* 40, 606–23. Reprinted in 1975a, vol. III, 70–92.

Durkheim, Émile. (1897a). *Le suicide: étude de sociologie*. Paris: Alcan. (Translated in 1951a.)

Durkheim, Émile. (1897e). Review of Labriola, Antonio, *Essais sur la conception matérialiste de l'histoire*. *Revue philosophique* 44, 645–51. Reprinted in 1970a, ch. 9. (Translated in 1978a, 123–130; 1982a, 167–174.)

Durkheim, Émile. (1898b). Représentations individuelles et représentations collectives. *Revue de métaphysique et de morale* 6, 273–302. Reprinted in 1924a, pp. 13–50. (Translated in 1953b, 1–34.)

Durkheim, Émile. (1900b). La sociologie en France au XIXe siècle. *Revue bleue*, 4th series, 12, 609–13, 647–52. Reprinted in 1970a, 111–36.

Durkheim, Émile. (1901a(i)). Deux lois de l'évolution pénale," *L'Année sociologique* 4, 65–96. Reprinted in 1969c, pp. 245–273. (Translated in 1978a, 153–80.)

Durkheim, Émile. (1901c). *Les Règles de la méthode sociologique*, 2nd. ed.Paris: Alcan. Translated in 1938b, 1982a.

Durkheim, Émile. (1901d). Lettre au Directeur de la *Revue philosophique*. *Revue philosophique* 52, 704. Reprinted in 1975a, vol. I, 52–53. (Translated in 1982a, 253–54.)

Durkheim, Émile. (1902b). *De la division du travail social*, 2nd. ed. Paris: Alcan. (Translated in 1933b, 1984a.)

Durkheim, Émile. (1907b). Lettres au Directeur de la *Revue néo-scolastique*. *Revue néo-scolastique* 14, 606–07, 612–14. Reprinted in 1975a, vol. I, pp. 401–405. (Translated in 1982a, 257–60.)

Durkheim, Émile. (1903a(i)). With Marcel Mauss. De quelque formes primitives de classification: contribution à l'étude des représentations collectives. *L'Année sociologique* 6, 1–72. Reprinted in 1969c, 395–461. (Translated in 1963b.)

Durkheim, Émile. (1908a(3)). L'inconnue et l'inconscient en histoire. *Bulletin de la société française de philosophie* 8, 229–245, 247. Contribution to discussion. Extracts reprinted in 1975a, vol. I, 199–217. (Translated in 1982a, 211–28.)

Durkheim, Émile. (1909d). Sociologie religieuse et théorie de la connaissance. *Revue de métaphysique et de morale* 17, 733–758, all of which except 754–58 was incorporated into the "Introduction" to 1912a. These missing pages are reprinted in 1975a, vol. 1, 185–88 and translated in 1982a, 236–40.

Durkheim, Émile. (1912a). *Les formes élémentaires de la vie religieuse*. Paris: Alcan. (Translated in 1995.)

Durkheim, Émile. (1919b). La Conception sociale de la religion. In *Le sentiment religieux à l'heure actuelle, edited by* F. Abauzit *et al.* Paris: Vrin. Reprinted in 1970a, 305–13.

Durkheim, Émile. (1924a). *Sociologie et philosophie*. Paris: PUF, 1974. (Translated in 1953b.)

Durkheim, Émile. (1925a). *L'Éducation morale*. Paris: Alcan. (Translated in 1961a.)

Durkheim, Émile. (1933b). *The division of labor in society*. Translation of 1893b/1902b by George Simpson. New York: Macmillan.

Durkheim, Émile. (1938b). *The rules of sociological method*. Translation of 1895a by Sarah A. Solovay and John H. Mueller, ed. by George E. G. Catlin. New York: Free Press.

Durkheim, Émile. (1951a). *Suicide: A study in sociology*. Translation of 1897a by J. A. Spaulding and G. Simpson. New York: Free Press.

Durkheim, Émile. (1953b). *Sociology and philosophy*. Translation of 1924a by D.F. Pocock. New York: Free Press/Macmillan, 1974.

Durkheim, Émile. (1961a). *Moral education*. Translation of 1925a by Everett K. Wilson and Herman Schnurer. New York, NY: Free Press/Macmillan.

Durkheim, Émile. (1963b). With Marcel Mauss. *Primitive classification.* Translation of 1903a(i) by Rodney Needham. Chicago: University of Chicago Press.

Durkheim, Émile. (1969c). *Journal sociologique.* Edited by Jean Duvignaud. Paris: PUF.

Durkheim, Émile. (1970a). *La science sociale et l'action.* Edited by J.-C. Filloux. Paris: PUF.

Durkheim, Émile. (1975a). *Textes.* Edited by Victor Karady. Paris: Les Éditions de Minuit. These three volumes provide the original pagination of those of Durkheim's publications that are included.

Durkheim, Émile. (1978a.) *Emile Durkheim on institutional analysis.* Edited and translated by Mark Traugott. Chicago: University of Chicago Press.

Durkheim, Émile. (1982a). *The rules of sociological method and selected texts on sociology and its method.* Translation of 1895a and other works by W.D. Halls. New York: Free Press.

Durkheim, Émile. (1984a). *The division of labor in society.* Translation of 1893b/1902b by W.D. Halls. New York: Free Press.

Durkheim, Émile. (1995). *The elementary forms of religious life.* Translation of 1912a by Karen Fields. New York: Free Press.

Durkheim, Émile. (1997). *Montesquieu: Quid secundatus politicae instituendae contulerit.* Contains Latin original and English translation by W. Watts Miller and Emma Griffiths of Durkheim's Latin thesis originally published in Bordeaux by Gounouilhou in 1892. Oxford, UK: Durkheim Press.

Durkheim, Émile. (2004). *Durkheim's philosophy lectures; Notes from the Lycée de Sens Course, 1883–1884.* Translation of 1884a by Neil Gross and Robert Alun Jones. Cambridge, UK: Cambridge University Press.

Gluckman, Max. (1949–1950). Social beliefs and individual thinking in primitive society. *Memoirs and Proceedings of the Manchester Literary and Philosophical Society* 91, 73–98.

Godlove, Terry F., Jr. (1986). Epistemology in Durkheim's Elementary Forms of the Religious Life. *Journal of the History of Philosophy* 24, 385–401.

Godlove, Terry F., Jr. (1989). *Religion, interpretation, and diversity of belief: The framework model from Kant to Durkheim and Davidson.* New York: Cambridge University Press.

Horkheimer, Max, & Theodor W. Adorno. (1997). *Dialectic of Enlightenment.* New York: Continuum.

Jones, R.A. (1986). *Émile Durkheim: An introduction to four major works.* Beverly Hills, CA: Sage Publications.

Llobera, Joseph R. (1980). Durkheim, the Durkheimians, and their collective misrepresentation of Marx. *Social Science Information / Information sur les sciences sociales* 19, 385–411.

Lukes, Steven. (1973). *Emile Durkheim: His life and work.* New York: Penguin Books.

Paoletti, Giovanni. (2008). Some concepts of 'evil' in Durkheim's thought. In *Suffering and evil: The Durkheimian legacy*, edited by W.S.F. Pickering and Massimo Rosati. New York: Durkheim Press/Berghahn Books.

Parsons, Talcott. (1968/1937). *The structure of social action*. New York: Free Press.
Pickering, W.S.F. (1984). *Durkheim's sociology of religion: Themes and theories*. London: Routledge & Kegan Paul.
Pickering, W.S.F. (2008). The response of Catholic and Protestant thinkers to the work of Emile Durkheim, with special reference to *Les formes élémentaires*. *Durkheimian Studies / Études Durkheimiennes* 14, 59–93.
Pyysiäinen, Ilkka. (2005). Religion, *délire*, and counterintuitiveness. *Durkheimian Studies / Études Durkheimiennes* 11, 3–10.
Rosati, Massimo. (2008). Suffering and evil in the *Elementary Forms*. In *Suffering and evil: The Durkheimian legacy*, edited by W.S.F. Pickering and Massimo Rosati. New York: Durkheim Press/Berghahn Books.
Rosenberg, Alexander. (1980). *Sociobiology and the preemption of social science*. Baltimore, MD: The Johns Hopkins University Press.
Rueschemeyer, Dietrich. (1982). On Durkheim's explanation of division of labor. *American Journal of Sociology* 88, 579–89.
Schaub, Edward L. (1920). A sociological theory of knowledge.*Philosophical Review* 29, 319–39.
Schmaus, Warren. (1995). Explanation and essence in *The Rules of Sociological Method* and *The Division of Labor in Society*. *Sociological Perspectives* 38, 57–75.
Schmaus, Warren. (2003). Is Durkheim the enemy of evolutionary psychology? *Philosophy of the Social Sciences* 33(1), 25–52.
Schmaus, Warren. (2004). *Rethinking Durkheim and his tradition*. New York: Cambridge University Press.
Schmitt, Frederick F. (Ed). (2003). *Socializing metaphysics*. Lanham, MD: Rowman & Littlefield.
Sorel, Georges. (1895). Les théories de M. Durkheim. *Le Devenir Social* 1, 1–26, 149–80.
Therborn, Göran. (1976). *Science, class and society: On the formation of sociology and historical materialism*. London, UK: NLB.
Thompson, Kenneth. (1982). *Émile Durkheim*. Chichester, UK: Ellis Horwood, and London, UK: Tavistock.
Thompson, Kenneth. (1985). Introduction. In *Readings from Emile Durkheim*, edited by K. Thompson. Chichester, UK: Ellis Horwood, and London, UK: Tavistock.
Tooby, John, & Leda Cosmides. (1992). The psychological foundations of culture. In *The adapted mind: Evolutionary psychology and the generation of culture*, edited by Jerome H. Barkow, Leda Cosmides, & John Tooby. New York: Oxford University Press.
Turner, Jonathan. (1990). Émile Durkheim's theory of social organization. *Social Forces* 68, 1089–1103.
Wright, Robert. (1994). *The moral animal*. New York: Random House.

Religion and the Emergence of the Rule of Law[†]

Charles M. North and Carl R. Gwin

1. The Origins of Economic Growth

From our comfortable and relatively wealthy perches in the 21st Century, many of us in developed nations ask why so many nations are poor? Surrounded by wealth, we wonder how widespread extreme poverty can persist in so many places. We view the poor countries as the exceptional cases, and our own wealthier countries as the norm. But this perspective is rooted in our own circumstances and ignores the grand sweep of history. In the many millennia since *homo sapiens* first emerged, humankind's basic conditions have been characterized by subsistence-level living with short average life-spans. Only in the last few centuries has humanity begun to experience the widespread accumulation of wealth typical in a modern developed economy, and with this economic prosperity has come improvement in quality of life in many measurable ways.

So, the interesting question to ask is not *why are some countries poor?*, because poverty has been the norm for humanity for most of its existence. The interesting question is *why did any country ever get rich?* Economists and economic historians have proposed a multifaceted array of answers to this question. Any valid answer to *why did any country get rich?* must at least begin with the nations of Western Europe, because that is where the modern wealth-generating economy first got its start.

In this chapter, we examine the role played by the Medieval Roman Catholic Church in creating the institutions that generated the rule of law in Western Europe, planting the seeds that led to modern economic

† This research is funded in part by a grant from the John Templeton Foundation. For helpful comments, we thank Peter Boettke, Larry Iannaccone, and participants at a 2007 seminar at Baylor University and at the 2007 annual meeting of the Association for the Study of Religion, Economics, and Culture/Society for the Scientific Study of Religion. We also thank Nick Deere and Lori Keith for research assistance. The usual disclaimer applies.

growth. We consider "rule of law" to mean that a body of rules exists that is defined and enforced well enough to constrain arbitrary governmental actions, and that government itself has well-defined and enforced civil and criminal rules to govern social interactions. The chapter (which is a preliminary sketch of a long-term research project) begins by observing that the Roman Catholic Church was one of the primary producers of wealth in the medieval period (from 1000 to 1500 CE). The Church's wealth flowed in substantial part from monastic estates, whose heightened productivity likely resulted from cooperative behavior encouraged by the shared beliefs and social norms within the monastery. In the tenth century CE, secular authorities appropriated a large amount of monastic land and other Church properties. For this and other reasons, the Church embarked on a reform campaign in the latter part of the 11th century that asserted the power of the Pope over both the Church and the secular rulers.

The papal reform of the 11th century led to the emergence of ecclesiastical courts as the creators and interpreters of the Church's own canon law, and ecclesiastical courts were able to protect the Church and its holdings from appropriation by political rulers. Many canon law doctrines that shielded the Church from an arbitrary state ultimately made their way into modern Western law, providing protection of property and contract rights to individuals *vis-à-vis* the state in ways still felt today. In contrast to Western Europe, the religious authorities in other parts of the world lacked the power and authority of the Medieval Church relative to secular rulers, so that the various religious organizations of Eastern Europe, the Middle East, China, and India were not able to provide the same jurisprudential functions as the Medieval Church did.

We focus on the time period from 1000 CE to 1500 CE, because these are the years when Western Europe first began its ascendance to economic dominance.[1] In 1000 CE, across Europe and Asia, per capita

1 A starting point of 1000 CE puts us at a time when cross-regional differences along nonreligious dimensions (such as preexisting capital, accumulated technological innovations, and so forth) would be relatively smaller than during a later period–and likely were not in favor of Western Europe. The year 1500 makes a sensible endpoint for two additional reasons. Because 1500 predates the Protestant Reformation, using it as an endpoint eliminates problems of disentangling the effects of the Protestant Reformation (as asserted by Max Weber, among others) from the larger effects of Western Christianity. (For discussion of the role of Protestantism in the emergence of modern economic growth, including

economic development was basically equal in all regions, with most regions existing at a subsistence level. Five hundred years later, Western Europe had moved ahead of the rest of Eurasia. David Landes (1999, 29) described Europe's ascent:

> Europe was lucky [to have favorable geographical features], but luck is only a beginning. Anyone who looked at the world, say a thousand years ago, would never have predicted great things for this protrusion at the western end of the Eurasian landmass that we call the continent of Europe. In terms popular among today's new economic historians, the probability at that point of European dominance was somewhere around zero. Five hundred years later, it was getting close to one.

Using modern geographic definitions, Angus Maddison (2001) estimated real GDP per capita in each of the major regions of Europe and Asia for the years 0, 1000, and 1500. These estimates are set forth in Table 1. Little change occurred in GDP per capita over the first millennium, and the income levels of most regions of Eurasia were basically even in 1000. Landes (1999, 342) even said that in 1000 China was developmentally "well ahead" of any other region – "and certainly of Europe." Timur Kuran (2004a, 124) made a similar statement about the Middle East: the Islamic world was ahead of the West in the tenth century and had clearly fallen behind by no later than the seventeenth century.

Table 1. GDP Per Capita in Europe and Asia, 0–1500 CE (1990 International Dollars)

Region	GDP Per Capita			Average Growth Rate	
	0	1000	1500	0–1000	1000–1500
Western Europe	450	400	774	-0.01	0.13
Eastern Europe	400	400	462	0.00	0.03
Former USSR	400	400	500	0.00	0.04
Japan	400	425	500	0.01	0.03
China	450	450	600	0.00	0.06
India	450	450	550	0.00	0.04
Other Asia	450	450	565	0.00	0.05
Entire World	**444**	**435**	**565**	**0.00**	**0.05**

Source: Maddison (2001), Tables B-21, B-22

a brief discussion of the rule of law, see Robert Nelson's chapter in this volume.) In addition, some scholars have argued that Western Europe's economic ascendance is attributable to its exploitation of the colonial system (e.g., Pomeranz 2000). Using an endpoint of 1500 moots such arguments because it predates the colonial period.

Between 1000 and 1500, Western Europe caught up to and then passed the rest of Eurasia. As shown in Table 1, Maddison estimated that the average annual growth rate in real GDP per capita in Western Europe was 0.13 percent. Although this long-run growth rate is paltry by modern standards, it nevertheless is more than double the growth rate of China, the next-fastest-growing region. Pounds (1974, 97–98) reported that trade between Western Europe and the eastern end of the Mediterranean changed in character between 1000 and 1500. At the beginning, Western Europe was an importer that paid for its purchases in bullion; by the end, Western Europe was increasingly exporting processed and manufactured goods to the Middle East while importing raw materials. As a result, in 1500, Western Europe's real GDP per capita was 29 percent higher than in China, 37 to 41 percent higher than in India or the rest of Asia, 55 percent higher than in Japan and the region of the (now) former USSR, and 68 percent higher than in Eastern Europe.

There are many reasons for this early divergence in relative levels of development across regions. Geographical advantages mattered: Europe had a more temperate climate, rainfall patterns more amenable to cultivation, and fewer parasites than existed in tropical regions. Europe had big, strong animals such as horses and oxen that proved to be a key energy source for agriculture and for transportation. Also, Europe's array of natural barriers, like rivers and mountains, made for smaller natural political units, which meant there were more autonomous polities with their own rulers. More competition among rulers meant that there was less of a chance to be arbitrary in governance, because citizens could vote with their feet by moving to a better-run neighboring principality (Jones 2003, 105–08, 226; see also Diamond 1999).

Differences in weather variability may also have played a role in Europe's ascent. Jones (2003, Chapter 2) argued that India and China were subject to more severe environmental uncertainty (such as floods, droughts, storms, etc.) than Western Europe, making capital more prone to being destroyed in the Asian regions. Thus, India and China faced a relatively higher disincentive to invest in capital, which deterred growth in income per capita. Jones also argued that the higher risk of natural disasters placed a premium on family size in Asia relative to Europe, because a larger family would increase the available labor to recover after natural disasters. Combining this effect with a disincentive to invest in human capital, Jones contended that the Asian regions would have featured an emphasis on quantity over quality in decisions on bearing and rearing children (2003, 15–21, 226–27).

But geography by itself cannot explain why Europe's relative economic success began during the first half of the second millennium rather than at some other time. Jones (2003) attributed early European economic development to several factors. First, the emergence of factor markets for land and labor made resource allocation much more responsive to pricing incentives (2003, xxi, xxxv). Second, European societies managed to curtail the degree of predatory taxing behavior by the governments, an effect helped by the fact that the number of states in Europe never shrank to one (2003, xxxvi).

Landes pointed to several additional factors that led to Western Europe's ascendance between 1000 and 1500 CE. Most obviously, technological innovations mattered. The three-field system of crop rotation and the development of iron tools for clearing forest and plowing Western Europe's heavier soil were critical for European development (Landes 1999, 41). He also claimed that Europeans had a higher regard for property rights than the people of other Eurasian regions, beginning with the Greek tradition of democracy and strengthened by subsequent influences (Landes 1999, 32–36). For example, Germanic customs arose in a nomadic community, in which clear individual ownership extended only to whatever a person could carry. The political fragmentation that existed after the fall of the Roman Empire deterred growth of the kind of authoritarian political power that could confiscate private property on a whim. And the Judeo-Christian tradition was based on Old Testament laws that clearly recognized private property and meted out punishment for violations of another's property. Knowledge of the Jewish laws spread with the translation of scripture into the vernacular among various "heretical" movements, including the Waldensians and Lollards during the medieval period.

Though he pointed out some of the ideological origins of property rights among Europeans, Landes did not provide compelling reasons why the rulers in medieval Europe would ever have protected these property rights. Nor did Jones fully explain why Europeans managed to curtail governmental predation. We fill this gap in existing analyses by explaining how the Church had both the incentives and the ability to stand up to secular authorities by developing a system of law that protected property from arbitrary appropriation by the state.

2. Religion and Economic Growth

We are hardly the first to suggest a connection between religion and economic growth. Max Weber set forth his well-known hypothesis in *The Protestant Ethic and the Spirit of Capitalism* (cf. Robert Nelson's chapter in this volume). Weber's thesis was that the spirit of modern capitalism is best characterized by a work-oriented ethic that regards labor as something to be done for its own sake, and not merely for the consumption it permits. He further argued that this ethic is most clearly articulated by "ascetic" Protestantism, particularly Calvinism. Thus, Weber argued that Protestantism was central to the rise of the "spirit of capitalism," if not capitalism itself.

While Weber's hypothesis is interesting and has attracted substantial attention, it has also been regarded as historically inaccurate. For example, Stark (2004, 465–68) summarized the work of several scholars who have found that capitalistic enterprises predated the Protestant Reformation by centuries. Moreover, Stark said that the work ethic that Weber attributed to Protestantism had previously been present in medieval Catholic monasticism and had been enacted in the laws of twelfth-century Italian city-states (which prohibited conspicuous consumption and luxurious lifestyles). Weber was likely correct that a new "ethic" was needed for a market capitalist economy to arise, but that ethic was not attributable solely to Protestantism.

In recent years, economists have been turning their attention to the role that religion and religious institutions play in the economic process. Barro and McCleary (2003) found that national aggregate measures of religious attendance and beliefs had significant effects on rates of economic growth in the late 20th century. Similarly, Guiso, Sapienza, and Zingales (2003) concluded that, on average, religious beliefs were associated with economic attitudes that favor economic growth. Richardson and McBride (2009) showed that religion provided a basis for cooperative behavior in medieval guilds where secular incentives were not up to the task. In a cross-sectional sample of 207 countries, North, Gwin, and Orman (2009) examined correlations between religious heritage and the level of rule of law in 2004. They concluded that the rule of law was significantly higher in countries whose largest religious group in 1900 was Protestantism, Catholicism, or Hinduism. Table 2 presents data from North, Gwin, and Orman (2009) on mean GDP per capita in 2001 for countries based upon their largest religious groups in the year 1900. There are substantial differences in GDP per capita across religious groups, perhaps suggesting that there are variations in economic development that are linked in some way to religious heritage.

Table 2. GDP per Capita in 2001 by Countries' Largest Religious Group in 1900

	Number of Countries	Mean GDP per Capita
African Ethnoreligion	36	$2,067
Asian Ethnoreligion	8	15,088
Buddhist	8	6,025
Catholic	53	13,030
Hindu	4	4,800
Islam	41	6,091
Orthodox	13	7,223
Pacific Island Ethnoreligion	6	2,583
Protestant	38	16,545

Source: North, Gwin, and Orman (2009)

Whether and how religion is linked to economic growth is still an open question. North, Gwin, and Orman (2009) suggested one plausible linkage – different religions are correlated with varying levels of rule of law, and rule of law is a well-known correlate of economic growth (e.g., Scully 1988; Knack and Keefer 1995; Barro 1997, 2003; La Porta et al. 1998; Rodrik 1999). We now explore in detail one causal avenue for this linkage from religion to rule of law to economic growth in Western Europe: the development of law in the ecclesiastical courts of the Medieval Church, and the subsequent influence canon law had on the secular law of Western Europe.

3. Church Property, Ecclesiastical Courts, and an Emerging Rule of Law

Jones (2003, xiv) noted that, among all of the Eurasian landmass, only Western Europe "managed the politically remarkable feat of curtailing arbitrary power, thus reducing risk and uncertainty, encouraging more productive investment, and promoting growth." In fact, he attributes much of "the European miracle" to this accomplishment:

> Economic development in its European form required above all freedom from arbitrary political acts concerning private property. Goods and factors

> of production had to be free to be traded. Prices had to be set by unconditional exchange if they were to be undistorted signals of what goods and services really were in demand, where and in what quantities (2003, 85).

Why was Europe able to accomplish this feat, while no other region of the Eurasian landmass did? Our answer begins with the dual nature of the Medieval Church. As a way of understanding the differences in what motivated various individuals within the Church, Stark (2003, 40–46) categorized the Medieval Church into two distinct segments: a "Church of Power" and a "Church of Piety." According to Stark, the Church of Power was "the main body of the Church as it evolved in response to the immense power and wealth bestowed on the clergy," whereas the Church of Piety was "made up of those who were still committed to the moral vision of early Christianity." Economic historian Douglass North also recognized this dual nature of the Medieval Church, describing it as both "the top-heavy bureaucracy of the late Roman Empire and the major center of material wealth, selling salvation in return for treasure and land" and "the Church of asceticism, extreme austerity, hermit life, and devout missionaries" (1981, 125). To somewhat oversimplify, the Church of Power resided in the papacy and the episcopate – that is, in the clergy who made up the main hierarchy of the Church. In contrast, the Church of Piety was centered in the monks who made up the various monastic orders and had submitted themselves to a more austere and pious existence than those in the Church of Power.[2]

Combining a deeper examination of the Church of Power and the Church of Piety with the excellent work of Harold Berman (1983), we offer an answer to why Western European countries were able to curtail the arbitrary power of the state: the centralized transnational hierarchy of the Roman Catholic Church provided a counter-balance to the power of the secular princes and developed a system of canon law that ultimately led to limits on the power of the state under secular law. The Church managed this feat despite having no real political authority only because (1) the Church of Power was willing to exercise

2 The labels "Church of Power" and "Church of Piety" are useful generalizations more than complete descriptions of reality. There must have been some pious clergy within the Church hierarchy, and there also must have been some power-hungry monks within the monasteries. But the basic scheme seems reasonable–piety should have been greater in the monastic estates due to the greater sacrifice required to be part of a monastic order.

whatever persuasive authority it had over the masses in its struggles against the secular powers, and (2) as discussed in the following sections, the Church of Piety provided credibility to the Church as a whole upon which the Church of Power could rest its persuasive authority.

This symbiotic relationship between the two parts of the Church was possible in Western Christendom because of the emergence of a centralized bureaucracy within the Church during the papal reforms of the 11th and 12th centuries. The centralized bureaucratic hierarchy distinguishes Western Christendom from the other major religions of Europe and Asia, none of which had a similar centralized authority that was distinct from the state.

3.1. Wealth Worth Fighting For

The Church was a major landholder in Medieval Europe. Even during the later years of the Roman Empire, the Church already owned a significant amount of land (Pounds 1974, 17). "Before the year A.D. 900, the Church directly owned approximately one-third of all cultivated land in western Europe, including 31 percent of such land in Italy, 35 percent in Germany, and 44 percent in northern France" (Ekelund et al. 1996, 8, citing Herlihy 1961, 86).

The Church had acquired much of this land during the eighth and ninth centuries, when the Merovingian and Carolingian rulers had given large amounts of land to the Church through commendation. The Church also gained property during the eighth and ninth centuries through bequests. However, the haphazard nature of property acquisition by abbeys, monasteries, and other Church entities led to piecemeal layouts, as evidenced by the handful of surviving inventories of property held by ninth century monasteries. There is evidence, though, that the abbeys and monks consolidated their holdings by selling faraway parcels and acquiring property closer to home, and they also took steps to systemize production and impose manageable administrative units (Pounds 1974, Chapter 2).

By 1200, though, the Church's ownership of cultivated land in Western Europe declined to 15 to 20 percent. Half of this decline occurred between 900 and 1000 due to direct seizures of Church properties by various local rulers – with monasteries being the hardest hit – as well as leases from the Church to laymen (Herlihy 1961, 92–93). By

1000, the Church clearly saw itself under attack from secular rulers and needed a way to defend itself.

The Church's substantial tracts of land provided a tempting target for kings and princes looking for sources of revenue. Herlihy's (1961) estimates suggest that appropriations of Church properties may have reduced Church land holdings by as much as one fifth between 900 and 1000. The Medieval Church needed a mechanism to protect itself from these types of appropriations of property, and it found that mechanism in its own court system.

3.2. Ecclesiastical Courts and the Papal Revolution

Ecclesiastical courts were Western Europe's first modern legal system. They were the outgrowth of several revolutionary changes within the Church during the latter half of the 11th century. Most important was the reform of the papacy itself. From the time of Constantine to about 1000 CE, Roman Catholic clergy were more subject to the control of emperors, kings, and feudal lords than to the pope. Secular authorities appointed the clergy and provided them with funds. Beginning in the 10th and early 11th centuries, reformers within the Church sought to remove the secular influence and the corruption that accompanied it. The reform movement was centered in the monasteries, especially the Abbey of Cluny in France, and sought a number of reforms – such as stopping the buying and selling of Church offices ("simony") and ending clerical marriage – that linked bishops and priests into local politics (Berman 1983, 88–91.)

The papal revolution began in earnest with the selection of Pope Leo IX in 1049, who imposed celibacy on the clergy, opposed simony, and argued for the right of the Church to select its own leaders. Leo IX also formed a party within the Church to support his proposed reforms, and this group was led by a young monk named Hildebrand. In 1059, a council in Rome, called by Pope Nicholas II, declared that the Roman cardinals, rather than the Holy Roman Emperor, had the authority to select the pope. In 1073, Hildebrand was elected pope, and he became Pope Gregory VII. More than any other pope of the era, Gregory represents the reform movement of the 11th century. In 1075, Gregory declared greater authority for the papacy than it had ever wielded. He asserted that the Pope was supreme over the Church, including the right of the Pope to appoint bishops, and over all Christians. He also asserted authority over the secular rulers, including the emperor; Gregory declared that the Pope had the authority to remove the emperor from office (Berman 1983, 94–95). Of course, declaring these things and making them happen were different matters. Berman summarized Gregory's plight as follows:

> Lacking armies of its own, how was the papacy to make good its claims? How was it to overcome the armies of those who would oppose papal supremacy? And apart from the problem of meeting forceful opposition, how was the papacy to exercise the universal jurisdiction it had asserted? How was it effectively to impress its will on the entire Western Christian world, let alone Eastern Christendom, over which some claims of jurisdiction were also made?

An important aspect of the answers to these questions was the potential role of law as a source of authority and a means of control (Berman 1983, 95).

Thus, the ecclesiastical courts began to develop a system of law that was to govern the Church's internal and external relationships at both an individual and a corporate level. Control was centralized in Rome, and a new clerical hierarchy arose that Berman described as "the first translocal, transtribal, transfeudal, transnational class in Europe to achieve political and legal unity" (Berman 1983, 107–08).

The other major revolution that prompted the emergence of the ecclesiastical courts within the Church of Power was the development of a Scholastic approach to the study of law. Three factors combined to spark a new approach to law as a subject of study separate and distinct from the study of theology or other fields: (1) a rediscovery in about 1080 CE of the Roman law code compiled under emperor Justinian in Constantinople around 534 CE, (2) the emergence of a particular style of dialectical scholarship under the Church's so-called "scholastics," and (3) the growth of universities, beginning in Italy in the latter half of the 11th century. The canon lawyers developed a theory of law that sought to synthesize the various rules from Roman law, Church decrees, Greek philosophy, and more into a body of rules based on consistent principles that could evolve and grow as new situations arose. Underlying the whole was the canonists' assumption that natural law was supreme to all other forms of law, so that the ecclesiastical courts could reject laws of both the Church and secular rulers if such laws were inconsistent with natural law as ascertained by the ecclesiastical courts (Berman 1983, 120–64).

Prior to the emergence of the canon law and the ecclesiastical courts, much of the law in Western Europe had been based on custom. Such law might be beneficial or not, but it had an aura of sacredness to it because it was part of a long-standing cultural custom. The canon law substituted its own preference for natural law in place of the sanctity of custom. According to Berman (1983, 145), "The theory that customs must yield to natural law was one of the greatest achievements of the canonists." In large part, this achievement was significant because it had the effect of elevating laws over persons and laid the foundation for the idea of rule of law.

The canon law developed bodies of law governing a variety of subjects based upon the principles of the supremacy of natural law and the supremacy of the Church over all secular authorities. Ecclesiastical courts came to assert jurisdiction over cases based on the identity of the people involved in the dispute ("personal jurisdiction") and on the subject matter being disputed ("subject-matter jurisdiction"). They also asserted jurisdiction over matters in which the parties had voluntarily chosen to submit the dispute to ecclesiastical courts and matters where there was a failure of justice itself in the secular courts. A summary of the matters within either the personal or subject-matter jurisdictions of ecclesiastical courts shows that a wide array of legal disputes came under the ambit of the canon law. The ecclesiastical courts asserted personal jurisdiction over all suits involving

- clergy and members of their households;
- students;
- crusaders;
- "wretched persons," including poor people, widows, and orphans;
- Jews, in cases against Christians; and
- travelers, including merchants and sailors, when necessary for their peace and safety.

The subject-matter jurisdiction of the ecclesiastical courts extended to cases arising out of

- administration of the sacraments;
- testamentary matters;
- benefices, including church property;
- oaths, including pledges of faith; and
- sins meriting ecclesiastical censures.

From these lists, it is easy to see how the Church's courts asserted jurisdiction over matters involving property and contract rights. Cases involving inheritance, marriage, Church property, and more would have put many property disputes within the ecclesiastical courts' declared jurisdiction. Canon law courts determined contract rights in cases involving oaths and in contract disputes involving persons within the personal jurisdiction of ecclesiastical courts. In addition, ecclesiastical courts also had the chance to develop the substance of family law, the law of inheritance, and criminal and tort law (Berman 1983, 221–24).

Today, we know that effective rule of law is an important piece of the story of economic development. Many of the ideas generated in the medieval canon law courts have shaped our modern law in ways beneficial to economic growth. The transmission of legal rules from canon law into secular law began almost immediately after the establishment of the law faculty at the University of Bologna in the 12th century, as the lawyers who spread from Bologna to the rest of Europe were trained in the canon law and its methods. In this way, the secular law was influenced dramatically by the style and form of the canon law (Berman 1983, 162).

A few examples from Berman (1983) will suffice to show how canon law concepts and methods became part of our modern secular law. First, the Church subjected itself to a body of corporate law by which it governed itself. The ecclesiastical courts were the arbiters of this canon law of the corporation, and even the Pope was bound to follow the orders of the courts. This early modeling of the Church as a corporate body with its own existence separate from any individual and subject to the rules that created the corporation provided a model for secular governments that were similarly corporate in conception and limited by their own rules. The Magna Carta is one such set of rules, having been drafted in large part by the Archbishop of Canterbury (Berman 1983, 205–15.)

Second, in the canon law, marriage evolved from a sacrament that could be conducted without a priest into a body of contract law. The canon law of marriage valued the presence of freely-given consent to the marriage contract, and required the absence of mistake, duress, or fraud in the formation of the marriage contract. Such ideas were not only the foundation of modern law of marriage, but also of modern contract law (Berman 1983, 227–28). The defenses of mistake, duress, and fraud, formulated in ecclesiastical courts, continue to be an important part of modern contract law.

Third, ecclesiastical courts were never fully successful in wrestling away jurisdiction from secular courts over devises of land upon the death of the owner. In response, the canon law developed the instrument of the *inter vivos* trust as an alternative to a testamentary devise of land. The concept of the trust eventually carried over into secular law and in England became part of the jurisdiction of the court of chancery, the royal court of equity. One key innovation in the canon law was the *cy pres* doctrine, which is still the law in much of the United States (Berman 1983, 234–36). The modern *cy pres* doctrine allows courts to modify the terms of a charitable trust if its original purposes become impossible, impracticable, or illegal to perform. This doctrine – originated in the canon law – is notably absent in the Islamic laws of the *waqf*, as described in Kuran (2004b). The *waqf* was a form of charitable trust under Islamic law, but the resources committed to the *waqf* were required to be used forever for their initially-designated purposes, lest the *waqf* be handed over to the state. Kuran (2004b) argued that the static nature of the *waqf* served for centuries as a hindrance to economic development in Islamic lands. In contrast, the *cy pres* doctrine developed in the ecclesiastical courts permitted the purpose of property held in trust to change when the original purpose of the trust became impossible or illegal, thereby assuring that no resources would be held in perpetuity in uses that would eventually become socially inefficient.

The ecclesiastical courts were a revolutionary innovation run by the Church of Power. They had jurisdiction over Church property, including the monastic estates within the Church of Piety that generated so much wealth for the Church and that had come under attack in the century before the papal reforms. The Church had both the motive and the method to protect itself against the arbitrary encroachments of the state. But why did anyone – particularly the rulers – do what the ecclesiastical courts said? Before we can answer this question, we first must discuss the idea of economic cooperation within the context of the monasteries of the Church of Piety.

3.3. Cooperation and Productivity

In the jargon of game theory, "cooperation" occurs when people work together for their mutual good, even though it is possible for each person to gain a little extra by being more selfish. A classic example of cooperation is the Infinitely Repeated Prisoner's Dilemma, in which two players play the "stage game" in Figure 1 over and over forever.[3] The stage game gives each player two strategic choices – Cooperate or Defect. The numbers in each cell represent payoffs to Player 1 and Player 2, respectively, for the combination of strategies associated with the cell. The traditional solution approach to this game is the Nash equilibrium, which occurs in any cell where neither player can improve his payoff by switching to another strategy. Players prefer higher payoffs to lower ones.

		Player 2 Cooperate	Defect
Player 1	Cooperate	2,2	0,3
	Defect	3,0	1,1

Fig 1. A Prisoner's Dilemma Game

One defining characteristic of the Prisoner's Dilemma is that "Defect" is a dominant strategy for both players. That is, no matter what Player 2 chooses to do, Player 1 can get a higher payoff by choosing "Defect." The same is true for Player 2. As a result, the unique Nash equilibrium of the stage game is for both players to defect, yielding payoffs of (1, 1) to the players.

Of course, both players could obtain better payoffs of (2, 2) if they were to play (Cooperate, Cooperate). This combination of actions is not a Nash equilibrium in the stage game, though, because either player could obtain an even higher payoff by playing "Defect" in response to the other player's "Cooperate." The crux of the problem of cooperation is how to overcome the short-term incentive to defect in settings like the Prisoner's Dilemma.

One example of a Prisoner's Dilemma-like setting is team production, where it is often the case that all that can be clearly measured is the total output of the team. If a team shares the profit from its output, any individual worker could slack off without lowering the entire team's output by much. Thus, there is a strong temptation for individual work-

3 In this chapter, we discuss cooperation among players known to each other in advance. The chapter in this volume by Bulbulia and Schjoedt examines from a social neuroscience perspective how cooperative behavior can emerge at a societal level among people who do not know each other in advance.

ers to shirk and thereby "free ride" off of the labor of others. In a medieval estate, agricultural output depended in part on how hard individual serfs decided to work in the manor's fields. If all the serfs worked hard, then the output would be higher, the manor would be wealthier, and some of that wealth could (perhaps) be shared with the serfs by a benevolent lord. But, for any single serf, there was an incentive to shirk; one person's reduction in effort would have no observable effect on total output, but that one person would certainly enjoy working a little less hard. The problem, of course, is that output does fall if every serf follows his incentive to shirk, and widespread shirking makes everyone worse off – even if the workers share the joint output.

If a Prisoner's Dilemma is infinitely repeated, strategies exist that can sustain a Nash equilibrium in which both players choose to cooperate in every period of the game. Robert Axelrod's well-known *The Evolution of Cooperation* studied cooperation within the context of a Repeated Prisoner's Dilemma. Axelrod organized computer simulations of Repeated Prisoner's Dilemmas to determine what types of strategies led to higher payoffs in such settings. He concluded that the strategies that were more successful were those that (1) did not cheat first, (2) were willing to dispense proportionate punishments for cheating by others, (3) were thereafter able to forgive those acts of cheating, and (4) were easy for other players to recognize (Axelrod 1984, 54). North and Taylor (2004) pointed out noteworthy similarities between what Christian scriptures teach about how to interact with other people and the traits of the strategies that Axelrod found to be successful. However, North and Taylor did not discuss whether Christian teachings might have encouraged cooperation in the past, and thereby fostered economic growth.[4] This paper takes on those questions in the context of the monastic estates of the medieval period.

4. Cooperation in Monastic Orders and Estates

The monasteries of Western Europe grew wealthy in part because they benefited from cooperative behavior within their walls. This cooperation was rooted in the devotion and religious ethic characteristic of

4 Similarly, North and Taylor (2004) did not examine whether the doctrines or sacred texts of other religions might also be capable of encouraging cooperative behavior.

the Church of Piety. Shared beliefs and social norms provided a substitute for monitoring costs within the monasteries, allowing them to spend more resources in production.

Our analysis of monastic production from a principal-agent perspective is an important addition to the work of Ekelund et al. (1996), who viewed monasteries and parish churches as downstream suppliers of a monopoly Church's product. Because of this relationship, some typical principal-agent problems arose between the upstream Church hierarchy and the downstream monasteries, and the Church resolved such problems by making monks and parish priests into residual claimants of certain forms of revenue flows over which those clergy had the greatest control. Even so, Ekelund et al. (1996, 53) contended that workers in the monasteries faced a strong incentive to shirk because production was often done in teams, creating the chance to free ride off of other team members. However, Ekelund et al. did not consider how shared religious beliefs and social norms among the monks could have induced higher effort levels with lower monitoring costs, thereby reducing the free rider problem.

Christian scripture contains numerous teachings that should encourage cooperative behavior. The "Golden Rule" instructs Christians on how to treat others: "Do to others as you would have them do to you." (Luke 6:31) Christian scripture also posits a broad conception of one's brother; indeed, Christianity can be read to say that no one is truly "other." For example, in the Parable of the Good Samaritan (Luke 10:29–37), the "neighbor" is a Samaritan, an ethnic group of half-breeds who were viewed with contempt by the Jewish society of Jesus' day. Similarly, in Acts 10, the Apostle Peter has a vision instructing him to eat unclean food, ultimately leading Peter to see that the gospel is meant to go beyond ethnic Jews. Acts 16 describes the Apostle Paul's vision of a man of Macedonia calling Paul to preach the gospel to the Gentiles. In Galatians 3:28, Paul writes, "There is neither Jew nor Greek, there is neither slave nor free, there is neither male nor female; for you are all one in Christ Jesus." Admittedly, we are glossing over some important exegetical and historical matters here, but it is fair to say that the core of the Christian religion was very open to people that typical Jews of New Testament times would have considered "unclean" or "other."

With a Golden Rule ethic and an openness to others, interactions between truly faithful followers of Christianity should have led to the type of cooperative behavior that can fuel economic success. Of course, whether such behavior should have emerged and whether it actually did emerge are wholly separate questions. The medieval period in church history was characterized by clergy of dubious morals, by a series of Crusades against "others" in the Middle East, and by second-class treatment of Jews and other ethnic minorities throughout Western Christendom. Nevertheless, if there were clusters of individuals who actually tried to follow the Christian teachings described above, then such clusters should have prospered financially as well as spiritually relative to others around them. The monks living in the monasteries composed just these sorts of clusters. They were more inclined than most to know and follow Christian teaching on how to interact with others. In the closely-knit communities of the monasteries, it would have been apparent that the monastic order could best prosper if all its members contributed cooperatively to the group's work.

Many of the monastic orders were organized around the Rule of St. Benedict, which specified how the monasteries were to be organized and operated and also provided rules to govern the daily activities of the monks. (Ekelund et al. 1996, 42) The main economic goal of the Rule was to make the monastery self-sufficient and self-contained, to assure both the material and spiritual well-being of the monks. The Rule placed high importance on community and required monks to abide by a vow of obedience to the abbot, the head of the monastery. Benedict's Rule was notable for the balance it introduced into monastic life. Monks were allowed sufficient food to sustain their strength, proper clothing to stay warm in cold climates, and sufficient sleep (7–8 hours a night) to sustain health. The work day was split fairly evenly among prayer and liturgical duties, manual labor appropriate to the monk's skills and abilities, and study of Scriptures and spiritual writing. Even so, monks were expected to keep to their vows of poverty, chastity, and obedience. In all, the Rule of St. Benedict laid down a set of expectations that, if followed, would have eliminated many of the principal-agent problems identified by Ekelund et al. The superior productivity of the monastic estates suggests that these principal-agent problems were in fact resolved.

Douglass North (1981, 125) noted that "[m]onasteries were frequently the most effective farming centers in the Middle Ages." There are two important reasons for the increased productivity of the monastic estate: monasteries were able to generate more food and other goods than the monks themselves needed, and they invested these surplus resources into productive capital and improved technology. The available evidence suggests that monasteries were already generating surpluses in the early Middle Ages. There are few surviving records of monasteries from the eighth and ninth centuries, so inference about the entire set based on the surviving sample is obviously imperfect. Nevertheless, one very large monastic estate in north-central Italy (St. Giulia, near Brescia) received far more income in kind – both food and non-food items – from its possessions than the monastery could consume, and the monastery was likely selling its surplus at market to provision the towns in its region (Pounds 1974, 64).

Similarly, the tenants of the monasteries of the Low Countries, northern France, and Germany were weaving surplus cloth for export (Pounds 1974, 106, 306–07, 315). Within a few hundred years, monasteries were substantial wool traders, and there was substantial demand for their woolen cloth because of its high quality (Ekelund et al. 1996, 52). Indeed, the monasteries were the original loci of manufacturing activity in the eighth and ninth centuries, making their own cloth, salt, timber, and iron. This monastic dominance of manufacturing did not last, though. From the tenth through the twelfth centuries, manufacturing shifted from the peasant laborers in the monasteries to specialized workers in urban centers (Pounds 1974, 283–84, 333, 340). Nevertheless, the early dominance of monastic estates in the manufacturing realm is evidence of their ability to generate agricultural surpluses larger than other types of estates.

How did the monasteries generate these surpluses? Typically, monasteries followed a life cycle. In the earliest phase, they were centers of religious devotion sustained primarily by their own production of food, clothing, and so on. Over time, the monasteries were able to produce more than they needed for their own support, and so they turned to trading in the market as a means of selling surplus output. As would be expected in a market economy, monasteries "began to operate like agricultural firms" (Ekelund et al. 1996, 43). They invested in commercial vineyards and began raising sheep and other animals on lands that were of marginal planting value. The monasteries of the Cistercian Order developed a specialized class of monks called the *conversi*, lay brothers who performed much of the manual labor of the monastic estate. This permitted a degree of specialization by the various types of monks, which increased not only agricultural output but also the amount of devotional activities among the choir monks. (Pounds 1974, 172; Ekelund et al. 1996, 43–45, 51)

The monastic estates that used *conversi* also were better able to adhere to the three-field system of crop rotation than were either secular manors or monastic estates that relied on peasant labor.[5] From a consumer's standpoint, the main problem with the three-field system is that the spring-sown crops (oats and barley) make less-appealing bread than wheat or rye. Barley could be made into beer; oats were fed to horses and used when needed for human consumption as porridge or for beer when barley was unavailable. Because of the better command over the labor force, abbeys using *conversi* were able to enforce use of the three-field system, thereby producing more crops and better-fed horses (which in itself enhanced productivity). In contrast, manors relying on peasant labor often had to limit themselves to a two-field system in order to grow more of the bread grains that the peasants themselves wanted (Pounds 1974, 190–93).

Thus, monastic estates were more productive than other manors in part because the benefits of cooperation allowed them to produce more output. But the monasteries also used this surplus to invest in capital that enhanced the productivity of all the workers. Ekelund et al. (1996, 53–54) said that the monasteries had an incentive to develop labor-saving technologies and more efficient farm-production techniques, in order to allow the monks to meet their spiritual obligations. According to Landes (1999, 58), monastic estates made early use of extensive power machinery to perform the tasks of the estate. In addition, the surplus wealth of the monasteries allowed them to clear large amounts of forest land and to reclaim marshland, which "necessitated not only a considerable expenditure, but also the employment of a large body of workers. In the reclamation of the coastal marshes, especially those of the Low

5 The three-field crop-rotation system splits the estate into thirds. On one-third, an annual crop (such as wheat or rye) is sown in the fall and harvested the following fall. Another one-third of the estate lies fallow for half of the year, and then a spring-sown crop (like oats or barley) is planted for harvest in the fall. The final third is left fallow, and animals graze there, so that the soil is nourished both by natural replenishment and from animal manure. Thus, two-thirds of the estate is put into production each year, and harvests are increased. (Pounds 1974, 190–93.) The three-field system contrasts with the older two-field system, in which half of the field is used to grow an annual crop while the other half is left fallow. Under the two-field system, only half of the estate is used for production of a crop in any given year, while in a three-field system two-thirds of the estate is productive in any given year. Yet, in both systems, all parts of the estate are fallow for one-half of the crop-rotation cycle.

Countries, the monasteries played a prominent role" (Pounds 1974, 172–73).

The heavy plow was another form of capital that was relatively more available to the monastic estates because of their greater wealth. As a technological innovation, the heavy plow was most valuable in the hands of an organization with a highly cooperative workforce, like a monastery. Pounds describes the heavy plow as "a cumbersome instrument, fitted with wheels which controlled the depth to which the share cut into the soil; a coulter, which made a vertical cut through the soil, and a mouldboard, which undercut the sward and turned it over" (Pounds 1974, 194). Light plows did little but scratch the surface of the earth without turning over the soil. In contrast, the heavy plow was able to cut into the soil, turn the sod, and bury the weeds. The heavy plow required a team of animals to pull it and at least two men to control the animals and the plow. Using horses in combination with oxen increased the speed of plowing, thus making spring-sown oats valuable as horse feed to the plow's owner. A heavy plow was difficult to turn around at the end of a furrow, which led to fields being cultivated in longer, thinner strips (a "furlong"). The heavy plow created economies of scale in agricultural production. The tracts farmed individually by most peasant families were too small to sustain a full team, and the plow was too expensive for a peasant family to own (Pounds 1974, 55–56, 195–96). Thus, the heavy plow necessitated a communal effort at plowing; when it was used, the heavy plow spurred large increases in agricultural productivity. It would have been most productive in larger, well-organized communities characterized by cooperative behavior, such as the monastic estates.

Finally, the monasteries probably also had higher quality workers (i. e., better human capital) because of their ability to select their own members. Both choir monks and *conversi* came from outside the Church and had to go through a rigorous selection process before being admitted into the order of monks. It is also likely that some initiates came from boys who had grown up as orphans within the monasteries, and that the monks retained the better workers while allowing the less productive ones to depart the monastery upon attaining majority.

In summary, most evidence suggests that monastic estates were more productive than other types of estates. Cooperative behavior within the monastery generated higher effort levels without having to increase monitoring costs. The monasteries also were early adopters of technological innovations that added to the productivity gains made possible by increased cooperation. And the religious character of the monastic estate made use of these technologies more effective. The three-field system could be implemented because of the better control over the workforce, and the higher surplus from cooperative behavior likely generated the initial wealth needed to adopt the heavy plow and various water-driven machines. The monastic estates of the Church of Piety were a great source of wealth for the Church as a whole, a fact that necessitated action by the Church of Power to protect the Church's wealth from secular rulers. As already discussed, the Church used its own courts to provide that protection, but why did anyone follow the orders of the Church's courts?

5. The Authority of the Ecclesiastical Courts

The penalties for violations of canon law were mainly limited to religious sanctions, ranging from minor acts of penance up to the extreme punishment of excommunication (Ekelund et al. 1996, 62, 65). Without backing from political rulers, the Church did not have any way to implement its orders by force. Instead, for religious sanctions to be followed, the Church had to maintain the credibility of its spiritual teachings so that both the penitent and the society around him feared the Church's ability to control spiritual outcomes. If neither the masses nor the rulers believed the Church's message regarding sin and salvation, then the punishments available to the ecclesiastical courts – being entirely religious in nature – were doomed to fail. Had the Medieval Church consisted only of the Church of Power, it is likely that the Church would not have had sufficient credibility with rulers and the masses to give teeth to its religious sanctions. It was the Church of Piety that gave credibility to the Church as a whole through its devotion to the people, through delivery of religious and social services, and through its relatively ascetic lifestyles. A symbiotic relationship thus existed between the two "churches:" the Church of Piety generated credibility and authority among the Christian populace for the Church of Power, and in return the Church of Power used its power in general and its court system in particular to protect the Church of Piety from abuse and appropriation of resources by secular political forces.

The ecclesiastical courts also used other strategies to enhance their own credibility. Clergy were held to higher standards of conduct than laypersons in similar cases. Medieval canonists concluded that the

Pope could be removed from office under canon law, placing a check even on the head of the Church (Berman 1983, 158, 191). By holding its own membership to higher standards than everyone else, the Church built credibility for its court system and reinforced its role as protector of rights against an arbitrary state.

Of course, the Church of Power could not forever rely on the Church of Piety to build credibility. Monasticism declined with feudalism. The Black Death dramatically reduced the population during the 1300s, so that the price of labor increased relative to the value of land. With laborers in short supply, markets for labor emerged to provide peasants with work opportunities beyond the manor. To retain agricultural workers, manorial lords altered their relationships with peasants, giving peasants more and more control over the land that they farmed and paying them for service on the demesne. These changes in relations between lord and servant, caused by the emergence of free markets for labor, constituted the ultimate destruction of the feudal system (North and Thomas 1973). Similarly, the opportunity cost of becoming a monk increased dramatically, leading to a decline in the size and influence of the monasteries. But by the time these things happened in the late medieval period, the foundation of rule of law was laid. Berman (1983, 24) wrote that the various European revolutions that followed the papal revolution – the Protestant Reformation and the English, French, and Russian revolutions – all built upon the framework of the canon law. In this way, the canon law revolution of the 11th century was perpetuated into modern times by the legal systems in most of the developed world. Limitations on the state were created, and the modern economies of Western Europe began truly to be built.

6. The Need for Comparative Analysis

Up to this point, we have presented a hypothesis – that a symbiosis between the two medieval "churches" was critical in allowing ecclesiastical courts to lay the foundation for the modern rule of law – and presented evidence in favor of that hypothesis. What remains to be done is to test the hypothesis with some form of "control group." Ideally, we would have reliable and meaningful measures for Medieval Europe and Asia of things like the relative power of church and state, the nature of secular and religious court systems, and beliefs about religious systems, which would allow us to perform statistical analyses. But we do not have such data. Instead, the best option is to conduct comparative case study analyses, of which we will provide a brief sketch below.

In performing this comparative analysis, we ask only whether other cultures and civilizations in Europe and Asia could have had their religious organizations contribute to an emerging rule of law. If other religious organizations in Eurasia had circumstances similar to those in the Medieval Church, then our hypothesis implies that similar legal innovations should have occurred in those regions. On the other hand, evidence that the Medieval Church was unique in important ways that contributed to the emergence of the canon law system would support our hypothesis.

The key feature of the Medieval Church that allowed it to become a legal innovator was its "translocal, transtribal, transfeudal, transnational" scope (quoting Berman 1983, 108). The Church's integrated hierarchical nature, transcending political boundaries, generated for the Church a degree of influence and authority not held by clerics in other regions of the world. As a result, there was no other religious organization in the rest of the world that had the Medieval Church's ability to provide a counter-balance to the power of secular rulers. A few examples will provide some evidence, but each one still needs to be further investigated.

We begin with Eastern Europe. One possible alternative hypothesis to the one we raise is that Christianity as a whole was conducive to economic growth. The fact that Eastern Europe languished in the Medieval period while Western Europe grew suggests that, if religion provided preconditions to economic growth, the process was peculiar to Western Christianity. One thing that was very different in Eastern Christianity was the relationship between the various political authorities and the Orthodox Churches. Of course, the Eastern Churches go back to the founding of Christianity. After Rome fell and the Roman Church slowly learned to fill the governance gap left behind, the eastern half of the Roman Empire lived on in Byzantium. Whereas the Western Church developed Latin rites and traditions, the Eastern Churches were rooted in Greek. And if the Greek Church was centered anywhere, it was in Byzantium at the center of the empire.

The model of church and state in the Byzantine Empire was markedly different from what emerged in Western Europe in the wake of the papal reforms of the 11th and 12th centuries. Beginning with Constantine, the emperor became protector of the church and had authority over its earthly aspects. The priests possessed spiritual but not temporal authority over the church (Chidester 2000, 161–63). With the eastern priesthood subordinate to the emperor in temporal matters, there was little need for a full and robust body of church law.

As Eastern Christianity expanded throughout Eastern Europe, the Byzantine church-state model went with it. The Patriarch in Byzantium never gained authority over all of the other Orthodox churches in the way the Pope had done. What resulted, then, was a system in which each important political entity had its own Orthodox Church with its own patriarch, each of whom was head of his own Church. The various national Orthodox churches of Europe (such as the Greek, Russian, Bulgarian, Romanian, and Serbian churches) were in cooperation and fellowship with each other, but they never became the "translocal, transtribal, transfeudal, transnational" organization that Berman (1983) described. The Orthodox Churches never were in a position to be a counter-weight to their respective political powers. As a result, they could not have developed a body of law in the same way that the Western Church did.

Islam was born when Muhammad received a series of revelations from Allah through the angel Gabriel during the 7th century CE. In Muhammad's lifetime, he was not only a spiritual leader but also a temporal ruler as well. Religion and government were united in the person of the Prophet (Smith 1991, 229). Though Muhammad died in 632, a decade after assuming temporal leadership in Medina, the model for "church-state"[6] relations was already set. Religious and temporal power were merged, first in the Prophet, then in the series of "Rightly Guided" caliphs from 632 to 661, followed by the Ummayyad and Abbasid dynasties, and ultimately in the Sultan of the Ottoman Empire. Stated simply,[7] no Islamic hierarchy ever emerged that paralleled the organization of the Roman Catholic Church, and political and religious power were merged throughout much of Islamic history. These two facts made it impossible for Islam to experience the same religion-led legal innovation that occurred in Western Europe, because it would have required the caliph to stand up against himself.

The story of "church" and state in China is conceptually similar to that of Islam: the Chinese emperor was also a religious leader and thus

6 We use the term "church" in this section of the chapter only as a convenient shorthand for the various religious organizations discussed.

7 Timur Kuran has written extensively on the subject of underdevelopment in the Islamic world. Some examples include Kuran (2004a) and Kuran (2004b). He dealt specifically with legal formation in Kuran (2005, 789–99).

was unlikely to counter-balance his own power. Additional research is needed on Buddhist monasticism in China to explore the potential for the monks to build a power base separate from the emperors.

India followed a different path, in that large parts of India were ruled by Islamic invaders for a substantial part of the time period in question in this chapter (1000–1500 CE). Even so, many Indians retained their own religious beliefs rather than converting to Islam. North, Gwin, and Orman (2009) found that countries that were Hindu in 1900 had significantly higher levels of rule of law in 2004 than countries whose largest religion in 1900 was Islam, African tribal religion, or Orthodox Christianity. Whether this finding has any basis in the religious history of India is another part of our long-term project.

In summary, it is likely that, among Eurasian civilizations, only Western Europe had a religious environment that would allow a religious organization to do what the Medieval Catholic Church did – set itself up as having authority to develop its own legal system that was binding on the secular political powers.

7. Conclusion

In this chapter, we add to the overall understanding of the many reasons why modern economic growth happened first in Western Europe by emphasizing the under-appreciated role of the Roman Catholic Church. The Church's teachings, if followed, led quite naturally to increases in cooperative behavior within the Church. The gains from cooperation emerged most clearly within the monastic estates of the Church of Piety, which grew wealthy because they out-produced their secular manorial counterparts. This growing wealth drew the interests of the secular rulers, who began appropriating Church lands between 900 and 1000 CE. In response, the Church of Power reformed itself during the late 11th century under several popes, including Gregory VII. In the process of these reforms, the Church of Power increased its own levels of piety, asserted its authority over the secular rulers, established a transnational bureaucracy with the sway and influence to stand up to secular authorities, and developed its own legal system from which to enforce and enshrine these reforms. The canon law system provided an effective and comprehensive legal system in Western Europe, where none had really existed, and the Church was able to use this court system to guard itself and others against arbitrary secular rulers.

Of course, courts cannot enforce their own decrees; they must derive their legitimacy from somewhere. The ecclesiastical courts – themselves part of the Church of Power – gained legitimacy among both the princes and the paupers in part because of the goodwill built up by the Church of Piety. In summary, the Church of Power had ambition, but to fulfill its ambition it needed both the wealth and the credibility generated by the asceticism and service of the Church of Piety, both of which were made possible by the monasteries' surplus production. The Church thus protected the legal rights of both parts of its dual nature through a court system whose credibility was derivative of that of the Church of Piety. The canon law and the ecclesiastical courts thus developed laws that restricted the power of the state as against property holders (including the Church itself), and these legal principles were eventually put into the law of most countries of Western Europe. In this way, the Medieval Church's efforts to protect itself from princes and rulers led to a rule of law based on limited government – an innovation that paved the way for Western Europe's economic ascendance.

References

Axelrod, Robert. (1984). *The evolution of cooperation.* New York: Basic Books.

Barro, Robert. (2003). Determinants of economic growth in a panel of countries. *Annals of Economics and Finance* 4, 231–74.

Barro, Robert. (1997). Determinants of economic growth: A cross-country empirical study. Cambridge, MA: MIT Press.

Barro, Robert J., & Rachel M. McCleary. (2003). Religion and economic growth across countries. *American Sociological Review* 68, 760–81 (October).

Berman, Harold J. (1983). *Law and revolution: The formation of the Western legal tradition.* Cambridge, Mass.: Harvard University Press.

Chidester, David. (2000). *Christianity: A global history.* New York: HarperCollins.

Diamond, Jared. (1999). *Guns, germs, and steel: The fates of human societies.* New York: W. W. Norton & Co.

Ekelund, Robert B., Jr., Robert F. Hébert, Robert D. Tollison, Gary M. Anderson, & Audrey B. Davidson. (1996). *Sacred trust: The Medieval Church as an economic firm.* New York: Oxford University Press.

Fukuyama, Francis. (1995). *Trust: The social virtues & the creation of prosperity.* New York: The Free Press.

Gilchrist, J. (1969). *The Church and economic activity in the Middle Ages.* London: St. Martin's Press.

Guiso, Luigi, Paola Sapienza, & Luigi Zingales. (2003). People's Opium? Religion and economic attitudes. *Journal of Monetary Economics* 50, 225–82.

Herlihy, David. (1961). Church property on the European continent, 701–1200. *Speculum* 36(1), 81–105 (January).

Jones, Eric. (2003). *The European miracle: Environments, economies and geopolitics in the history of Europe and Asia.* 3rd Ed. Cambridge, UK: Cambridge University Press.

Knack, Stephen, & Philip Keefer. (1995). Institutions and economic performance: Cross-country tests using alternative institutional measures. *Economics and Politics* 7(3), 207–27 (November).

Kuran, Timur. (2005). The absence of the corporation in Islamic law: Origins and persistence. *American Journal of Comparative Law* 53(4), 785–834.

Kuran, Timur. (2004a). *Islam and mammon: The economic predicaments of Islam.* Princeton, NJ: Princeton University Press.

Kuran, Timur. (2004b). Why the Middle East is economically underdeveloped: Historical mechanisms of institutional stagnation. *Journal of Economic Perspectives* 18(3), 71–90.

Landes, David S. (1999). *The wealth and poverty of nations: Why some are so rich and some are so poor.* New York: W. W. Norton & Co., Paperback Ed.

La Porta, Rafael, Florencio Lopez-de-Silanes, Andrei Shleifer, & Robert W. Vishny. (1998). Law and finance. *Journal of Political Economy* 106, 1113–55 (December).

Maddison, Angus. (2001). *The world economy: A millennial perspective.* Paris: OECD Development Centre.

North, Charles M., Carl R. Gwin, & Wafa Hakim Orman. (2009). Religion, corruption, and the rule of law. Working paper.

North, Charles M., & Beck A. Taylor. (2004). The biblical underpinnings of tit-for-tat: Scriptural insights into Axelrod's *The Evolution of Cooperation. Faith & Economics* No. 44 (Fall).

North, Douglass C., & Robert Paul Thomas. (1973). *The rise of the Western world: A new economic history.* Cambridge, UK: Cambridge University Press.

North, Douglass C. (1981). *Structure and change in economic history.* New York: W. W. Norton & Co.

Pomeranz, Kenneth. (2000). *The great divergence: China, Europe, and the making of the modern world economy.* Princeton: Princeton University Press.

Pounds, N.J.G. (1974). *An economic history of Medieval Europe.* London: Longman.

Richardson, Gary, & Michael McBride. (2009). Religion, longevity, and cooperation: The case of the craft guild. *Journal of Economic Behavior & Organization* 71, 172–86.

Rodrik, Dani. (1999). Where did all the growth go? External shocks, social conflict, and growth collapses. *Journal of Economic Growth* 4, 385–412 (December).

Samuelsson, Kurt. (1993 /1961). *Religion and economic action: The Protestant ethic, the rise of capitalism, and the abuses of scholarship.* Trans. E. Geoffrey French. Toronto: University of Toronto Press.

Scully, Gerald W. (1988). The institutional framework and economic development. *Journal of Political Economy* 96(3), 652–62 (June).
Smith, Huston. (1991). *The world's religions: Our great wisdom traditions.* San Francisco: HarperCollins.
Stark, Rodney. (2004). SSSR Presidential Address, 2004: Putting an end to ancestor worship. *Journal for the Scientific Study of Religion* 43(4), 465–75 (December).
Stark, Rodney. (2003). *For the glory of God: How monotheism led to Reformations, science, witch-hunts, and the end of slavery.* Princeton: Princeton University Press.
Weber, Max. (1992/1930). *The Protestant ethic and the spirit of capitalism.* Trans. Talcott Parsons. London: Routledge.

Max Weber Revisited

ROBERT H. NELSON

1. Introduction

When even the most extraordinary of events have become familiar, it is easy to lose sight of their true momentous quality. In the past 200 years, extraordinary is an understatement for the basic change in the human material condition on earth. An average person today in the developed parts of the world lives better in most material respects than a royal family of 300 or 400 years ago. Extending a life through quadruple by-pass heart surgery, flying from New York to London in six hours, holding a direct telephone conversation from Washington to Beijing, routinely eating a diverse diet of foods from all around the world, seeing events unfold in real time throughout the world by television – all these and many other familiar items of our existence today would have been regarded as virtual miracles in the not-so-distant past.

The turning point was 1800. Economic historian Gregory Clark reports that there was no large improvement in the living standards of the great majority of the people living in England until 1800. Indeed, for the world as a whole "the average person in … 1800 was no better off than the average person of 100,000 BC." Life expectancy was 30 to 35 years, "no higher in 1800 than for hunter gatherers." It was not until the nineteenth and twentieth centuries that there occurred "the first break of human society from the constraints of nature, the first break of the human economy from the natural economy" – the moment when very large numbers of people first overcame the state of material deprivation that had always previously characterized human existence for the great majority.[1]

There is no more important historical question than the following: how and why did this happen? The central events are familiar enough. Signs of a rapidly growing material productivity first appeared in Hol-

---

1 Gregory Clark, *A farewell to alms: A brief economic history of the world* (Princeton, NJ: Princeton University Press, 2007), pp. 195, 1, 33.

land in the seventeenth century. The leading edge of economic change shifted to England in the eighteenth century, setting the stage there for the industrial revolution in the nineteenth century. By the beginning of the twentieth century it was the United States that was leading the way into the new economic world. After World War II, the nations of the European Union came to rival the United States economically. In Asia at the same time, Japan was the first to join the new economic world. By the end of the century, China and India – along with a number of other smaller Asian nations – were following in this path.

Seen over the perspective of 200 years, all this is nothing short of astonishing. Although his writings helped to set the stage for the new economic world, Adam Smith had little inkling of the events to come – his world was the late eighteenth century before the real economic takeoff began. Karl Marx was the first great economist (great in historical impact, if not always analytical insight) who both saw clearly the extraordinary material advances taking place in the nineteenth century and attempted to offer a systematic explanation. While he offered many accurate observations, and newly focused attention on some critical issues, his theory of economic history was in the end a failure. The success of Marxism was instead as a new category of secular economic religion – drawing on apocalyptic and other familiar themes of Christianity, thus establishing a powerful religious resonance in western civilization that attracted many millions of faithful.[2] As the distinguished American theologian Paul Tillich once said, Marx was "the most successful of all theologians since the [Protestant] Reformation."[3]

After Marx, the next great economist to address directly the causes of the material transformation of the human condition was Max Weber (1864–1920). Although Weber is now regarded mainly as a sociologist, he was part of the German school of economic history and his first chaired professorship was in economics. Weber's treatise on *The Protestant Ethic and the Spirit of Capitalism* appeared in two articles in 1904–05 (followed by a modestly revised edition in 1920).[4] Weber assumed, reasonably enough, that a significant part of the explanation must lie in the

2 See Robert H. Nelson, *Economics as religion: From Samuelson to Chicago and beyond* (University Park, PA: Pennsylvania State University Press, 2001).

3 Paul Tillich, *A history of Christian thought: From its Judaic and Hellenistic origins to existentialism* (New York: Simon and Schuster, 1967), p. 476.

4 Max Weber, *The Protestant ethic and the spirit of capitalism*, trans. Talcott Parsons (New York: Charles Scribner's, 1958). This translation is based on Weber's 1920 revision.

events of preceding centuries that set the stage. Following Marx, Weber framed his treatise as an explanation for the rise of "capitalism" (although Marx himself had seldom used this precise term).

Rather than the rise of capitalism, however, a broader and more accurate term is "new economic world" – to think of the material transformation of the nineteenth and twentieth century as merely a matter of the accumulation of "capital" and of the interactions of "capitalists" and "workers" (and other economic classes in earlier historic eras) is much too limiting. The full workings of an economy cannot be understood outside the full institutional framework – including even the religious side of life – in which it functions. As Weber argued, the ideas in the minds of human beings are a large economic "parameter" (to use some contemporary economic jargon). Indeed, strictly speaking, there is no "economic order" but only a "social order" that may include a very large economic dimension. A full understanding of even narrowly economic outcomes can not be achieved outside the consideration of law, politics, technology, psychology, philosophy, religion, and other elements of society (however great the challenge that this may pose to the current disciplinary boundaries of the academy).

Yet, as a matter of historical fact, Weber did frame his treatise as an analysis of "capitalism." It may have been because he was conforming in this respect to the intellectual trends of the late nineteenth and early twentieth century, a period when a total economic determinism often dominated intellectual discourse. If Weber hoped to receive serious attention for his work, it would be important to frame his efforts in this context, offering an improvement on (but not an outright rejection of) the Marxist understanding. While not going as far as Marx, Weber did in fact accept (reasonably enough) the partial validity of an economic determinism. It was certainly true that economic facts could significantly influence the intellectual and political events of the times. However, unlike Marx and many other total economic determinists, Weber saw that ideas could also significantly influence economic events. Indeed, as it seemed to Weber, religious ideas rivaled any other explanatory factors. The continuing interest in Weber's writings reflects the fact that he gave an atypical answer – that now seems prescient – for his time. William Schweiker, professor of theological ethics at the Divinity School of the University of Chicago, summarized the thinking as of 2009: "For many reasons, … Protestants helped to advance modern democratic political forms as well as the spread of capitalist economies."[5]

Weber, in short, was analyzing a much broader question than the specific behavior of capitalists and workers. Writing at the beginning of the twentieth century, he was saying that the astonishing material transformation of the nineteenth century – and continuing through the twentieth century, although Weber of course could not know of that – had been caused in significant part by an earlier basic change in the way the people of Europe – or at least the Protestant parts of Europe – viewed the world. The rise of the new economic world was in significant part a story in the history of religion.

2. Protestantism and Economic Winners

Weber's initial interest in the economic importance of Protestantism was stimulated by his observation that in the Germany of his times – as well as other European countries – there was a disproportionate number of Protestants among the most economically successful. As he described the question to be explored in *The Protestant Ethic and the Spirit of Capitalism*, it was that "the occupational statistics of any country of mixed religious composition brings to light with remarkable frequency … the fact that business leaders and owners of capital, as well as the higher grades of skilled labour, and even more the higher technically and commercially trained personnel of modern enterprises, are overwhelmingly Protestant" – far out of proportion to their numbers in the population.[6] This historical observation admittedly had been made before Weber and has been affirmed many times since.

In 1967, for example, the British historian Hugh Trevor-Roper commented that "even in Catholic countries, like France or Austria, it was Protestants who throve and built up industry. And it is indisputable that extreme forms of Protestantism were popular among industrial workers." Moreover, it was not all Protestants equally but especially Calvinists, the main objects of Weber's attention. Thus, in the France of Cardinal Richelieu, he "relied largely on [Protestant] Huguenot

5 William Schweiker, "Protestant ethics," in Jan Peil and Irene van Staveren, eds., *Handbook of economics and ethics* (Northampton, MA: Edward Elgar, 2009), p. 407.

6 Weber, *The Protestant ethic*, p. 35.

men of affairs. His bankers were French Calvinists." The domination by Calvinists "does not appear in France only. We have seen it in Lutheran Denmark and Lutheran Sweden" where Calvinists, although few in number, were economically prominent. All in all, "in Catholic as in Protestant countries, in the mid-seventeenth century, we find that the Calvinists are indeed the great entrepreneurs. They are an international force, the economic *elite* of Europe. They alone, it seems, can mobilize commerce and industry and, by so doing, command great sums of money, either to finance armies or to reinvest in other great economic undertakings."[7]

More recently, Walter Mead, senior fellow at the Council on Foreign Relations in New York, has written on the interaction of economics and religion in the history of Great Britain and the United States. With respect to the role of Calvinists, Mead observes that "Anglo-American history certainly provides Weber with support. The merchants of England were much more likely to be Calvinists than the general population; in the United States it was the most Calvinist regions – like New England and its daughter communities in the Middle West – that were most responsible for America's rapid development." The vast majority of Americans in the early years were Protestant but it was in particular the "Calvinist Presbyterians of New Jersey and Congregationalists of greater New England" who led the way economically.[8]

Weber was speaking mainly of the economic success of Protestants as individuals. It is possible also to speak of nations as historically "Protestant," "Catholic," or another religion (reflecting the predominant historical faith of the population, and recognizing that the present religious beliefs may have changed significantly from the past). Looking back over their history, even though they have had many individual Catholics, the following nations can be assigned unambiguously to the Protestant category: England, Holland, the Scandinavian nations, and the United States. The following nations can be assigned unambiguously to the Catholic category: Italy, Spain, Portugal, Ireland, Belgium, and Austria (this is obviously not an all-inclusive list). Germany and Switzerland are less clearcut but on balance belong in the Protestant category.

7 Hugh Trevor-Roper, *The Crisis of the seventeenth century: Religion, The Reformation, and social change* (Indianapolis, IN: Liberty Fund, 1999 – first ed. 1967), pp. 6, 8, 11–12.

8 Walter Russell Mead, *God and gold: Britain, America, and the making of the modern world* (New York: Knopf, 2007), p. 242.

Over the past 30 years, the British economic historian Angus Maddison (since 1978 a professor at the University of Groningen in Holland) has accomplished a remarkable task: compiling the most complete long run historical set of national economic data ever available (and that Weber of course did not have, although his sense of the economic situation in Europe matches fairly closely the Maddison findings).[9] In 1820, as shown in Table 1, two Protestant nations, Holland and England, were the economic super stars of Europe. Each had an income per capita almost 50 percent above that of the nearest other nation.[10] Other than these two nations, there is a surprising similarity of economic status in Europe, whether the nation is Protestant or Catholic. The incomes per capita of Catholic Italy, Spain and France were in 1820 not all that different from Protestant Germany, Switzerland, and Sweden. Four smaller nations, two Catholic and two Protestant, however, lagged – Portugal, Ireland, Norway and Finland.[11]

By 1900, around the time that Weber was writing, the picture had changed. Two of the leading Catholic nations, Italy and Spain, had joined the ranks of the economic laggards (the decline was, to be sure, only relative, as both experienced significant absolute increases in national income per capita over the course of the nineteenth century). Holland had fallen precipitously in relative economic status, now

9 Maddison's estimates of national income per capita are available at his web site. Go to http://www.ggdc.net/maddison/.

10 Estimates of national income for a year as distant as 1820 require a number of assumptions and depend critically on the relative prices employed. Economic historians Jan de Vries and Ad van der Woude compare income per capita for Great Britain and Holland from 1700 to 1850, using prices in Dutch guilders from the eighteenth century. They estimate that in 1750 income per capita in Holland was about 50 percent greater than in Britain. However, they show Britain catching up with Holland by 1790, several decades earlier than Maddison estimates, although on the whole broadly consistent with his calculations. See Jan de Vries and Ad van der Woude, *The First Modern Economy: Success, Failure, and Perseverance of the Dutch Economy, 1500–1815* (New York: Cambridge University Press, 1997), p. 707.

11 Maddison is unable to provide national income estimates for 1820 for Russia and Eastern Europe. The first year for which he provides such data is 1870 for most of the nations of Eastern Europe. In that year, Czechoslovakia and Hungary had incomes per capita greater than Portugal, the poorest nation in Western Europe, and about equal to Finland, the second poorest. In 2000, the income per capita of Russia was still only about one-third the western European standard and 22 percent of the United States income per capita.

Table 1. Per Capita GDP (1990 International Geary-Khamis dollars)

Protestant Nations	*1820*	*1900*	*1960*	*2000*
Denmark	$1,274	$3,017	$8,812	$22,966
Finland	781	1,668	6,230	19,532
Germany	1,077	2,985	7,705	18,982
Holland	1,838	3,424	8,287	21,609
Norway	801	1,877	7,204	25,133
Sweden	1,199	2,561	8,688	20,677
Switzerland	1,090	3,833	12,457	22,435
United Kingdom	1,706	4,492	8,645	20,159
*All Protestant***	*1,424*	*3,676*	*8,346*	*20,151*
Catholic Nations	*1820*	*1900*	*1960*	*2000*
Austria	1,218	2,882	6,519	20,689
Belgium	1,319	3,731	6,952	20,619
France	1,135	2,876	7,546	21,277
Ireland	877	2,736*	4,282	21,759
Italy	1,117	1,786	5,916	18,786
Portugal	923	1,302	2,956	13,812
Spain	1,008	1,786	3,072	15,622
*All Catholic***	*1,100*	*2,533*	*6,242*	*19,181*

* 1913
** Weighted. average (by population)

having an income per capital below Catholic Belgium. England ended the nineteenth century as the wealthiest country in the world but its relative economic superiority had declined sharply, and its income per capita was now only 10 percent above the rapidly rising entrant to the ranks of economic super stars, the United States.

In summary, in terms of national economic outcomes, the leading question as of 1820 was the much superior performance of Protestant Holland and England. What, if anything, had their Protestantism had to do with it? By 1900, it was the recent rise of the United States – also a Protestant nation – that commanded the greatest interest. The relative declines of Italy and Spain over the course of the nineteenth century also were notable: Was this due in any way to their Catholic heritage, or perhaps more to their Mediterranean climates and locations, or perhaps still other factors in their long histories?

Table 2. Per Capita GDP Relative to the United States (Percent)

Protestant Nations	1820	1900	1960	2000
Denmark	101 %	73 %	77 %	80 %
Finland	62	40	55	68
Germany	85	72	68	66
Holland	146	83	73	76
Norway	63	45	63	88
Sweden	95	62	76	72
Switzerland	86	93	109	78
United Kingdom	135	109	76	70
*All Protestant***	*113*	*89*	*73*	*70*
Catholic Nations	**1820**	**1900**	**1960**	**2000**
Austria	96	70	57	72
Belgium	104	91	61	72
France	90	70	66	74
Ireland	69	51*	37	76
Italy	88	43	52	66
Portugal	73	31	26	48
Spain	80	43	27	55
*All Catholic***	*87*	*61*	*55*	*67*

* 1913
** Weighted average (by population)

3. What Weber Said

Scholars are not immune to their own incentives. To write in full support of Weber's analysis and conclusions is not likely to attract much professional attention – or to lead to a professorship. Other scholars have no doubt been influenced by their own fundamental disagreement – virtually a religious disagreement – with the large role that Weber assigned to religious ideas in shaping history. One easy way of attacking Weber is to erect a straw man of his thesis, and then to proceed to demolish it. For example, some authors have correctly observed that Calvinism regarded high wealth and luxurious living as a violation of God's commands, indeed as virtual temptations of the devil. How, then, they argue, could Weber be correct to say that Calvinism provided strong religious encouragement to large profits? It is important, therefore, to understand precisely what Weber did say and did not say.

Weber devoted large portions of *The Protestant Ethic and the Spirit of Capitalism* to the idea of the "calling." A distinctive feature of Calvinism was its view of an all-powerful God who could not be influenced in any way by human actions – including the critical determination of whether a person was or was not among the saved. Calvinist theology offered the most extreme Protestant rejection of the Catholic theology that allowed "works" to have a role in salvation. God for Calvin had thus simply predestined some people (unfortunately a minority) for salvation and the others to eternal damnation. Moreover, it would be impossible for any human being to know in which category he or she fell, however good or bad their behavior might seem by ordinary human standards, or indeed any other human criteria. God's thinking in matters of salvation must remain simply a great and inscrutable mystery, known only to Him.

Weber argued that, whatever the theological merits of such a view, it was a psychologically untenable belief for an ordinary member of the human species. If literally believed, if nothing whatsoever mattered in matters of salvation, it might easily lead to a deep fatalism, a lack of moral commitment, and a withdrawal from the world – or perhaps instead to a selfish individualism in pursuit of many worldly pleasures. The later Calvinist response (if not that of Calvin himself), as Weber found, was to see success in a calling as a "sign" (but not a guarantee) of God's favor. For the good Calvinist, those who were saved would have an inner peace of mind and grace that would manifest itself in worldly accomplishments in pursuit of a calling. In a great paradox, the religious success of Calvinism may have lain significantly in the fact that its popular understanding brought back salvation by good works in spades. However much Calvin himself might have been horrified by the thought, one might even say that the later evolution of Calvinism ended up with a stronger statement of salvation by works than the original version of the Catholic Church itself.

A good Calvinist thus had the strongest religious encouragement to pursue success in a business enterprise, among other possible callings, with full religious fervor. A high level of profits might in practice serve as the best indicator of a future in heaven. High profits, however, could also pose a grave new threat. If a newly successful businessman began to live a life of pleasure and luxury, the prospects for his eternal soul might be endangered – as had happened to many ex-Calvinists. It was not necessary, however, for the businessman to live in poverty. A devout Calvinist whose calling was in business should be as successful – should make as large a profit as possible – within the bounds of acting ethically in his relations with others. He should not, however, use the profits for any grand pleasures for himself or his family.

There were two main options. The most likely was to reinvest the profits in the business, thus boosting the total level of capital investment, creating further profits and investment, and establishing a cycle of profit making and investment obviously calculated to help to create a new economic order (often referred to as "capitalism"). Another option, also pursued by many Calvinists, was to give the money away (perhaps most likely to occur in the later stages of life). As Weber emphasized, regarded from a utilitarian point of view of maximizing personal happiness and enjoyment – perhaps the outlook of most people in the history of the world – the Calvinist businessman was behaving altogether "irrationally." He was supposed to work very hard, impose on himself a severe personal discipline throughout his life, and yet should not want or get much practical benefit – in this world at least. Calvinism in this way produced, as one might say, a whole new human species of "ascetic entrepreneur and businessman."

It amounted, as Weber observed, to a transfer of the religious zeal of the monk to the practical affairs of the world. Not only a few select people of exceptional religious devotion but all people must live and act according to the religious principles of the monastery. As it has frequently been said of Protestantism, its followers were "the priesthood of all believers." As Weber wrote about the ethic promoted by Calvinism,

> [It] acted powerfully against the spontaneous enjoyment of possessions; it restricted consumption, especially of luxuries. On the other hand, it had the psychological effect of freeing the acquisition of goods from the inhibitions of traditionalist ethics. It broke the bonds of the impulse of acquisition in that it not only legalized it, but ... looked upon it as directly willed by God. The campaign against the temptations of the flesh, and the dependence on external things, was ... not a struggle against rational acquisition, but against the irrational use of wealth.[12]

This was the core argument of *The Protestant Ethic and the Spirit of Capitalism*. But Weber also developed many other important themes in a less organized fashion, a main reason for the continuing wide interest in his work. Gathered together appropriately, as will be described below, some of Weber's lesser themes can be cumulated to form larger theses – sometimes identified by Weber in passing, sometimes never mentioned explicitly by him (leaving it to his later readers to do the work

12 Weber, *The Protestant ethic*, p. 171.

of interpretation). One area of particular interest was the tension between the individual and the community in Calvinism.

A 2003 study of the impact of Calvinism describes it as having brought about a "disciplinary revolution" in early modern Europe. In comparing Catholicism, Lutheranism and Calvinism, Philip Gorski notes that "while all three confessions advocated discipline – both religious and social – it was the Calvinists who did so with the greatest fervor and consequence." Calvinism also "gave particular emphasis to the conformity of the church – indeed the entire political community – with scriptural law." For the Calvinists, the purpose of their tight social discipline "was not so much to punish individual sinners as to expunge sin from the Christian community."[13]

Thus, on the one hand, Calvinism, like all Protestantism, was deeply individualistic – the new relationship with God was that of an individual without any church intermediaries. On the other hand, Calvinism offered a powerful sense of common membership in a religious community. God had instructed that a Calvinist community should be a model of righteousness and virtue. The original Puritans who came to Massachusetts in the seventeenth century saw themselves as building a "city upon a hill" as a beacon for all the world. As Weber notes, and similar to the Jews (Calvinism and Judaism were close cousins in many respects), the Puritans saw themselves as "God's chosen people" in the fulfillment of his plans for the world.[14] Ironically in light of the individualism of the formal theology, a Calvinist community was likely to be more cohesive and to exercise stricter collective discipline than its Catholic counterpart – as Weber recognized while choosing not to make this a central message of *The Protestant Ethic and the Spirit of Capitalism.* Calvin's Geneva was at least as close to the medieval as the modern spirit of political and economic freedom in its manner of governance.

13 Philip S. Gorski, *The disciplinary revolution: Calvinism and the rise of the state in early modern Europe* (Chicago: University of Chicago Press, 2003), pp. 20, 21.
14 Weber, *The Protestant ethic*, p. 166.

4. Weber's Early Critics

Criticism of Weber's thesis emerged almost as soon as it appeared among German scholars such as Felix Rachfahl, Werner Sombart, Georg Simmel, and Lujo Brentano.[15] Rachfahl argued that the laity among the Catholic faithful were also encouraged to hard work and ascetic discipline, much in the manner of a Calvinist pursuit of a calling. Sombart found that the Jews historically were the more important factor in the rise of capitalism, also pointing to counter-examples such as Leon Battiste Alberti, a very successful Florentine merchant whose work ethic and other values closely resembled those found by Weber in Calvinism. Brentano cited the example of Jacob Fugger who well before the Reformation exhibited a dedication to making very large amounts of money simply for its own sake. Others argued that the discoveries of the Americas had shifted economic activity in Europe away from the Mediterranean, and towards the Atlantic (and only by coincidence toward Protestant nations such as Holland and England).

In England, R.H. Tawney in 1926 became one of the first to address the Weber thesis in *Religion and the Rise of Capitalism.*[16] He disagreed with Weber's argument that the Protestant Ethic had itself caused the rise of capitalism, stating that "if capitalism means the direction of industry by owners of capital for their own pecuniary gain, and the social relations which establish themselves between them and the wage-earning proletariat whom they control, then capitalism had existed on a grand scale both in medieval Italy and in medieval Flanders."[17] But Tawney still found a large role for Calvinism in economic history, partly because the workings of a capitalist economy had helped to reshape Calvinism itself. Its evolving religious precepts, including importantly the idea of "the calling" that Weber emphasized, gave additional ethical support and legitimacy to capitalism. Economics and religion thus interacted and reinforced one another to create a powerful impetus that at first had yielded the political and economic institutions of Holland and England and then spread to wider parts of the world in the nineteenth and twentieth centuries.

---

15 See Malcom M. MacKinnon, "The longevity of the thesis: A critique of the critics," in Hartmut Lehmann and Guenther Roth, eds., *The Protestant Ethic: Origins, evidence, contexts* (New York: Cambridge University Press, 1993).

16 R. H. Tawney, *Religion and the rise of capitalism* (London: J. Murray, 1926).

17 Tawney, p. 84.

Another English reviewer, H.M. Robertson, in 1933 recast some of the themes of Tawney, again finding that capitalism first appeared in Italy, as well as pointing to the earlier presence within Catholicism of an ascetic commitment to worldly tasks.[18] In the years after World War II, the Swedish economic historian Kurt Samuelsson was among the strongest critics of Weber, declaring in 1957 that "'capitalism' and the 'capitalistic ethic' had existed long before the Reformation." Indeed, "viewed in the perspective of the history of ideas as a whole, the element of divergence from the corresponding Catholic world was from the beginning exceedingly slight." Belgium, a Catholic country, was also rapidly developing the institutions of capitalism in the sixteenth and seventeenth centuries. Samuelsson concludes that as a matter of economic history "wherever Weber saw Protestants and the Reformed church, other [non-religious] factors can be found that are far more obviously calculated to promote trade and industry, capital formation and economic progress." Indeed, the real key to the success of England, Holland, Scotland, and the northern part of Germany lay "in their location on ocean shores of transcontinental routes that were in use hundreds of years before the Reformation."[19] Samuelsson asserted that, contrary to Weber (and even the views of some of Weber's critics), religion and the rise of capitalism were simply two altogether unrelated subjects.

Other reviewers of Weber's work in the 1950s, however, were more approving. In 1958 a leading American intellectual historian, H. Stuart Hughes, saw Weber as an intellectual giant of the twentieth century who with Emil Durkheim was one of "the two most important founders of the discipline of sociology." Indeed, Hughes declares that Weber is "the only rival of Freud for the title of the leading social thinker of our century" (admittedly a greater compliment in 1958, when esteem for Freud was at its peak, than it would be today).[20] Hughes wrote with respect to *The Protestant Ethic and the Spirit of Capitalism* that:

18 H. M. Robertson, *Aspects of the rise of economic individualism: A criticism of Max Weber and his school* (Cambridge, UK: Cambridge University Press, 1933).

19 Kurt Samuelsson, *Religion and economic action: A critique of Max Weber,* trans. by E. Geoffrey French (New York: Harper Torchbooks, 1961 – first Swedish ed. 1957), pp. 48, 115.

20 H. Stuart Hughes, "Weber's search for rationality in Western society," in Robert W. Green, ed., *Protestantism, capitalism and social science: The Weber thesis controversy* (Lexington, MA: D.C. Heath, 1973), pp. 150, 158. This article is ex-

> [It] early became the most widely read of Weber's writings. And this popularity was unquestionably justified. Despite all the criticism to which it has been subjected, and the corrections of detail that is has undergone, The Protestant Ethic remains one of the great works of social thought of our time – an almost unique combination of imaginative boldness in its central hypothesis and meticulous scholarship in its documentation. In its careful balancing of the material and spiritual, it pursues an argument of a subtlety that has frequently thrown the overhasty reader off track.[21]

By 1964, as Robert Green has observed, "no five-foot shelf could have held all the works published on the Weber thesis controversy."[22] Although there would be no diminution of interest, the character of much of the future commentary, however, would change. It is now often acknowledged that the specific importance of the Calvinist calling in Weber's thesis may well have been overstated. The economic impacts of Calvinism and other forms of Protestantism are still seen as powerful but they were in fact diverse and other features of Protestantism may have been equally or more important. In 1998, for example, the Harvard economic historian David Landes wrote that in England, "the Dissenters (read Calvinists) were disproportionately active and influential in the factories and forges of the nascent Industrial Revolution." While declaring his overall strong support for the Weber thesis, Landes shifts the emphasis somewhat: "The heart of the matter lay indeed in the making of a new kind of man: rational, ordered, diligent, productive. These virtues, while not new, were hardly commonplace. Protestantism generalized them among its adherents, who judged one another by conformity to these standards."[23]

5. The Dutch Case

In 1500, as Table 3 (also based on Maddison estimates) shows, Italy was the richest nation in Europe. Italy, however, was eclipsed by Holland in 1600 and the gap between Holland and Italy (and the rest of Europe as

---

cerpted from Hughes, *Consciousness and society: The reorientation of European social thought, 1890–1930* (New York, Knopf, 1958).

21 Ibid., p. 165.

22 Robert W. Green, "Introduction," in Green, ed., *Protestantism, capitalism and social science*, p. xiii.

23 William S. Landes, *The wealth and poverty of nations: Why some are so rich and some so poor* (New York: Norton, 1998), p. 177.

well) continued to grow during the seventeenth century. By 1700, Holland's income per capita was 70 percent greater than that of England, its closest economic rival.[24] Italy and Belgium, two Catholic countries, in 1700 also had incomes per capita below but similar to England. The rest of Europe fell even much further behind the Dutch. As of 1600, Catholic Europe was still richer than Protestant Europe, but that was no longer true in 1700. By then, the weighted average (by population) of the incomes per capita of the Protestant nations of Europe exceeded that of the Catholic nations by 14 percent. This gap would become larger and persist for three centuries until the late twentieth century.

The most rapid period of Dutch growth was from the 1580s to the 1660s. As economic historians Jan de Vries and Ad van der Woude report, Holland "grew quickly in strength, dominated the economy of Europe, and constructed a trading empire that spanned much of the world." By 1650, Holland had the highest wage rates in Europe, partly reflecting the fact that it was able to maintain "the highest overall level of total factor productivity for the better part of the seventeenth and eighteenth centuries." In the first half of the seventeenth century, for example, agricultural productivity increased by 80 percent. As a result of these and other economic advances, de Vries and van der Woude conclude that the United Provinces of Holland in the seventeenth century "can lay claim to being the first modern economy by virtue of continuity (it has been a modern economy ever since) and by virtue of establishing the conditions for economic modernity over much of Europe."[25]

Dutch productivity increases were based in part on the accumulation of large stocks of investment capital. Holland benefited as a common destination for French Huguenots, Antwerp merchants, Italian capitalists, Spanish Jews, and other wealthy individuals fleeing limits on their economic freedoms and other forms of state and church control elsewhere. But most of the Dutch investment was generated internally. De Vries and van der Woude report on the example of Louis Trip, a

---

24 More precisely, we mean the "United Kingdom," but I will use "England" in this chapter in the broadest sense, unless speaking specifically of Scotland or some other subunit of the United Kingdom.

25 Jan de Vries and Ad van der Woude, *The first modern economy: Success, failure, and perseverance of the Dutch economy, 1500–1815* (New York: Cambridge University Press, 1997), pp. 668, 693, 673, 693.

Dutchman who invested 46,000 guilders in two family businesses in 1632, saw them double:

> in value in fifteen years, and then increase six-fold in the next decade, leaving him with assets of greater than 600,000 guilders in the 1660s – all this possible partly because he spent less than 10 percent of his annual income for consumptive purposes. He would seem to be, in short, a capitalist as described by Weber, and there were many more of his kind in Holland. Investment was also encouraged by a proliferation of Dutch "institutional, technological, and organizational improvements" that, among other encouragements to economic growth, significantly "reduced transactions costs," thus helping to generate large profits.[26]

Table 3 Income per capita (1990 International Geary-Khamis dollars)

Protestant Nations	1500	1600	1700
Denmark	738	875	1,039
Finland	454	538	638
Germany	688	791	910
Holland	761	1,381	2,130
Norway	610	665	722
Sweden	695	824	977
Switzerland	632	750	890
United Kingdom	714	974	1,250
All Protestant*	692	862	1,085
Catholic Nations	**1500**	**1600**	**1700**
Austria	707	837	993
Belgium	875	976	1,144
France	727	841	910
Ireland	526	615	715
Italy	1,100	1,100	1,100
Portugal	606	740	819
Spain	661	853	853
All Catholic*	817	914	951

* weighted average (by population)

At one point, De Vries and van der Woude examine directly the role of Calvinism in the economic rise of the Dutch Republic. They find that Calvinism was a significant factor but not precisely in the way postulated by Weber. For one thing, many of the Protestants of Holland were not in fact devout Calvinists; they might be critical of the Catholic Church, and advocates of major religious and other institutional changes in Eu-

26 Ibid., p. 670.

rope, but their thinking was often more in the humanistic vein of Erasmus. Cities such as Amsterdam attracted large numbers of the economic and religious refuges of Europe who brought a wide range of unorthodox views. Hence, as de Vries and van der Woude conclude, the evidence is weak for the direct "influence of Calvinism in rationalizing personal life," as Weber had theorized.[27]

They reject, however, any suggestion that Calvinism was irrelevant to the economic success of Holland. For one thing, the very existence of an independent and free Holland resulted from the fierce religious struggle – lasting 80 years – of Dutch Calvinists against Spanish Catholic rule. Calvinism also helped to frame even among "the humanists among the urban elite … [a new understanding of] themselves" in Dutch society. The Calvinist way of thinking "furnished the merchant, artisan, and, indeed, all commercial people a basis upon which to claim a legitimate place in the Christian polity" of Holland. De Vries and van der Woude conclude that "without the inner-psychological and outer-political 'fixing agent' of Calvinism, the claims of merchants to govern in a Republic would have been difficult to justify – to themselves as much as to others." Coming close to the Weber formulation, the Calvinist influence also encouraged successful Dutch businessmen "to avoid the destructive temptations of the secular life through an ascetic discipline," continuing in the zealous pursuit of ever greater economic successes.[28]

But departing somewhat from Weber, de Vries and van der Woude find that the political role of Calvinism may also have been an important factor in that it exerted a powerful "influence in rationalizing public life," serving to encourage the many institutional and organizational improvements devised in Holland from the sixteenth to the eighteenth centuries. In short, Weber's specific thesis relating to the Calvinist theology of predestination and the calling may not have been the decisive factor in the rise of the Dutch economy but "what cannot be doubted is the important impress left by Calvinism" on a number of important features of the Dutch state and on the self-concept of the individual Dutch businessman, all this contributing significantly to the rise of Holland as the "first modern economy," the richest country in Europe through the seventeenth and eighteenth centuries.[29]

27 Ibid., p. 169.
28 Ibid., p. 168, 169.
29 Ibid., pp. 169, 172, 707.

6. Protestantism as Agent of Social Transformation

In an extreme form of economic determinism such as Marxism, the essential explanations are all material. The content of ideas and all the rest of society follow from the economics – in Marxism, the mental illusions of a "false consciousness" (such as religion) merely correspond to the workings of a particular stage of economic history. Although the economics profession today does not carry things this far, it has long believed that the economy can be studied independent of political, psychological and other non-material elements of society. There are "laws" of economic events to be discovered that are analogous to the laws that control the natural world – and economists should also expect to develop precise mathematical formulations of these laws.

A transformation of the astonishing magnitude of the new economic world of the nineteenth and twentieth centuries, however, must encompass every element of society.[30] In 1968, a leading Israeli sociologist, S.N. Eisenstadt, argued that Weber's full argument is better understood in such a broad framework, as a study in the ability of Protestantism to transform a whole society in all its respects, not just the economic behavior of its members. Eisenstadt notes that different religions can have varying capacities to bring about – intentionally or unintentionally – "the transformation of social reality" in all its economic, political, legal, and other aspects. Protestantism, moreover, has a particularly high transformative capacity among religions, even though "all the scholars who have dealt with the matter seem to agree that the transformative potential seems not to be connected to a single tenet of the Protestant faith."[31]

It is nevertheless clear that one of "the most important [factors is] … its strong combination of 'this-worldliness' and transcendentalism." Protestantism has a special way of redirecting religious energies to radically altering the practical affairs of this world. A second key factor is "the strong emphasis on individual activism and responsibility," causing lay Protestants to work devotedly for improvements in the world. A third factor is "the direct relationship of the individual to the sacred

30 See Karl Polanyi, *The great transformation: The political and economic origins of our times* (Boston: Beacon, 1957 – first ed. 1944).

31 S. N. Eisenstadt, "The Protestant ethic thesis in an analytical and comparative framework," in S.N. Eisenstadt, *The Protestant ethic and modernization: A comparative view* (New York: Basic Books, 1968), p. 10.

and to the sacred tradition," as found above all in Protestantism, and which "minimizes the extent to which individual commitment is mediated by any institution, organization, or textual exegesis." This element encourages individuals to dedicate themselves to "the possibility of continuous redefinition, a possibility which is further enhanced by the strong transcendental emphasis that minimizes the sacredness of any 'here and now,'" and thus opens the way to whole new ways of conceiving the workings of religion and every other part of society.[32] Taking its cues from Luther's initial bold act of rebellion, Protestantism offered almost an institutionalization of the habit of radical change.

Although beginning with Luther, these features were characteristic most of all of Calvinism. For the Calvinist faithful, Eisenstadt writes, they redefined their whole "conception … of the social world and of their own place in it." This reconception of individual and collective identity was not limited to the economic side of life but encompassed all aspects. Rather than changes in the economic side of life, as emphasized by Weber, an even greater consequence – especially in the earlier part of the Protestant Reformation in the sixteenth century – may have been in the political realm. Protestant, and especially Calvinist, communities were characterized by a great autonomy and self-sufficiency from the larger state. Thus, as Eisenstadt writes, "the basic theological tenets of Luther, Zwingli, and Calvin themselves – however marked were the differences in their attitudes toward political constitutions – contained some very strong reformulations of the relationships between state and 'society,' between rulers and ruled, and of the scope and nature of the political community." Although Weber gave less attention to the political consequences of Protestantism, "the first institutional aspect … which Protestantism tended to transform was the central symbols, identities and institutions of the political sphere."[33] Even much later, as compared with the other countries of Europe, the institutional differences found in Holland and England – the two European Protestant nations of conspicuously greatest economic success – were greater in terms of their political systems than their economic systems.

32 Ibid., pp. 10, 11.
33 Ibid., p. 11.

7. The Consequences of Religious Competition

Eisenstadt focuses on the influence of ideas so he does not address two other factors that may have been even more important in making Protestantism a powerful agent of social transformation. First, there was the very fact of the Protestant Reformation itself. Catholic theologians have often used a different term, referring to the "Protestant Revolution."[34] Protestantism did in fact provide a revolutionary example for Europe. In a real sense (more likely to be noted by a Catholic historian), and although Luther did not directly command any armies, he precedes Cromwell, Robespierre, and Lenin. In 1500, the Catholic Church had held a religious monopoly in Europe for a thousand years; whatever its many failings, it had survived and anchored Christian Europe for all that time. It was an act of immense daring to declare that the Catholic Church was not merely fallible but that secession from the Church was a real and legitimate option – or even an obligation if the Church had betrayed its true mission. It would be no less bold today, for example, for a citizen of the United States to declare that there exists a right of sovereign secession – indeed mandated in certain circumstances – from the American nation-state.[35] Luther not only made such a heretical statement (for his and our time as well) but acted forcefully to make it happen.

Once Luther had set the precedent, to be sure, it would be successfully followed by many within Protestantism itself. After Luther's great secession, it was difficult to say why one Protestant group should not also be free to secede from another. Indeed, by 1600 there was a multiplicity of Protestant churches, ranging from the Anglican Church in England to numerous minor sects throughout Protestant Europe – a state of affairs that continues to the present day. As Catholic theologians have often lamented, the institutional practices of Protestantism create a state of "free choice" in religion. If a church can in some sense be analogized to a firm, Roman Catholicism before Luther was a religious monopoly, while Protestantism then created a "free market" in religion

34 John W. O'Malley, *Trent and all that: Renaming Catholicism in the early modern era* (Cambridge, MA: Harvard University Press, 2000).

35 In 1861, the American south did of course make such a statement but Lincoln and the north ruthlessly suppressed it in the Civil War, the greatest military cataclysm in all of American history. In the sixteenth century, Rome attempted a similar suppression and had considerable success in restoring many newly Lutheran areas to Catholic authority, but many other areas successfully resisted.

(also leaving the Catholic Church in many religiously pluralistic nations as just another religious competitor).[36]

The consequences for religion of the contrasting organizational structures of Roman Catholicism and Protestantism were large. In economics, a free market is almost inevitably more dynamic than a monopoly; the pace of economic innovation and change is more rapid where there is free and open competition. Religious change is not much different; if I do not like my current Ford, I can always buy a Toyota, and the same holds true for my exercise of religious choice. Then, if religious change can cause economic change, as Weber argued, economies in nations with Protestant religions will tend to be more dynamic as well. Since every economic system requires some form of religious legitimation (if often in our own day provided by forms of secular religion), the economies in Protestant societies will be able to adapt more quickly to new market forces, technological changes, and other altered circumstances.

This goes far to explain why, as has often been observed, Protestantism in the modern age has been more susceptible than Catholicism to the modern forces of secularization. It is in significant part due to the competitive organizational structure of Protestant religion. As new scientific discoveries and other events challenged or even undermined many traditional Christian beliefs, Protestant religion in the modern era could adapt more easily and quickly, as compared with Catholic religion. This did not require every denomination of Protestantism to change rapidly but merely some of its branches that would then gain many new adherents. Another apt analogy is to Darwinist evolution; Protestantism, one might say, is a Darwinist form of religious adaptation, while Catholicism offers a single large religious bureaucracy that in principle can evolve only through internal processes of change. Modern ideas thus more rapidly penetrated Protestant theology and practice (as a whole, even as some particular Protestant denominations defined their position in the "religious market" by a wholesale rejection of modern trends).

This is not to suggest that Protestants were (or are) any less devout than Catholics. Indeed, it was probably more often the contrary. Each Protestant could find a branch of the Christian faith that both proclaimed to possess an absolute truth of the world and this truth would

36 See Laurence R. Iannaccone, "Introduction to the economics of religion," *Journal of Economic Literature,* 36 (September 1998), 1465–96.

correspond closely to the religious sensibilities of the individual member of the faithful. If the theology of the Catholic Church seemed to be in error, there was not much a good Catholic could do. If the theology of a Protestant denomination seemed in error, a person could often simply switch to another church. In short, just as a free economic market matches goods and services with widely varying individual tastes, Protestantism can reach a similar result in the religious domain. Deeper religious conviction and greater piety among the Protestant faithful – at least on average – is to be expected, even as the range of strongly held Protestant convictions may be more diverse.[37]

8. Warfare as Agent of Change

Unfortunate as it was, the reality is that another important historical impact of the Protestant Reformation was the widespread religious warfare in Europe that followed, reaching a peak with the Thirty Years War from 1618 to 1648. In some German states, as much as 50 percent of the total population is estimated to have died. Throughout Germany, the loss of life may have been as high as 30 percent. Germany was convulsed economically and politically during this period as armies marched back and forth across its territory, destroying property and leaving states intermittently subject to Catholic and Protestant rule. Normal life was impossible. War also encouraged authoritarian rule; in war individual freedoms easily become a luxury no longer seen as affordable. The Thirty Year War set Germany back several decades from the normal course of economic development.

37 Protestantism might also be analogized to a decentralized system of many local governments, while Catholicism is like a centralized system of one government for the whole nation. Using an economic model, the economist Charles Tiebout once famously demonstrated how in a decentralized system the levels of public services would closely match the consumer tastes of the residents of each locality, as people entered and left, thus sorting themselves out according to income and tastes for local public services, and generating a system of more homogenous localities. Such a result would be more difficult or even impossible to obtain in a monolithic state or national system where public services would be similar everywhere. Protestantism might be said to offer a similar "Tiebout solution" in the religious domain. See Charles M. Tiebout, "A Pure Theory of Local Expenditures," *Journal of Political Economy* 64 (October 1956), 416–24.

There was, however, an unintended possible benefit from all this; after the fighting stopped, Germany had to be rebuilt. With the old order destroyed, the way was paved for a new order to be created, allowing for a degree of social transformation that is normally impossible in the face of many entrenched forces powerfully resistant to such change. After World War II, the two most rapidly growing nations in the world were Germany and Japan (admittedly, partly because they had new political systems imposed on them and the United States committed large resources to their rebuilding). On balance, the Thirty Years War may well have been a net detriment economically for Germany, including over the long run, but it would require a detailed analysis of all the long run factors to develop a full assessment.

Moreover, there were different economic impacts of the Thirty Years War – both short run and long run – among the nations of Europe. England did not escape the conflict altogether but, partly owing to the protections afforded by its island geography, it never had to worry seriously about outside invasion and in general suffered less than other European nations. It did have its own internal religious war within Protestantism, culminating in the Puritan Revolution, but the level of devastation paled before that in some parts of continental Europe. Holland was also largely spared the worst ravages of the Thirty Years War and in 1648 derived a great benefit; it finally emerged as an independent nation, as a weakened Spain, after 80 years of fighting to prevent Dutch secession, finally had to concede Holland's independence. Sweden under Gustavus Adolphus intervened militarily in Germany with great success, while avoiding any destructive warfare on its own soil, leaving Sweden at the end of the Thirty Years War as a newly powerful European nation. Thus, at its conclusion the fierce religious warfare of the early to mid seventeenth century left three nations, all Protestant, better off relative to other European countries. War exceeds even a free market in its ability to bring about radical social transformation – an unintended and unfortunate consequence of the Protestant Reformation.

9. Protestantism and Social Discipline

In its struggles with Spain, Holland was able to fend off a much larger nation state partly because the Dutch showed remarkable discipline and organization. England in the sixteenth century had had its own successes in fending off Spain, defeating the Spanish Armada (with some help from the weather). The Sweden of Gustavus Adolphus, as noted, was a similarly effective fighting state. Some of the more recent reviewers of the Weber thesis have argued that another main consequence of the Protestant Reformation was in fact the strengthening of discipline and in general of state capabilities in the Protestant nations of Europe, relative to Catholic Europe. This inevitably would have major consequences for the political and economic history of Europe.

Philip Gorski, a recent commentator on *The Protestant Ethic and the Spirit of Capitalism*, writes that "Calvin understood church discipline as a form of witness through which God's will and majesty were made manifest in the world."[38] Thus, much as an individual might obtain a sign of his or her favor before God through success in a calling, there could also be a collective sign of God's favor. Worldly success would be important to Calvinists both at the individual and the community levels. When the Calvinist community and the state overlapped, the Calvinist state was likely to be less corrupt, to impose tighter moral standards, and to be more administratively efficient, as compared with its Catholic counterparts. (The Catholic state, however, was more likely to be disciplined and efficient in carrying out the task of expunging heresy from its midst.)

The Calvinist emphasis on the self-discipline of the individual also served to create "more obedient and industrious subjects" whose self discipline made it possible to put them to use by the Calvinist state "with less coercion and violence." Those who work with great zeal for a collective purpose – doing it their own free will – are likely to serve the state more effectively than those who are simply ordered to do so. In Calvinist political bodies, there thus appeared a "new infrastructure of governance" that was put at the service of the early modern state, resulting in an overall "intensification of governance."[39]

If the most famous Weber thesis related to the impact of Calvinism in the business world, Gorski sees another important message in that the process of increasing state capacities was also "unleashed by the Protestant Reformation." Understanding this newly emerging form of early modern state "helps explain why two of the least centralized and least monarchical states in the early modern world – the Netherlands and England – were also among the most orderly and powerful" of Europe-

38 Gorski, *The disciplinary revolution*, p. 21.
39 Ibid., xvi.

an states.[40] Beginning in the seventeenth century, they gave their citizens more freedom but also could count on greater individual allegiance. They effectively built a physical and social infrastructure that directed and enhanced the most constructive state use of individual freedoms from the bottom up.

As Gorski acknowledges, while they are embedded at various places, Weber in the *Protestant Ethic and the Spirit of Capitalism* did not develop such political arguments in a systematic way. In a 1919–20 essay on "The Protestant Sects," however, he came closer. As Gorski describes Weber's argument then, "what distinguished the ecclesiastical polity of the ascetic churches and sects ... was that they all possessed a system of congregational discipline, ... which was quite different from the system of ecclesiastical discipline practiced by the Catholic Church and other hierocratic denominations, such as Lutheranism and Anglicanism." In the Calvinist and other Protestant denominations with similar internal practices, "discipline was enforced by the laity, was communal in character, and focused on the moral qualities of the individual believer. It was public and it was imposed by one's peers" in the church. In the Catholic system of church governance, by contrast, "discipline was enforced by the clergy, was authoritarian in character, and was triggered by specific offenses. It was private and it was applied by the priestly class."[41] The internal communal discipline of the Calvinist congregation proved to be more effective than the external commands of the Catholic hierarchy (or of the Catholic state working in close coordination with the Catholic Church).

As such attitudes were secularized in the eighteenth century, the Protestant habits of disciplined study, self – improvement and self – education were transferred to the workings of the emerging modern state. It made, for example, for better informed voters who were better able to distinguish among the political charlatans and the politicians with real claims to leadership skills. By contrast, those who grew up in a Catholic society had little historic religious experience to draw upon in biblical study, church participation and other lay responsibilities for church leadership and management. The results were visible in the nineteenth and twentieth centuries in the longstanding political disorders of Italy and Spain (until they joined the European Union) and that still continue in much of Latin America today.

40 Ibid., xvi, xvii.
41 Ibid., 27.

10. Weber's Grand Narrative

In 2005, the centenary of the publication of *The Protestant Ethic and the Spirit of Capitalism* arrived. In a chapter in a celebratory volume, the American sociologist Donald Nielsen interpreted Weber's most important message as the statement of an original "philosophy of history." The use of the term "capitalism" was so fluid that it was hard to say any longer what it might even mean. Except perhaps for a few hardcore members of the economics profession, interest in exclusively material understandings of society was declining, with Marxism–the most extreme form of determinism–now rapidly becoming a leftover of a bygone era. According to Nielsen, Weber's insights were still very relevant to our own times because, when seen in their totality, *The Protestant Ethic and the Spirit of Capitalism* portrays the rise of the modern economic world as one element of a much larger "grand narrative" that charted "the transformation from medieval to modern culture" in Europe.[42]

In presenting this grand narrative, Nielsen finds that–by assembling the insights of diverse parts of *The Protestant Ethic*–Weber develops "his history into a coherent whole through the use of a variety of narrative devices, including ideas of historical reversal, revival, and return, as well as inner transformation and others," in a process covering "over a half millennium of history as well as aspects of the histories of a half dozen nations, including England, America, France, Germany, Italy and Holland."[43] *The Protestant Ethic* includes, as Nielsen describes it, a sophisticated portrayal of "the structure of medieval religious consciousness."[44] The medieval outlook had the following features:

> In the medieval worldview, it was thought impossible for these groups [among the laity] to lead a rational, disciplined existence. Instead it was assumed that since they were in the world, occupied the natural status of mankind in a fallen state, and caught up in worldly pursuits, they would inevitably sin and, therefore regularly require the system of canon law, confession, and penance that the church provided for the remission of sins. The effect of the confessional was "to relieve the subject from personal responsibility for his conduct ... and thus of the full rigor of ascetic demands." A

42 Donald A. Nielsen, "The Protestant ethic and the spirit of capitalism as grand narrative: Max Weber's philosophy of history," in William H. Swatos, Jr. and Lutz Kaelber, eds., *The Protestant ethic turns 100: Essays on the centenary of the Weber thesis* (Boulder, CO: Paradigm Publishers, 2005), pp. 54, 56.

43 Ibid., p. 56.

44 Ibid., p. 57.

> perfect moral existence was impossible for those living in the world. On the other hand, for those wishing to pursue a more perfect spiritual life, one less accommodated to the world, the various monastic orders were held out as a method sanctioned by the Church to achieve this higher goal.[45]

As a key step along the path of the social transformation of the Western world, the Protestantism Reformation fundamentally altered this basic way of thinking about religion and society. As Weber emphasized, the Reformation worked to redirect the religious ethic of the monastery to the entire social order, thus giving an asceticism, rationalism, and intense commitment of religious energies to the practical affairs of the world. It was related to the large emphasis that Weber gave to the whole psychological "issue of motivation:"[46]

> Religious ideas about salvation, when linked to existential settings, can shape motivations and influence conduct. However, this is hardly all of Weber's account. Calvin and his followers also emphasized the problem of idolatry. This religious idea, the avoidance of glorification of the creature and the creaturely, plays an interesting role in Weber's narrative. The religious notion of idolatry represented a revival of the Old Testament "taboo against any humanization of God" and is paralleled by the Puritan ban on the deification of the creature. It has sweeping social, economic, and political consequences. It gave the Puritans leverage to oppose any "ennoblement" of their middle-class lifestyle. This meant opposition to luxury, creaturely enjoyments, sports, entertainments, and amusements, as well as any display beyond the minimum required for a modicum of allowable human comfort. It also set them against any political authority that usurped the place of God.[47]

Thus, as Nielsen interprets *The Protestant Ethic and the Spirit of Capitalism*, it traces the basic transformation from a medieval Catholic to a seventeenth-century Puritan way of thinking about the world–with all the attendant large consequences for western political and economic history. The final step in the grand historical narrative presented by Weber is the gradual secularization of the Puritan worldview in the eighteenth century. Weber takes Benjamin Franklin as a leading example of this shift towards a more modern but still in its essence Calvinist consciousness. As Nielson comments, "Franklin's spirit of capitalism expresses an ethic, rather than the lack of one. It does not result from a stripping

45 Ibid., p. 58.
46 Ibid., p. 63.
47 Ibid., pp. 63–64.

away of ethical restraints, nor does it express a universal human motivation such as greed." The origins of Franklin's ethic are to be found "rooted in the soil of earlier Protestant asceticism, but by Franklin's time the ethic has shed its religious hull."[48]

It is yet another stage of historical transformation. In this case new tenets of secular religion have emerged from old religion to reshape the ways of thinking–and behaving in economic domains–of the eighteenth and nineteenth centuries: "Franklin's ethic was inherited from ascetic Protestantism but already contains the germ of utilitarianism. [From Protestantism] it lacks the eudemonistic emphasis on 'the greatest happiness' and refuses to admit that the greatest good is whatever is most useful. Franklin is not Jeremy Bentham." But he is headed in that direction: "By calling attention to the utilitarian elements already found in Franklin's thought, as well as to the deeper roots of these elements in Protestant teachings, Weber creates a historical narrative of religious and ethical ideas whose phases unfold from one another in fluid, but by no means 'linear' succession," moving from medieval times to the end of the eighteenth century.[49]

As part of this grand narrative, the Protestant ethic also helped to pave the way for a new ethic of political and economic freedom that gradually emerged in the Calvinist societies of northern Europe. It had been learned originally in the Calvinist and other pietistic sects in which all members participated equally. The minister, deacons, and other leaders of the Calvinist churches were democratically chosen. The members of the Calvinist congregation gathered together every Sunday (sometimes more often) to study the Bible and to discuss important religious questions. Indeed, throughout Protestant Europe one found "regular Bible reading, daily journals, moral log books, and rigid control over time," all these techniques serving to enhance the individual capacities and "self-discipline" of the faithful (the level of "human capital" in contemporary economic language). This followed directly from Protestant theology as each member of the faithful was responsible for learning the full message of the Bible and carried the burden of maintaining his or her own individual relationship with God.

As such elements were secularized, and reflecting also the basic individualism of the Protestant religious consciousness and the Puritan defense of the rights of the believer against any excessive claims of the

48 Ibid, pp. 66–67.
49 Ibid., p. 67.

state, it opened up the way for modern freedoms, setting the stage for the industrial revolution and the evolving new economic world of the nineteenth century. Adam Smith might be regarded as a new, secular version of an "economic Calvinist," advocating the independence from the state for businessmen that Calvinism demanded for the religious true believer. Professional economists have mostly ignored the large Protestant backdrop to *The Wealth of Nations.*[50] But the distinguished German theologian Ernst Troeltsch (a contemporary and close friend of Weber) recognized this long ago, writing in 1912 that,

> the great ideas of the separation of Church and State, toleration of different Church societies alongside of one another, the principle of Voluntarism in the formation of these Church-bodies, the (at first, no doubt, only relative) liberty of conviction and opinion in all matters of world-view and religion. Here are the roots of the old liberal theory of the inviolability of the inner personal life by the State, which was subsequently extended to more outward things; here is brought about the end of the medieval idea of civilisation, and coercive Church-and-State civilization gives place to individual civilisation free of Church direction. The idea is at first religious. Later, it becomes secularized.... But its real foundations are laid in the English Puritan Revolution. The momentum of its religious impulse opened the way for modern freedom.[51]

Weber's "grand historical narrative" in *The Protestant Ethic and the Spirit of Capitalism* goes no further than the end of the eighteenth century and the existence by then among Calvinists in Holland, England, the United States and elsewhere of new ways of thinking about the world that would spread more widely and have even greater economic consequences in the next two centuries to come. Owing in significant part to the impact of Protestantism, the stage was set for an altogether unprecedented advance in the human material condition from 1800 to 2000. But in *The Protestant Ethic and the Spirit of Capitalism*, Weber did not himself give much attention to the economic events of the nineteenth century (others of Weber's writings did deal more with this economic history).[52]

---

50 One exception is A. M. C. Waterman, "Economics as theology: Adam Smith's Wealth of Nations," *Southern Economic Journal* (April 2002).

51 Ernst Troeltsch, Protestantism and progress: A historical study of the relation of Protestantism to the modern world (Boston: Beacon Press, 1958 – first English ed. 1912), pp. 125–26.

52 See Max Weber, *Theory of social and economic organization*, trans. A. M. Henderson and Talcott Parsons (New York: Oxford University Press, 1947) and Max Weber, *General economic history*. Trans. by Frank Knight (New York: Transaction Books, 1981 – first ed. 1927).

His contribution in *The Protestant Ethic* was to bring us to the starting point of the great economic takeoff.

11. Other Impacts of Protestantism

Thus far, the discussion has mostly focused, following Max Weber's example, on the consequences of Protestantism for the ways in which Europeans thought about themselves and the world. But there were other more mundane ways in which Protestantism could have a significant – if unintended – political and economic impact. As noted above, the Protestant Reformation was not only about theology. It was also about the ways churches were governed, their manner of interaction with the faithful, the education of the faithful, and the sexual and marital practices of both the clergy and the laity, among many other elements of church organization and operation. Indeed, the Protestant Reformation in a number of such areas made changes that were just as radical as in Christian theology.

Mass Literacy – Owing significantly to the imperative for every member of the faithful to be able to read and discuss the Bible, Protestantism put a high premium on achieving mass literacy. Historian David Landes comments that "good Protestants were expected to read the holy scriptures for themselves" and therefore Protestants stressed "instruction and literacy, for girls as well as boys." Sweden in the eighteenth century was among the first nations in Europe to achieve near universal reading (but not writing) literacy, not through formal education but through "home-based instruction ... for primarily religious purposes."[53] By contrast, there was no corresponding expectation that the Catholic laity had to be able to read. Indeed, Catholics "were explicitly discouraged from reading the Bible."[54] In southern Italy and Spain at the end of the eighteenth century literacy was still less than 25 percent.[55]

Today in Europe, virtually 100 percent literacy is the norm. But all the Protestant nations historically achieved high levels of literacy well before Catholic nations. In 1875, male literacy in Protestant England,

53 Harvey J. Graff, *The legacies of literacy: Continuities and contradictions in Western culture and society* (Bloomington, IN: Indiana University Press, 1987), p. 224.

54 Landes, *The wealth and poverty of nations*, p. 178.

55 David Vincent, *The rise of mass literacy: Reading and writing in modern Europe* (Cambridge, UK: Policy Press, 2000), p. 9.

Holland and Prussia was 80 percent, 90 percent and 95 percent, respectively. In Catholic Austria, Belgium, Italy, and Spain, it was 60 percent, 60 percent, 35 percent, and 30 percent, respectively. Women fared even relatively worse in Catholic nations. Female literacy in 1875 in England and Holland was 80 percent and in Prussia in 1880 (the first year for which data are available) was 95 percent. Female literacy in Belgium, Italy and Spain in 1875 was 50 percent, 25 percent and 20 percent, respectively, and in Austria in 1890 (the first year available) was 70 percent. France in the second half of the nineteenth century achieved higher levels of literacy than other Catholic nations but French reading and writing levels were still below the Protestant nations of Europe.

Following Gutenberg's development of the printing press around 1440 and the resulting much lower cost of reading material in the centuries that followed, a high level of literacy assumed an increasing practical economic significance. Printed material is much more efficient than an oral tradition in communicating ideas, technical methods – and indeed anything that can be put down in symbolic form on paper – over longer distances in time and space. Printing, combined with growing literacy, thus accomplished a communications revolution. Among the early consequences was to spread Protestant ideas across Europe with a new speed and accuracy, facilitating the successes of the Reformation itself. A Protestant nation was like a population today that is computer literate, while the ordinary people in Catholic nations remained "computer illiterate" until a considerably later time. If computer literacy is important today, being able to read and write was probably even more important economically in earlier centuries.

A high level of mass literacy creates not only a large economic asset (a much higher level of "human capital," as economists say) for a society but is also a major asset for the workings of a democracy. Reading and writing facilitated the creation of an informed body of voters by allowing wider communication to occur among people separated by larger geographic distances. It also helped to create of common sense of community and interest in participating in politics across wider geographic areas. If the citizens of a nation are reading many of the same books, magazines, and other materials, they are likely to develop a stronger collective sense of identity as a nation and to feel a greater sense of responsibility for its future policies and actions.

Confiscations of Catholic Church Property – After King Henry VIII of England broke away from Rome in 1533, he confiscated the lands of the Catholic Church – by some estimates around 25 percent of the total area of England. Many of the lands were then given away or sold, shifting them into ownerships where they were more likely to enter the commercial system. This positive economic outcome, moreover, was not limited to England. As economic historians Nathan Rosenberg and L.E. Birdzell report, in "Catholic countries, a substantial portion of the land was owned by ecclesiastical foundations and so was not available for purchase in the usual course of trade. The dispossession of these foundations, in the countries that became Protestant, added appreciably to the land and mineral resources available for exploitation by the merchant class."[56] Writing in 2005, Philip Gorski similarly notes that "by dissolving monastic properties and abolishing the monastic orders, the Protestant Reformation changed the structure of landholding" in ways that encouraged economic growth.[57]

In Utrecht in Holland, for example, de Vries and van der Woude report that 31 percent of "land within the city walls had been in the hands of churches, monasteries, brotherhoods, immunities and the like. The Reformation transferred most of it to the city and to secular owners, thereby setting in motion a rigorous restructuring of urban land use." Utrecht took over several monastic structures that "proved highly attractive as industrial sites for space-intensive industries." Indeed, "the recycling of old [Catholic] religious structures played a prominent part in the industrial development policies of several Dutch cities."[58]

Increasing the Supply of Labor – The rise of Protestantism tended to increase the supply of labor in a country in several ways. First, the priesthoods, orders, and other clerical groups of the Catholic Church represented a large number of men and women removed from the ordinary economic side of life. Second, becoming a priest required long study and a longer period of withdrawal from even clerical work functions. A second important influence on the supply of labor was the number of religious holidays. The Catholic Church tended to have more holidays when normal work was suspended, as compared with Protestant faiths. In the seventeenth century in the United States, for ex-

56 Nathan Rosenberg and L. E. Birdzell, Jr., *How the West grew rich: The economic transformation of the industrial world* (New York: Basic Books, 1986), p. 134.

57 Philip S. Gorski, "The little divergence: The Protestant Reformation and economic hegemony in early modern Europe," in Swatos and Kaelber, *The Protestant ethic turns 100*, p. 168.

58 De Vries and van der Woude, *The first modern economy*, p. 169.

ample, both the Puritans and Quakers abolished even Christmas as a holiday. Historian David Hackett Fischer reports that "in company with other groups of radical Christians, including the Puritans in New England, Quakers [in middle America] ... abolished many religious holidays." They did this partly for religious reasons "because these celebrations seemed corrupt and 'needless' to them, and also for a deeper reason. 'All days are alike holy in the sight of God.'"[59] Just as there should be no special Catholic priesthood distinct from the laity, all Protestant men and women were required to live all the time according to the highest religious standards. The more radical forms of Protestantism thus also rejected the Catholic classification of the calendar into ordinary days and other days of special religious devotion.

Gorski agrees that this was another significant factor contributing to the economic "divergence" in the early modern era between the Protestant North Atlantic and the continental Catholic parts of Europe. As he writes, "by decreasing the number of religious holidays and lengthening the average work day, the Protestant Reformation increased the effective supply of labor."[60]

The Economic Effects of a Celibate Priesthood – The priests and nuns of the Catholic Church not only withdrew from the daily routine activities of work but also from marriage and reproduction (in contrast to Martin Luther, for example, who had six children, four of whom survived into adulthood). This meant at least some decline in future total population, depending on the size of the clerical groups (often large in the Middle Ages). Perhaps more important, the clergy provided much of the intellectual leadership of both Catholic and Protestant societies. Catholic countries in effect created a Darwinian system in which they were intentionally removing many of their most educated – and often among the most intelligent – members of society from the reproductive pool. If the human evolutionary process has any application within a time span of centuries, this was likely to have a negative political and economic impact.

Aside from the well documented and significant role that hereditary factors play in intelligence, family background and experience also have a significant influence on intellectual development. In a Catholic nation, the clerical classes could not directly contribute to the future develop-

59 David Hackett Fischer, *Albion's seed: Four British folkways in America* (New York: Oxford University Press, 1989), p. 561.

60 Gorski, "The little divergence," p. 168.

ment of the society through the intense personal interactions among parent and child. By contrast, in Protestant nations the intellectual leadership often came disproportionately from ministers and then from their children when they reached adulthood. An American historian notes, for example, that in early Puritan Massachusetts "genealogists have remarked on 'the vast number of unions between the members of the families of Puritan ministers.' One commented that 'it seemed to be a law of social ethics that the sons of ministers should marry the daughters of ministers.'" These unions, moreover, created a closely linked group of families that provided much of the leadership class – a social network of ministers and their families that represented "the cousinage that governed Massachusetts." They "went to the same schools, visited constantly with one another, joined in the same working associations, and dominated the life of the Bay Colony for many generations" – indeed, maintaining a "regional hegemony" that lasted until well into the nineteenth century.[61]

Protestants and Science – In the 1930s the American sociologist Robert Merton sought to understand the historically unprecedented development of science in England in the seventeenth century. Like many intellectuals of that period, his initial assumption was that religion and science would be in conflict. He was therefore surprised to discover that many leading English scientists – indeed a quite disproportionate number relative to the total English population – came from Puritan backgrounds, and many of them were still devout as scientists. He assembled his findings in *Science, Technology and Society in Seventeenth Century England*, offering what might be described as a Weber thesis of science.[62] The Protestant Reformation, and especially Calvinism, had given a large boost not only to the rise of capitalism, but also to the rise of western science.

As in other areas, there were multiple factors. The Catholic Church had established Aristotelian and other orthodoxies as its official teachings. The Protestant Reformation, however, in rejecting the authority of the Catholic Church opened the way for new scientific thinking. Anthony Waterman reports, for example, that in the eighteenth century an effort was made to extend "Newton's method into all possible lines of human inquiry." In Britain, "establishment thinkers quickly grasped

61 Fischer, *Albion's seed,* pp. 40–41.

62 Robert K. Merton, *Science, technology and society in seventeenth century England* (New York: Howard Fertig, 2001 – first ed. 1938).

the apologetic importance of natural theology, and Newton was made not an enemy but an ally." However, things moved more slowly in France where "Cartesian physics continued to be preferred to Newtonian until the middle of the [eighteenth] century." Part of the reason was that "the natural theology associated with Newton's cosmology was feared by authority in France down to the [French] Revolution as tending to deism." Scottish critics considered that in France the Catholic Church "discourages inquiries into nature, lest by having our views enlarged, we may escape her bonds."[63]

A second impact on scientific discovery reflected the character of Protestant theology. All of Christian theology saw the biblical Creation in the first days as a reflection of God's thinking; nature was in a real sense a mirror of the mind of God. To study nature was therefore to learn about God. For Catholics, however, similar forms of religious learning could also be obtained from a long history of Church writings and from visiting the great cathedrals and wonderful artwork of Catholic history. But the Protestant Reformation in principle rejected such forms of learning, allowing instruction of the faithful in only two ways – by reading the Book of the Bible and by visiting and experiencing the "Book of Nature," both forms of communication directly from God without any Catholic or other church intermediaries.[64]

Calvin thus wrote in his great systematic statement of his theology, *Institutes of the Christian Religion*, that "the knowledge of God [is] sown in their minds out of the wonderful workmanship of nature." For those able to turn away from the "prodigious trifles" and "superfluous wealth" that occupy the minds of so many, it will be possible to be "instructed by this bare and simple testimony which the [animal] creatures render splendidly to the glory of God." Human beings must show respect for the natural world because it is especially in its presence that they can find "burning lamps" that "shine for us … the glory of its Author" above.[65] As Calvin believed, God had created the world a mere six

---

63 A. M. C. Waterman, "The changing theological context of economic analysis since the eighteenth century," *History of political economy* 40 (annual suppl.) (2008), pp. 126, 127.

64 See Robert H. Nelson, *The new holy wars: Economic religion versus environmental religion in contemporary America* (University Park, PA: Pennsylvania State University Press, 2010), Part III.

65 Hugh T. Kerr, ed., *Calvin's Institutes: A new compend* (Louisville, KY: Westminster/John Knox Press, 1989), pp. 26–27, 99.

thousand years ago, and it was still possible to see in nature His handiwork, altered only in minor ways since the Creation.

To this strong religious motive for studying nature was added the strict discipline and capacity for hard work of the Calvinist faithful. In England, as Merton found, the result had been a great boost to the development of science: "Among the original list of members of the Royal Society in 1663, 42 of the 68 for whom religious information pertaining to religious leanings is available, were clearly Puritan." There was in general a clear "affinity between Puritanism, Baconianism and the new science." Even as far back as the seventeenth century eminent people had taken "the occasion to comment upon the close connection between the reformers of religion and of science." Merton found similar connections in other parts of Europe as well, observing that "all available evidence points in the same direction, Protestants, without exception, form a progressively larger proportion of the student body in those schools which emphasize scientific training, whereas Catholics concentrate their interests on classical and theological training." Merton concluded that "ascetic Protestantism generally emerges as an emotionally consistent system of beliefs, sentiments and action which played no small part in arousing a sustaining interest in science," not only in the seventeenth century but "even in the nineteenth century, their divorce was not final."[66]

Among those exposed in his youth to a large Puritan influence was Isaac Newton, whose view of nature "portrays a powerful God of dominion akin to the view of divine Providence espoused by John Calvin."[67] Similar to Calvin, Newton wrote that "we see the effects of a Deity in the creation and therefore the proof of a Deity."[68] Stephen Snobelen, a contemporary student of Newton, states that he "avers that an empirical study of nature will lead the student inductively toward God."[69] Indeed, that was the purpose not only of Newton's voluminous theological writings but of his *Philosophiae naturalis principie mathematica*, announcing to the world in 1687 the workings of gravity and the solar

---

66 Merton, *Science, technology and society in seventeenth century England*, pp. 114–15, 128, 136.

67 Stephen D. Snobelen, "Isaac Newton: His life and religion," in Arri Eisen and Gary Laderman, eds., *Science, religion, and society: An encyclopedia of history, culture, and controversy, vol. 1* (Armonk, NY: M. E. Sharpe, 2007), p. 365.

68 Newton, quoted in Snobelen, "Isaac Newton," p. 365.

69 Snobelen, "Isaac Newton," p. 365.

system. Showing the mathematical unity of the universe was for Newton the best way to illuminate for the world a path to God.

Protestantism and Higher Education – The same forces that encouraged science in Protestant societies also worked to promote the development of institutions of higher education. Unlike many past differences between Catholic and Protestant nations, this gap has persisted even into the twenty-first century. Indeed, the lists of the top ranked institutions of higher education in the world are today dominated by universities located in historically Protestant nations. There are at present two leading rankings of world universities, one released by Shanghai Jiao Tong University in China and the other by the Times Higher Education supplement in London. While there is inevitably a considerable subjectivity involved in such efforts, the Shanghai and London rankings, based on different methodologies, nevertheless show broadly similar results. Among the universities that were ranked in the top 100 in the world in 2008, Protestant nations, led by the United States (with by itself about half of the total number of universities in each ranking), dominated.

In the Shanghai rankings (which heavily weight publications and other evidence of productivity in the natural sciences, admittedly a historic weakness of Catholic universities), only four among the top 100 universities in the world were located in 2008 in historically Catholic nations (all of them in France).[70] England and Scandinavia (with ten and eight universities, respectively) each had more top 100 universities than the entire Catholic world. With a population of only 17 million, Holland had three universities in the top 100 of the Shanghai rankings. There were none in all of Catholic Latin America.

In the London results for 2008 (which put a greater emphasis on international peer review), the results overall are similar, except that England increases its representation from 10 to 17 universities in the top 100.[71] France now has only two top ranked universities but Belgium and Ireland have one each, again leaving the grand total for all historically Catholic nations at four (and, again, none in Latin America). In the

70 The China rankings are issued by Shanghai Jiao Tong University. See http://www.arwu.org/rank2008/ARWU2008_A(EN).htm .

71 The London rankings are issued by the Times Higher Education supplement, see http://www.timeshighereducation.co.uk/hybrid.asp?typeCode=243&pubCode=1&navcode=137.

London rankings, Scandinavia has five universities in the top 100 and Holland alone has four.

Among the large number of American universities in the top 100 in both the Shanghai and London rankings, many have strong historic connections to Protestantism. Harvard was the first American university in 1636, the result of a bequest by Puritan clergyman John Harvard of his 400 books and 800 pounds (half his total wealth). The seventeenth century Puritans of New England, as historian David Hackett Fischer reports, "had an obsessive interest in learning" that carried over to higher education.[72] Yale in 1701 was a new Puritan university in Connecticut and Princeton in 1746 in New Jersey was Presbyterian (the Scottish branch of Calvinism). Although most early American universities were founded with strong Protestant religious connections, another wave of newly created universities in the mid to late nineteenth century were non-denominational, founded to promote the development of the natural sciences and other expert professional fields. There was still a connection to Protestantism in these cases, however, because the funding was frequently donated by a leading industrialist or other wealthy Protestant. As noted above, Calvinism had long taught that a good Christian could make large amounts of money but that it should not be spent in large sums for personal enjoyments. Rather, it should be reinvested or given away.

Among leading American universities today, Cornell University was founded in 1865 by a wealth Protestant businessman, Ezra Cornell, a partner of the inventor of the telegraph, Samuel Morse. Stanford University was founded in 1885 by Leland Stanford, a descendant of Massachusetts Puritans and a founder of the Central Pacific Railroad. The University of Chicago was founded in 1890 by John D. Rockefeller, a descendant of French Protestant Huguenots and a devout Baptist all his life. Carnegie Mellon University was founded by steel magnate Andrew Carnegie in 1900, an immigrant from Scotland who was not himself a devout Christian but did believe devoutly in the Calvinist teaching of making money to give it way – and did precisely that with almost all of his immense wealth. Duke University moved to its present location in 1892 and received a large bequest in 1924 from another successful Protestant businessman, tobacco industrialist James Duke. Strikingly, although around 50 American universities are found in the top 100 in the world in both the China and Shanghai rankings, and Roman Catholics

72 Fischer, *Albion's seed*, p 531.

make up about 25 percent of the United States population, none of the top ranked American universities in 2008 had a strong historic connection to Catholicism.

Protestantism and the Rule of Law – Another important consequence of Protestantism was to promote the rule of law. Indeed, the Puritans felt a special affinity for the Old Testament, where the Jews had entered into a covenant with God. They extended this idea not only into the human relationship with God but into all areas of life. Relationships within the church, between husband and wife, between man and God, among businessmen, and in all walks of life were seen by the Puritan faithful as contractual in nature, agreements made among freely acting individuals. A contract was, as political scientist Michael Walzer comments, "the highest human bond" for a Puritan. Contracts must be, one Puritan minister wrote, "a voluntary relationship between persons about things wherein they enjoy a freedom of will and have a power to choose or refuse."[73] When such ways of thinking were extended into the political domain, the state came to be seen as the product of a voluntary contract. As the contract was spelled out between ruled and ruler, it would take in part the form of a system of well defined laws. Such a contractual view of the state – and of the individual rights of property ownership as protected by the state – would exert a large influence on the modern world through the writings of an English Puritan, John Locke.

In *Religion, Order and Law*, David Little, professor of religious studies at the University of Virginia, finds a large impact of Puritanism in the development of a system of law in England in the late sixteenth and the seventeenth centuries.[74] In the seventeenth century, James I, Charles I, and other Stuart kings attempted to assert various new royal prerogatives, extending from religious to political and economic matters. It was a period generally of increasing absolutism in Europe, especially the Catholic parts of the continent. In England, the Puritans were the fiercest in their resistance to such assertions of new state powers and their insistence on legal protections against arbitrary state actions. In the end, this led to the Puritan Revolution and the beheading of Charles I in 1649.

---

73 Michael Walzer, *The revolution of the saints: A study of the origins of radical politics* (New York: Atheneum, 1974), pp. 301, 214.

74 David Little, *Religion, order and law: A study in pre-revolutionary England* (Chicago: University of Chicago Press, 1984 – first ed. 1969).

The greatest English legal authority of the early seventeenth century, whose writings as both a practicing jurist and legal theorist would later significantly influence the development of English law, was Edward Coke. Little finds that "it was Coke who, in case after case, decided against the restriction of trade, against the long-existing political and economic controls, and at once encouraged and reflected the emergence of new values and a new conception of social order. It was he who, like so many of his fellow jurists, embodied a predisposition to disallow any extension of restrictive practices to the new [economic] conditions which were developing on every side."[75]

Coke admittedly did not appeal to Calvinist theology to reach his legal conclusions. Rather, he based his arguments on English legal tradition, asserting that new claims to state authority violated the historical legal relationships between the governors and the governed of England. Yet, as Little finds, this was mainly a ruse; Coke was really "unconsciously disguising his [radical legal] innovations in the clothes of the past." The real grounds of Coke's thinking lay elsewhere; indeed, Coke's (and others) "impulses within legal thought toward a spirit of free and autonomous economic activity, untrammeled by the traditional legal and political constraints, manifests a 'rich congruence' with some of the conclusions that emerged from the Calvinist Puritan pattern of order." In England, a new rule of law emerged "out of its Calvinist heritage, … [which] introduced a conception of social life with profoundly disruptive implications for English society, a conception that had certain affinities with the characteristics of capitalism."[76]

Indeed, the workings of a free market are, except for warfare or natural disaster, the most radical force for change known to human history. The market rapidly sweeps aside any obstacle to the pursuit of greater efficiency and higher profits. That is the underlying reason for much of the strong opposition historically to a market system – it creates too many immediate losers. But the Puritan influence undercut the legitimacy of the market opponents; as Little reports, Puritanism favored "a dynamic conception of social change that envisions a *new* society living by a *new* law." By contrast, the tendency of the Tudors and Stuarts in England was "to encourage 'court-bound capitalism' in direct opposition to a free market." The Stuarts sought "political absolutism [which] is no more suited to rational capitalism than are the patterns of medieval

75 Ibid., pp. 30–31.

76 Ibid., p. 31.

industrial life." Not only Cromwell and his armies but also English law were mobilized to combat any such tendencies to arbitrary state control. "Against the background of the Middle Ages and the age of the Tudors, Coke's [legal] determinations in the field of industrial activity amounted to a pronounced departure from tradition. … The foundations were laid here – however incomplete they might be – for the emergence of a free market economy some two centuries later."[77]

12. Protestant Reformation or Counter-Reformation?

In *The Protestant Ethic and the Spirit of Capitalism*, Weber made many passing observations with respect to the character of Roman Catholic religion but did not attempt a systematic analysis. He noted, for example, the historic preoccupation of the Catholic church with maintaining strict control in matters of religious belief, even as it was more tolerant of ordinary human sinfulness – as Weber commented, the Catholic policy was one of "punishing the heretic, but indulgent of the sinner." The Catholic priest "dispensed atonement, hope of grace, certainty of forgiveness, and thereby granted release from that tremendous tension to which the Calvinist was doomed by an inexorable fate, admitting of no mitigation – except perhaps by lifelong success in a calling." The result for a good Catholic was often a "very human cycle of sin, repentance, atonement, release, followed by renewed sin," ending in a final confession that could in itself be sufficient to relieve the burden of sin as death approached.[78]

The messages of Catholic faith were therefore less likely to lead to a rationally disciplined life dedicated to a worldly objective – whether of making large amounts of money or of making the world a better place. Yet, the Catholic ethic could encourage greater profit seeking in other ways. It would seem that a Catholic businessman should have fewer concerns – whatever the official teachings of the Church might say – if his profit making yielded an abundance of riches that could then be sinfully misspent on a corresponding life of luxury. A later confession or other act of atonement – perhaps a large donation to a religious cause – could easily enough resolve the matter in the eyes of the Catholic Church. If even seeming good Calvinists were secret utilitarians at

77 Ibid., p. 220.
78 Weber, *The Protestant ethic*, pp. 36–37, 117.

heart (an assumption that the economics profession today takes for granted), the strict ascetic requirements of Calvinism could act as a significant discouragement to a life of disciplined labor working towards high profits. As Weber had said, good Calvinists were supposed to be irrationally hard working but what if many Calvinists were actually more rational than they admitted publicly. They might well decide not to work so hard and so long.

In pre-Reformation Italy the Medici's amassed great wealth, using it even to obtain high positions in the Catholic Church, including the Papacy itself. There were many other examples of large successes in business in Catholic Europe, resulting in large accumulations of wealth. As long as its authority was not directly challenged, the Catholic Church easily tolerated this and many other kinds of behavior. Indeed, the Protestant Reformation was initially a reaction against such Catholic moral laxness; the Reformers wanted to restore the simple piety of early Christianity, before the Catholic Church had succumbed to riches and other earthly temptations. Luther in fact was harsh in his condemnations of the pursuit of profits and the resulting corruptions of high living. Based on this history, one might easily conclude that the Catholic Church would pose few obstacles to the gradual emergence of a new economic order in the modern world – and that Protestantism might in fact be the greater problem.

But the Protestant Reformation, ironically, also had a large impact on the Catholic Church – a subject on which Weber has few things to say. In response to the Protestant challenge, there followed the Council of Trent in the mid sixteenth century and then a full Counter-Reformation throughout Catholic Europe, led by Spain. Although the Catholic Church of 1500 might have posed few obstacles to the rise of capitalism in Europe, this was perhaps less true of the Catholic Church of 1600, and still further removed from the Catholic Church of 1700. It was not only Protestantism that had become more disciplined following the Reformation but the Roman Catholic Church also showed a new commitment to enforcing Catholic theology and morality.

In 1967 the British historian Hugh Trevor-Roper criticized *The Protestant Ethic and the Spirit of Capitalism* on just such grounds. He argued that "the Roman Catholic religion, as medieval history had shown, was perfectly compatible with capitalist expansion." But the rise of Protestantism changed the Catholic Church as well. It was no longer as tolerant of divisions within its ranks. Thus, while critical of the Catholic Church, the followers of Erasmus, unlike Luther, had sought reforms from within. By the 1550s, however, "the popes of the Counter-Reformation drove the Italian Erasmists over the Alps." In the decades to come Rome became the headquarters of "the Church of the princely system, and in society, the Church of a 'feudal,' official system. It was also exclusively tied to these systems. Its old elasticity had gone, intellectually and spiritually as well as politically." It neither understood nor could accommodate the looming forces of rapid intellectual and social change. Rather, as Trevor-Roper observed, "without heresy, without variety, it was the Church of one form of State and one form of society only." After the Counter-Reformation, Catholic defenders "harped on the essential unity of Church and State. The Catholic Church was the Church of their State."[79]

Trevor-Roper finds that in the wake of Luther there was in fact a "reinvigoration of the [Catholic] Church" as new religious orders such as the Jesuits were founded and "new forms of charity, new devotions, new methods of propaganda bring new resources to the Church and increase its possessions in mortmain." It was also accompanied by a "reinvigoration ... of the State" but as time passed "the newly established society, feeling itself vulnerable and threatened [by the Protestant heresy], becomes intolerant and turns out the uncomfortable, unassimilated elements in its midst. The obstinate survivors of the old reforming party are expelled, and the State settles down to enjoy its security ... in the [now] happily united Church-state."[80] It was a pattern that Trevor-Roper found could "easily be illustrated" in all the Catholic states of Italy, Spain, Flanders, Bavaria, and Austria. With respect to education, for example, as Harvey Graff writes, "the Counter Reformation in Italy represented the triumph of ecclesiastic monopoly over education. ... Counter Reformation forms of schooling tended to be narrower in their popular base than the [earlier] municipal school foundations. Literacy, by all counts, declined [in Italy] over the sixteenth and seventeenth centuries."[81]

Thus, it seems that the Protestant Reformation may have contributed to the rise of capitalism but for a reason much different from the

79 Hugh Trevor-Roper, *The crisis of the seventeenth century: Religion, the Reformation, and social change* (Indianapolis, IN: Liberty Fund, 1999 – first ed. 1967), pp. 36, 39.

80 Ibid., p. 37.

81 Graff, *The legacies of literacy*, p. 189.

Weber thesis; the Protestant Reformation may have worked to change Catholicism in ways that undermined its prior flexibility and thus its compatibility with capitalism and the forces of the modern world. A newly energized Catholic Church looked backward rather than forward and now moved effectively to limit threats to its authority posed by modern ideas. If Luther and many other Protestants also looked backwards to early Christianity, there was no Protestant Pope to enforce a strict discipline among the wide range of Protestant churches and sects. It was not mainly Luther but above all Calvin whose thinking worked to promote the creation of the modern world.

Trevor-Roper recognized, to be sure, that he needed to address the case of France which in a number of ways was a large exception. But "as the great power opposed to Spain, France found itself opposed to the Counter-Reformation" and thus avoided many of its most rigid tendencies. Indeed, until expelled in the late seventeenth century, the French population included many Protestant Huguenots who were disproportionately represented among the economically successful in France. Spain, by contrast, could never have tolerated such a wide presence of Protestant heresy in its midst. For a long period France "received the fugitives of the Roman and Spanish Inquisitions; it published the works suppressed by the Roman censorship; and it benefited by the vast sales of Church lands carried out in the Wars of Religion."[82]

But a state of comparative religious toleration did not last indefinitely even in France. Partly owing to the spectacle just across the English channel of Oliver Cromwell and the Puritan Revolution, including the execution of the English king, the Catholics of France grew more fearful of the Protestants in their midst, finally expelling them altogether in 1685. Hence, even in France, the end result was a new authoritarianism under Louis XIV and then in the eighteenth century a "fatal union of Counter-Reformation Church and princely State."[83] It was a state of affairs only ended by the French Revolution, whose followers had been inspired to their religious fervor in part by Jean Jacques Rousseau, born to a Calvinist family in Geneva.

Trevor-Roper thus sees the rise of capitalism in three phases. From 1500 until 1620, Spain was still a "great world power," Catholic south Germany was still "the industrial heart of Europe," and Italy was "as rich and intellectually exciting as ever." The period from 1620 to

---

82 Trevor-Roper, *The crisis of the seventeenth century*, p. 37.
83 Ibid., p. 38.

1660 was then one of widespread warfare and of revolutionary change across Europe. At the end "Spain and Italy have become backwaters, both economically and intellectually." By 1700, "the dynamic centre" of Europe economically had shifted from the Catholic world to the Protestant world of England, Holland, and the cities of the Baltic. They were the centers of economic change through the eighteenth century – and in the nineteenth century it was still true that Protestantism "was the religion of progress," economically and otherwise.[84]

Trevor-Roper writes that when France in the nineteenth century finally moved to abandon the legacy of the Counter-Reformation and to rejoin the modern world, it was "by becoming 'Protestant' – that is, [it was] by accepting the rule of a 'Protestant' elite and a 'Protestant' ideology which convulsed the French Church, alarmed French Catholics and brought papal thunderbolts from Rome – that France caught up, industrially, with those Protestant neighbors which, two centuries before, had outstripped it. Such empirical evidence of the nineteenth century cannot be overlooked."[85] It was not that there was anything intrinsic to the fact of being historically a Roman Catholic or a Protestant nation; indeed, theologically both Catholicism and Protestantism changed greatly over time to the extent that the Roman Catholic religion of 2000 is probably closer theologically to Luther and Calvin than the mainstream Protestantism of 2000 (think about the issue of abortion where Roman Catholics and old fashioned evangelical Protestants are now close allies). But in the seventeenth century the Catholic Church allied itself with the authoritarian trends in Europe, to the detriment of its economic, political and intellectual vitality for several centuries – until the Second Vatican Council of the 1960s.[86]

84 Ibid., 2, 4.

85 Ibid., pp. 3–4.

86 Trevor-Roper did not have the benefit of the recent Angus Maddison estimates of national incomes in western Europe from 1820 onward. In light of that data, Trevor-Roper's economic history of France holds up on the whole but might have to be recast somewhat. As he suggested, Holland and England in 1820 had outstripped the rest of Europe economically, including France. But France already in 1820 had a similar income per capita to Protestant Switzerland, Germany and Sweden. Many countries in Europe, including Catholic France, then made progress in catching up with Holland and England in the nineteenth centuries. The leading exceptions were Catholic Italy and Spain which suffered significant relative economic declines that took them out of the economic mainstream of Europe by 1900. Unlike Italy and Spain, France started the nineteenth century in the European economic mainstream and remained there

When James II in the 1680s attempted to increase his royal powers, party by bringing back the Catholic Church in England, Englishmen of all stripes saw a mortal threat to their freedoms, ensuring in 1688 the easy triumph of William of Orange and the Glorious Revolution. In a study published in 1968, one year after Trevor-Roper's analysis, another distinguished European historian, Herbert Luthy, similarly notes that the Protestant Reformation commenced "during a period of almost breathtaking growth in Europe" in all fields, economic and otherwise. If anything, the Reformation initially arose in opposition to these tendencies, hoping to restore an earlier Christianity that was not as compromised by the new political and economic forces as was the Roman Catholic Church. Luthy observes that "all the evidence advanced in favor of Weber's thesis is taken from the eighteenth and nineteenth centuries," a period when the Protestant religion was recasting itself and even abandoning many of the original Lutheran and Calvinist theological formulations. Luthy agrees with Trevor-Roper that in matters of religion it was instead "the Counter-Reformation, as an authoritarian and total reaction against all manifestations of the free heretical spirit, which stopped all further progress and which, after the spiritual and material catastrophes of the Wars of Religion, prevented a resumption of such progress wherever it had been triumphant." Until the Counter Reformation, "progress had been common to all Europe" but in those Catholic regions where it came to dominate the cultural and religious life there followed "a sleep of death both economically and (even more) intellectually," including, for example, "the astonishing absence of Catholic Germany from the rebirth of German philosophy and literature that followed the Thirty Years' War." As Luthy observes, even many Catholic historians have agreed on the "appalling break [that] the Counter Reformation was in the cultural history of Europe and how deadly was the shadow cast" intellectually and economically for those areas where it prevailed.[87]

---

for the rest of the century. In 1900, although England had the highest income per capita in Europe, no one nation, Protestant or Catholic, could claim to be economically much better off than any other–although some were clearly inferior.

87 Herbert Luthy, "And once again: Calvinism and capitalism," in Eisenstadt, ed., *The Protestant ethic and modernization*, pp. 95, 96.

13. The Case of Latin America

Many Latin Americans have been deeply puzzled by their very poor economic performance in comparison with their large Protestant neighbors to the north, the United States and Canada. A substantial body of Latin American literature has by now been created to address this question – why at the end of the twentieth century did almost every Latin American nation have an income per capita less than 30 percent of that of the United States? Latin Americans saw themselves in the nineteenth century as following in the footsteps of the United States – including having won their own wars of independence – and often modeled their constitutions and other political institutions after those of the United States. Later, they often encouraged American investment and otherwise sought to emulate the economic successes of the United States. The failure of essentially every Latin American nation in this regard would be a main contributing factor to the deep "love-hate" relationship that has long characterized Latin American views of the United States.[88]

Octavio Paz – The Mexican Octavio Paz was the Nobel prize winner in literature in 1990, a former Mexican ambassador to India, and in general one of the leading twentieth-century intellectuals of Latin America. In 1979, he authored an essay on "Mexico and the United States." As Paz noted, there were large cultural differences between Mexico and the United States: "We are two distinct versions of Western civilization." Paz had little doubt about the historic reasons for these differences: "The distinct and divergent attitudes of Spaniards and English .... can be summed up in one fundamental difference, in which perhaps the dissimilar [political and economic] evolution of Mexico and the United States originated: in England the Reformation triumphed, whereas Spain was the champion of the Counter-Reformation."[89]

These cultural differences carried over into areas which can have a large impact on national economic outcomes. As Paz noted, "for the society of New Spain [colonial Mexico], work did not redeem, and had no value in itself. Manual work was servile. The superior man neither worked nor traded. He made war, he commanded, he legislated." In

88 See Carlos Rangel, *The Latin Americans: Their love-hate relationship with the United States* (New Brunswick, NJ: Transaction Publishers, 1987).

89 Octavio Paz, "Mexico and the United States," (1979) in Paz, *The labyrinth of solitude and other writings* (New York: Grove Press, 1985), pp. 357, 360.

the United States, a nation formed by a Protestant culture, it was much different: "For the Puritans and their heirs, work is redemptive because it frees man, and this liberation is a sign of God's choice." Paz sees in Puritanism a religion that promoted an individual relationship with God (individual justification "by faith alone"); an absence of any clerical hierarchy (a Protestant "priesthood of all believers"); a full worldly engagement in search of an earthly perfection of society; and a powerful internalized sense of ethical responsibility. In a later secular age, such a Protestant individualism and strong sense of personal responsibility would reappear as a religious commitment to the values of political democracy and open markets. As Paz comments, the foundations of political and economic successes in the United States were laid early in the nation's history – "in the small religious communities of seventeenth-century New England [where] the future was already in bud: political democracy, capitalism, and social and economic development."[90]

Without the same religious heritage, Mexicans could one day profess a dedication to open markets and democratic politics but the roots were shallow. The Catholic Church, as the sole hierarchical source of religious authority, imparted basic values that carried over to political and economic domains as well. As Paz notes, "the political centralism of the Spanish monarchy had religious orthodoxy as its complement, and even as its foundation." The Spanish Catholicism of the Counter-Reformation, the form of Catholicism that reached colonial Mexico, taught an "orthodoxy [that] prevented examination and criticism" – and inevitably this extended to other areas of life, going well beyond religion.[91] As Paz comments with respect to Mexico and the United States,

> If one considers the historical evolution of the two societies, the main difference seems to be the following: the modern world began with the Reformation, which was the religious criticism of religion and the necessary antecedent of the Enlightenment; with the Counter-Reformation and Neo-Thomism, Spain and her possessions closed themselves to the modern world. ... And so, though Spanish-American civilization is to be admired on many counts, it reminds one of a structure of great solidity – at once convent, fortress, and palace – built to last, not to change. In the long run, that construction became a confine, a prison.[92]

---

90 Ibid., pp. 364, 365, 371.
91 Ibid., pp. 367, 368.
92 Ibid., p. 369.

Claudio Veliz – A similar assessment was offered in 1994 by another distinguished Latin American writer, the Chilean Claudio Veliz. There had been throughout most of Latin America a long "economic malaise" that had been accompanied by a similarly lengthy and "perplexing failure to comprehend its causes." It was not difficult to recognize "the somber saga of sterility, silliness, and irresponsibility that has for so many decades shaped a considerable portion of the economic arrangements of Latin America."[93] The real question was why Latin Americans had put up with it so long – why had they seemingly been unable to alter these dysfunctional arrangements for the better, despite at least two centuries of disappointing economic results.

In this regard, Veliz is disdainful of most Latin America economists and others who have produced innumerable studies which, "although seldom devoid of erudition and invariably enriched by good intentions," have ended up as the "least effective [scholarly] undertaking ever engendered by public concern about the troubled circumstances of any major region of the world." The basic problem was that it was necessary to focus on "a stubborn cultural circumstance" characteristic of Latin American nations that nevertheless had "proved beyond the capacity of the [mainstream economic] authors and their seminars and committees to comprehend." As a starting point, similar to the views of Paz, it was necessary to understand that Latin American culture was inherited in large part from Spain and for Spain the "Counter-Reformation ... became the greatest and most enduring achievement of her impressive imperial moment." It was not just in the sixteenth and seventeenth centuries but the influence of the Spanish Counter-Reformation "largely dominates, even to this day, the lives of the Spanish-speaking peoples [in Latin America] almost as convincingly and pervasively as the dynamic asymmetries of the Industrial Revolution preside over the English-speaking world."[94]

Much like Paz, Veliz sees the Counter-Reformation as a "titanic endeavor ... to arrest change" in Spain and to bring change in society "forever to a halt" in order that "all manner of stable, predictable, traditional arrangements" can be maintained.[95] Nothing, however, could be more at odds with the workings of a free market. Under the normal

93 Claudio Veliz, *The new world of the Gothic fox: Culture and economy in English and Spanish America* (Berkeley, CA: University of California Press, 1994), pp. 191.

94 Ibid.,179, 178, 53.

95 Ibid., p. 200.

workings of the market, one business after another will be failing, displacing owners, workers, and even whole communities. Indeed, lacking a powerful normative sanction to give it legitimacy, a free market – or even a modestly regulated market – is not likely to survive for long. In eighteenth and nineteenth century England, Protestant individualism – reworked to a secular form in the free market theories of Adam Smith – provided the requisite religious blessing. But in Spain, and in its Latin American colonies, reflecting the deeply conservative impulses of the Counter-Reformation, the core religious influence worked the other way.

As Veliz thus comments, "the cultural tradition of the Spanish-speaking peoples … proved unresponsive … to industrial capitalism" and their governments often sought to repress the market forces for change. Socialism, progressivism and other collectivist ideologies in this sense were not a force for modernization – as many of their leading advocates proclaimed – but a conservative movement to limit the extremely rapid pace of social transformation that free markets were bringing about. Reflecting a fear of an unknown market-driven future, those peoples in Spain and Latin America whose values were shaped by a Spanish colonial history "appear to be sheltered (imprisoned?) by a magnificent past, unable to come to terms with a disappointing present," reflecting the inheritance of a Spanish Catholic culture that for centuries manifested "an overriding affection for persons rather than a respect for things; a reluctance to sever the cords of the safety net; … a distrust of novelty and, generally, a sturdy disinclination to step outside the dependable protection of the dome, even in this, our own century of modernity."[96]

Jose Ignacio Garcia Hamilton – In the early twentieth century Argentina was a large exception to the Latin American story. Indeed, it had an income per capita in 1910 equal to 80 percent of the United States – by far the highest in Latin America and comparable at the time to European nations such as France and Germany. But then stagnation set in, and from about 1930 the Argentine economy began a long and sharp decline in which it increasingly diverged from Europe and gradually converged with its Latin American neighbors. No other modern nation has ever suffered such a large falloff in relative economic status over such a long period. The loss of relative economic status in Argen-

96 Ibid., pp. 201, 202.

tina was most rapid in the 1980s, a period of great political turmoil and economic disappointment.

The citizens of Argentina have both been surprised by their economic failures of the twentieth century and at times have been at a loss to understand just how and why such events could ever have occurred. Indeed, as two leading experts on the Argentine economy commented recently, the nation's economic experience "has long presented a puzzle. … The puzzle is straightforward: how could a country that was once one of the richest in the world now be placed so poorly?"[97]

Argentina's unique economic history has attracted attention from economists around the world. Most have fared poorly, however, in explaining the results. This is partly because economists have long been trained professionally to focus on narrowly economic variables and to consider matters of politics and culture as lying in a separate domain – the professional subject area for other social scientists such as political scientists and sociologists. Argentina's severe economic problems, however, are not the result of some peculiar set of national policy decisions involving a set of strictly economic variables. Rather, they are the result of a highly uncertain and often very unfavorable political environment for business investment, resulting from Argentine national failures extending over many decades. Between 1930 and 1983, Argentina experienced 9 coup d'etats, military rule for 22 years, and in between mostly vulnerable and unstable civilian regimes. For much of this time there was economic mismanagement, matched by large blunders in other areas of governmental concern as well.

As a distinguished Argentine journalist, economic historian, and social critic, Jose Ignacio Garcia Hamilton accepts no limits on the explanatory factors he can explore. Indeed, Hamilton looks to politics and culture to explain the economic woes of Argentina and other Latin American nations. He is particularly concerned to understand the roots of a Latin American tendency towards failed democracies and the substitution of incompetent "authoritarian" governments in their place. In searching for explanations, Hamilton offers answers in basic agreement

97 Gerardo Della Paolera and Alan M. Taylor, "Introduction", in Paolera and Taylor, eds., *A new economic history of Argentina* (New York: Cambridge University Press, 2003), p. 1.

with Paz and Veliz in finding that the Spanish Catholic heritage of Latin America has played a critical role.[98]

As Hamilton (himself a Catholic) comments, "the Roman Church tells us, Catholics, that we must seek salvation within the institution. The phrase *extra ecclesiam, nulla salus* (outside of the Church there is no salvation) clearly sums up this concept." As a matter of religious upbringing, then, we "Catholics get used to depending on [Church] authority for taking important decisions – or even small ones. In our childhood seeing a film, for instance, depended on the opinion of the priest, the Bishop, or the Religious Commission for Film Qualification." By contrast, the members of Protestant churches "are given the Bible where they themselves must find the truth and the guidelines for their own conduct." As a result, Protestantism instills an attitude of individual questioning and responsibility for religious truth among the faithful; the Protestant faithful "acquire maturity … and get used to independence, freedom and the assumption of their duties and obligations."[99] These religious attitudes have then been carried over to secular domains such as the manner of individual participation in politics, providing a fertile ground for the practice of democracy.

Another personality trait widely observed in Argentina society – and in other Latin American countries – is a tendency to oscillate between acts of submissiveness and outbreaks of rebelliousness in dealing with authority. Hamilton considers that "whereas for Protestants dissent is natural, for Catholics it implies strain, tension to overcome the corset of rules which weighs them down." When they break loose, they go to the other extreme. For "Catholics [they normally] must seek or confirm their truth in an external, superior authority rather than in their own reflection or intimate decision." But this did little to advance a "collective

98 It should be noted that in the case of Argentina it differs from other Latin American nations, among other things, in the very large number of Italian immigrants. From 1860 to 1930, about half of all immigrants came from Italy (many from southern Italy), significantly altering the demographic composition of the Argentine population. Hence, since the early twentieth century it has been more accurate to speak of Argentine Catholicism as a blend increasingly of Italian with the previously dominant Spanish Catholic heritage. Also unlike many other Latin American countries, there is no remaining significant presence in Argentina of the original native American populations.

99 Jose Ignacio Garcia Hamilton, *El autoritarismo y la improductividad* (Buenos Aires: Editorial Sudamericana, 1991). The material cited is from an unpublished English translation made available to me by Jose Garcia Hamilton.

sense of responsibility" that "usually arises from free thinking."[100] A well functioning democracy, however, depended on just such a strong sense of individual responsibility among the general populace for the well being of the whole society, something in short supply in Argentine and Latin American culture.[101]

Hence, as Hamilton concluded, Argentina's political and cultural problems, and hence its economic problems as well, reflected a Catholic personality type that was less suitable as a cultural basis for a democratic system of government and for the maintenance of market freedoms. Growing up in an Argentine Catholic household, Hamilton noted "how many times ...we ... end up saying: 'I'll do it, anyway I can confess later,' using a psychological mechanism which consists in avoiding responsibility, and, simultaneously transfer our guilt outside ourselves."[102] A social dynamic was at work in Latin American countries that had too often produced a politically and socially self-destructive set of attitudes among the population:

> Sometimes when we are intimidated with so many restrictions and rules, we rebel violently and totally ignore order. One way or another, responsibility is non-existent. Either we secretly reject an internal set of rules, or we break it openly and violently. Be it as it may, it is an indifferent and hostile attitude towards an order that intimately does not belong to us, which is not really ours.
>
> Lack of responsibility is often seen at humbler levels. We, Latin Americans, for instance, think that cities should be clean, but we also think that it is the Government's job to clean them and we, as citizens, have no responsibility at all. As a rule, all is State responsibility, while we, citizens, have no duties whatsoever. And as everything must come from outside, from superior spheres, we also expect salvation more than solutions.
>
> Salvation ... is someone else's task, which does not demand work but luck or God's intervention. ... Salvation is external and infallible, because it is

100 Ibid.

101 In Argentina, reflecting the large number of Italian immigrants, this may also have significantly reflected a southern Italian Catholic influence. In *The Moral Basis of a Backward Society*, former Harvard political scientist Edward Banfield found a culture of "amoral familialism" in a southern Italian town he studied. The citizens of the town showed a strong sense of loyalty within their own family but felt little sense of responsibility to society outside their family circle. See Edward Banfield, *The Moral Basis of a Backward Society* (New York: Free Press, 1958).

102 Hamilton, *El autoritarismo y la improductividad.*

magic or it comes from extrasensorial worlds. … What is the use then of effort and responsibility?[103]

14. The Case of the United States

To the north of Latin America is the United States, the common object of Latin American observation and comparison. As much as any nation, the United States was until the twentieth century a Protestant nation. In 1750, there were 465 Congregational Churches (the leading Calvinist church then in the United States) and even 250 Quaker churches but the 30 Roman Catholic churches represented only a tiny presence. By 1850, the United States had experienced a massive wave of German immigration and its Lutheran churches numbered 16,403. There were now also 13,280 Methodist churches (an outgrowth of the proselytizing efforts of John Wesley in England in the eighteenth century) but still only 1,221 Catholic churches in total.[104] The first – and so far only – Catholic to be elected President was John F. Kennedy in 1960.

The early Protestants came to the United States in four great waves, three of them driven by religious persecution in England. The first large group came in the 1630s, Puritans who fled to Massachusetts to escape the attacks on their faith of King Charles I. As the Puritans in England gained strength in the 1840s, culminating in the Puritan Revolution, pressures to emigrate declined. It was then the turn of the Anglicans to flee from Puritan persecutions in the 1650s, many of them of high social standing in England who became the new aristocracy of Virginia. As followers in a new and seemingly radical religion, Quakers were often harshly suppressed in England, and fled in large numbers to the Delaware valley (including the current state of Pennsylvania) from 1675 to 1725. The fourth great Protestant emigration from 1725 to 1775 was driven by economic rather than religious motivations, the Scotch-Irish poor who came from Northern Ireland, Scotland and the northern border areas of England, and who populated the Appalachian frontier of America in the eighteenth century.

A leading American historian, David Hackett Fischer of Brandeis University, has documented the central role that these four Protestant

103 Ibid.

104 David Hackett Fischer, *Albion's seed: Four British folkways in America* (New York: Oxford University Press, 1989), p. 423.

groups played in early American history. In *Albion's Seed: Four British Folkways in America*, Fischer describes over more than 900 pages the specific religious beliefs, family practices, political organization, economic activities, and many other elements of what he sees as four distinct Protestant American cultures. As Fischer writes with respect to these cultures, down to the present "strong echoes ... may still be heard in the major dialects of American speech, in the regional patterns of American life, in the complex dynamics of American politics, and in the continuing conflict between four different ideas of freedom in the United States." Americans inherited the British suspicion of power in government and the strong commitment to maintaining their liberties, channeling it in their own ways that reflected the different circumstances of the new world. Fischer concludes that the interplay of the four Protestant cultures in the United States "created an expansive pluralism which is more libertarian than any unitary culture alone could be." The Protestant legacy "in early America remains the most powerful determinant of a voluntary society in the United States [even] today."[105]

The instigators of the American Revolution, following in the path of their Puritan forbearers in seventeenth century England, were the Massachusetts heirs to the Puritan tradition. Most of the fighting for the first two years of the Revolution occurred in Massachusetts where the English were resoundingly defeated. The fighting then shifted to the middle Atlantic colonies where the American forces were led by George Washington, a descendant of John Washington who came to Virginia in 1657 after his father (an Oxford-trained Anglican clergyman) had been "removed from his living by the Puritans."[106] The last stages of the war brought the Scotch Irish into the conflict where their historically violent culture and patriotic attitudes also made for an effective fighting force. (Of the four major Protestant groups, the Quakers – who commonly rejected violence – were the only ones not to play a large role in the success of the American Revolution.) Absent the Protestant Reformation, in short, the patterns and timing of settlement of North America, and the course of its history, including even the very creation of the United States, would have inevitably taken a much different course.

Of the four groups, the Massachusetts Puritans had the most enduring influence on American history – rivaled by the Virginia Anglicans

105 Ibid., p. 6–7.
106 Ibid., p. 214.

until the U.S. Civil War, but thereafter marginalized by the exclusion of the South from the American mainstream for a full century.[107] The political, economic, and indeed virtually every aspect of life in Puritan Massachusetts in the seventeenth century was shaped by religion. It is difficult today for many people to grasp the defining role played by Christian religion in western civilization until the Enlightenment (it might help to analogize the current role of "science" to the role of "religion" in times past). As Fischer writes, the true goal of the Massachusetts Puritans was a "Bible Commonwealth" that would be a "Calvinist utopia," not only satisfying their own local needs but giving wider testimony to the glory of God, shining a beacon for all mankind to follow. Other groups throughout history may also have professed very high ideals but it mattered more in Massachusetts because the residents were "staunch Calvinists" and for them "Puritanism was a form of social striving which labored obsessively to close the gap between ideals and actuality."[108]

Fischer summarizes the Massachusetts Puritan theology in "five words: depravity, covenant, election, grace, and love." The Puritan understanding of covenant and election were of special importance for economic matters. The Puritans "thought of their relationship with God (and one another) as a web of contracts," an approach to life easily extended to commercial affairs. Following the "doctrine of limited atonement," the Puritans believed that only "a chosen few" were among the elect, as chosen in advance by God, a "Calvinist creed [that] entered deep into the soul of New England." As Weber had observed with respect to Calvinism in Europe, such a theology fostered an anxious concern for one's fate in the hereafter and for any possible signs of being among the few that would be saved. Fischer similarly describes the Massachusetts brand of Calvinism as "one of the most harsh and painful creeds that believing Christians have ever inflicted upon themselves." For example, "the people of Massachusetts were trained by their ministers never to be entirely confident of their own salvation" – and any such confidence ironically was "one of the surest signs that one was not saved." A good Puritan could never entirely escape this dire

107 See Sacvan Bercovitch, *The Puritan origins of the American self* (New Haven, CT: YaleUniversity Press, 1975); and Kevin Phillips, *The cousins' wars: Religion, politics, civil warfare, and the triumph of Anglo-America* (New York: Basic Books, 1999).

108 Fischer, *Albion's Seed*, pp. 50, 52, 22, 85.

condition – a lifelong existence of ceaseless "wild swings of hope and despair" – but could at least seek relief from the stresses of the world in a life of hard labor and the pursuit of a calling that reflected "a spirit of restless striving for assurance" of being among the few elect.[109]

Fischer observes that in itself "the Puritan ethic was very far from the spirit of capitalism." The Puritans "did not glorify 'capitalist enterprise' – two terms which they would not have approved or even understood." If Puritan theology set the stage in Massachusetts for the rise of a modern economic world, it was as an unintended accident. The powerful Puritan "ethic of work" was not intended to promote business success but in practice it had this consequence. One economic historian observed that the "New Englanders became the Dutch of England's empire."[110] As Fischer elaborates,

> The structure of New England's carrying trade was similar in its structure and social function to that which developed on the borders of the North Sea, both in the Netherlands and in the East of England. The combination of mixed agriculture, small villages, and a high level of commercial activity were much the same in East Anglia and Massachusetts. So also was the combination of interior farming villages, and very small seaports that sprang up as thickly in New England as in the Thames estuary and the seacoast of East Anglian coast.
>
> In Massachusetts, this economic system was fully developed by the mid-seventeenth century. Thereafter, for many generations it changed mainly by becoming more elaborately the same. Historian Bernard Bailyn concludes that "the character of the economic system as it emerged in this period remained essentially the same until just before the American Revolution".[111]

If all this fits well with the Weber thesis, Fischer adds some complications. The Quaker variant of Protestant culture, for example, also worked powerfully to promote economic success. In England, as Fischer reports, "Quakers played a role far beyond their numbers in the industrial revolution. The great banking houses of England were those of Quakers." Much of the early industrial heartland of the United States would be found in Pennsylvania and parts of New Jersey and Delaware, areas originally settled largely by Quakers. In a whole variety of ways, as Fischer observes, American Quakers "provided an ethical and cultural

109 Ibid., pp. 23, 112–13, 116, 115.
110 Ibid., pp. 157, 156, 155.
111 Ibid., p. 155.

environment which strongly supported industrial and capitalist development."[112]

This was partly because the Quakers believed in a life of "extreme austerity. The Quakers, more than any major Protestant denomination, fostered a style of life which Max Weber called worldly asceticism – the idea of living in the world but not of it. Work itself became a sacrament, and idleness a deadly sin." The Quakers also believed that "wealth was not to be consumed in opulent display, but rather to be saved, invested, turned to constructive purposes. Restraints were placed on indulgence." While similar beliefs were also found in Puritan Massachusetts, "the most extended form … was found not among the Puritans with whom it is often associated but among the Quakers."[113]

Quaker theology, however, differed radically in many areas from Calvinist theology. The Quakers believed that, in principle, all people could be saved. Fischer comments that the Quakers "repudiated the Five Points of Calvinism." Quakers worshipped "a God of Love and Light whose benevolent spirit harmonized the universe." In contrast here again to the Puritans, the Quakers "always maintained an official hostility to formal doctrine and never required subscription to a creed." The Quakers formed tight communities of true believers but, unlike the Puritans, were tolerant of religious diversity in their midst – there were no witch-hunts or persecutions of heretics where Quakers ruled.

There was one important commonality between Puritans and Quakers, however, and this may have been more important for economic matters than the many other large theological differences. The Quakers believe in "the idea of serving God with one's best talents." Fischer observes that "this idea had developed from Martin Luther's concept of the calling (*beruf*), which had an important place in the cultural thinking of many Protestant denominations. It was exceptionally strong among the Quakers."[114]

As illustrated by the Quakers, Protestantism thus could in multiple ways encourage hard work, dedication to a cause, rebellion against state authority, a fierce independence of mind, the ability to read the Bible, and other traits conducive to a democratic political system and an open market economy. In *Albion's Seed*, Fischer provides a wealth

112 Ibid., p. 558.
113 Ibid., p. 556.
114 Ibid., pp. 426, 555.

of detail concerning the powerful shaping influences of the four Protestant cultures of North America, not only in economic matters but many other areas – influences that, while diminished, have still not disappeared even in the early years of the twenty-first century. His purpose is in part to refute what he sees as a mindless economic determinism that dominated so much of the thought of the twentieth century. As Fischer explains, he is searching "for a way beyond reductive materialist models (of both the left and the right)." He does not deny "the importance of material factors in history" but in the broader picture "they are only part of a larger whole, and that claims for their priority are rarely grounded in empirical fact."[115] The reductionist materialism of the twentieth century was in truth closer to a religion than to a science.

Fischer does not merely assert the need for a broader perspective but goes on to demonstrate it, drawing on a vast array of past American historical scholarship. As he shows, it is the force of American Protestant religion in its various forms that goes far to "explain the origins and stability of a social system which for [the past] two centuries has remained stubbornly democratic in its politics, capitalist in its economy, libertarian in its laws, individualist in its society and pluralist in its culture."[116] The United States has been a quintessentially Protestant nation. Seen in the full light of the American experience, Weber's thesis requires various refinements and addendums, but in his emphasis on the powerful shaping force of religion in economic history, he was on the whole correct.

15. Conclusion

As Table 1 above showed, the large economic gap between Protestant and Catholic nations could still be found in Europe as recently as 1960 but had largely disappeared by 2000. Several factors seem to be at work. The Second Vatican Council brought about a long awaited reconciliation of the Roman Catholic Church with the modern world. Reflecting his unhappy exposure to communism in his native Poland, Pope John Paul II looked more favorably on democracy and open markets than most of his predecessors. Protestant Europe had gone through a similar accommodation to modern trends much earlier. Thus, by the end of the twentieth century both Protestantism and Catholicism had

115 Ibid., p. x.
116 Ibid., p. 4.

made their peace with science and the modern age, reducing the religious differences – and the resulting economic consequences – between them. Perhaps not unrelated, both were also experiencing a sharp falloff in church membership and attendance, as a common secular culture increasingly challenged the traditional institutional roles of Christianity throughout Europe, including even Spain, Ireland, and other former European bastions of traditional Catholic faith.

An equally important factor in the economic convergence of Europe was the rise of the European Union, the most successful attempt to unify Europe since the medieval Roman Catholic Church.[117] The EU is also held together by a religion, in this case a form of secular economic faith. Although it owes much to the Christian heritage of Europe, this faith seeks a new heaven on earth – reached along a path of economic progress – instead of a heaven in the hereafter.[118] Indeed, Walter Meads speaks of the rise of a new secular "fourth faith" in Europe (and elsewhere around the world) that is a successor in the line of the three earlier Abrahamic religions of Judaism, Christianity and Islam.[119]

Perhaps, as one might say, the new and most vital "church" of Europe may now be the European Union. Even Catholic Europe looks increasingly to Brussels rather than to Rome for guidance in political and economic matters. Every member nation of the EU must maintain a free democratic political system and keep its markets open to competitors from all over Europe. In this respect, while the discourse of the EU is conducted in a secular language, it may be said to have brought about a significant "Protestantization" of all of Europe. It was Protestantism, and above all Calvinism, that paved the way for modern political and economic freedoms.

It took the genius of a Max Weber to keep alive in the twentieth century – a time in which economic explanations of history reigned supreme – the idea that religion is also a large explanatory force in its own right. Whatever the validity of the specific criticisms of Weber over the

---

117 One at least suggestive piece of evidence in this respect is that in the Americas the economic gap between the Protestant North and the Catholic south remained large even in 2000. Movements toward economic union in the Americas were less successful and intruded less on the traditional political independence of the individual nation states.

118 See Robert H. Nelson, *Reaching for heaven on earth: The theological meaning of economics* (Lanham, MD: Rowman & Littlefield, 1991).

119 Mead, *God and gold*, p. 282. See also Robert H. Nelson, *The new holy wars.*

past century, he was surely correct in this larger perspective. We are in his debt.

The Market, God, and the Ascetic Life

PHILIP GOODCHILD

1. The Divinity of the Market?

Is the market a god?

This might seem to be a somewhat unusual question for a philosopher of religion to pose. While much of contemporary human life might express a preoccupation with the behaviour of prices, it remains difficult to discern the actual rituals through which the market is worshipped. Nevertheless, even contemporary life remains subject to fate and fortune, and virtuous or prudent conduct is insufficient to guarantee the success of ventures without the cooperation of unseen powers frequently termed 'market forces'. 'Market forces' express the aggregate demand of the mass of participants in the market, and yet they have a propensity to become detached from the good will of all participants, who no doubt seek prosperity, when they become destructive in 'market corrections' or in the prioritizing of short-term profit over long term security. The 'market', should there be such a thing, is a transcendent cause. One cannot even locate the 'market': one may be familiar with traditional village market stalls, with markets on streets, with stock exchanges and specialist commodity exchanges, but each of these is affected by market forces from elsewhere, and such forces are difficult to locate.

Nevertheless, the market is invoked by some as that which may succeed, where governments fail, in delivering the common good. The market is invoked as the supreme institution that delivers effective human production and cooperation, ensuring material prosperity, the efficient allocation of resources, and maintaining and enhancing credit. It is in this sense that this transcendent cause functions as a god: it takes over some of the traditional functions of religion described by anthropologists. Are market 'corrections' as necessary, just and inevitable as the final judgement, or at least as the laws of physics? Recent turmoil in the global financial markets invites a critical approach to this issue: there has been a manifest failure to ensure prosperity, given the consequent recession, public sector debts and cutbacks; there has been a manifest failure to allocate resources efficiently, given the transfer of wealth to a failing financial sector in order to keep it afloat; and there has been a manifest crisis of credit. The 'invisible hand' of the market has been all too invisible, and, if operative at all, it has been working only in the most mysterious of ways, rewarding the incautious and punishing the prudent.

The theological question of the divinity of the market has two dimensions: in the first place, does anything like the mechanism of the market objectively exist, having a determining influence on human affairs? In the second place, failing a demonstration of the objective mechanism, is a subjective faith in the power and justice of the market promoted by economists and politicians who legitimise that faith in the manner of priests (Nelson 2001)? Is the market an objective reality or a belief system? This alternative revolves around the question of which is the more relevant mode of social causation: the efficient causality of the market mechanism, functioning as a mode of social physics, described with increasing mathematical accuracy from Walras' account of general equilibrium to the Arrow-Debreu model, or the final causality of human intentions and purposes, where behaviour is regulated and disciplined in line with belief. In general, modern thought has become familiar with two kinds of power: the power of fundamental physical forces such as gravity, electromagnetism and nuclear bonds, and the power of the human will, evident in speech, persuasion and action. These form the basis for two modes of explanation, and if theology paradigmatically explains the world in terms of the latter as narrative, intention and purpose, economics has aspired to attain the former, becoming a social science that explains the world as a mechanical effect of market forces by analogy with physics (Mirowski 1991).

Faith in the divinity of the market, then, in practice means faith in the primacy of economics, and the power of market forces. By contrast, faith in some significant degree of government planning and intervention, by contrast, is a faith in politics, and the power of intention and persuasion (Altvater 1993, 22). The contrast between these modes of causation is a contrast between a 'natural' and a 'revealed' theology, and the resolution of their respective primacies is a metaphysical and theological issue. However, their mutual complementarity is now widely acknowledged in a paradox described admirably by Robert H. Nelson:

> The market is based on the idea of the individual pursuit of self-interest. At the same time, however, a market system will work best if there is a clear limit to self-interest. The pursuit of self-interest should not extend to the various forms of opportunism, such as cheating, lying, and other types of deception, misrepresentation, and corruption found within the marketplace. … Another key consideration is that property rights, contracts and other legal arrangements should be fairly and consistently enforced. In short, the market must exist within an institutional and civic-value context that transcends individual self-interest and supports and encourages actions that have a wider benefit for the common good (Nelson 2001, 268).

The mechanics of rational self-interest must be set within the wider context of human integrity and trust. For this, as Joan Robinson explains, it is the honesty of other people that is necessary for one's own comfort, whereas the truly rational course of action for the individual is to act as an opportunistic free rider (Robinson 1964, 11–15). Francis Fukuyama has celebrated the role of trust inherent in society as a fundamental feature of economic well-being, where 'reciprocity, mutual obligation, duty toward community and trust' are based on habit rather than rational calculation (Fukuyama 1995, 11). Indeed, if social capital is fostered through religion and tradition, then the greatest utility maximizers are not the most rational ones (Fukuyama 1995, 37). Religion may even make a significant contribution to the creation of wealth (Atherton 2008).

Nevertheless, it is not enough to claim that market forces need to be bounded or supplemented by political activity and religious commitments in order to foster growth and efficiency. The argument to be pursued here is that neither approach effectively captures the mode of causation operative in the economic life of humanity. More fundamental than either in determining human conduct is neither mechanics nor purposes but another mode of thinking: what we count as significant, how we direct our attention, what becomes visible to us, what we record, and what we trust. It is a question of self-determination and self-discipline on the basis of what is noticed and thinkable. It is a question of metaphysics, or what we take as fundamentally real, and a question of belief, or what we take as fundamentally determinative. Philosophy is the study of reason as such, and a reason is what motivates us: it is a form of feeling; 'a reason is just a thought or perception that moves or engages us' (McGhee 2000, 28–29). Our reasons determine what we perceive and count as significant; our reasons also determine what we overlook. We become creatures of our reasons to the extent that they determine what we see of the world, how we conduct ourselves in the world, and how we trust the world to be. Then the critical approach to the divinity of the market requires that we determine what kinds of reasoning are involved in decisions on pricing, buying and selling.

It will be argued in what follows that the 'market', as such, does not exist: there are particular localities where people trade particular assets and commodities, facilitated by market-makers and financial intermediaries, but no single network of markets. Nor is human conduct determined by belief and purpose alone: there are real conditions that shape preferences, conditions consistent enough to have definite effects. The most significant of such conditions is not some ideal pervasive institution called 'the market' that has no standing in reality, but an actual pervasive institution that is its intimate correlate: the institution of money. Moreover, since money is a promise, a debt and an obligation, then it is a quantitative means of structuring belief. Money reunites the mechanical and the intentional, the objective and the subjective, but its mode of causation is distinctive. A metaphysical analysis of this mode of causation is illuminating for a conjunction of the economic and the religious.

2. A Matter of Choice

Economic theory is caught in a dilemma in its treatment of human agency. On the one hand, it assumes that human beings are autonomous rational actors intent on maximising their own self-interests and exercising free choice; on the other hand, it attempts to determine the laws that govern actual economic behaviour as though people behave entirely like fully determined particles (Lawson 1997, 8–11). Are human beings free and purposive agents who determine their own ends as preferences, or are human beings subject to external market forces? A traditional view is that where economics is the science of means, ethics is the science of ends (Collingwood 1926). Does economics invade the territory of ethics when it seeks to explain how human choices are determined? This dichotomy can be resolved only if the laws governing behaviour are also explicit reasons for free action: for example, seeking economic growth, allocating resources efficiently, and preserving creditworthiness seem to be criteria of rational conduct that apply to individuals, businesses, and governments alike. These reasons for economic conduct become self-reinforcing to the extent that they are conditions for prosperity and influence; those who are not rational actors, in this specific sense, will not remain significant actors for long. Nevertheless, it begs the ethical question to suppose that the 'irrational' actors, who do not remain influential in the market because they lose the power to express effective demand, are themselves not significant ends, or do not express ethical ends. The inversion of means and ends, where acquisition of means or of power becomes an end in itself, has been described as 'the very essence of all evil in society' (Weil 1956, 495). For it is the very condition by which good ends are subverted. For this reason, economic theory has to present market forces as serving the free choice of ends, a choice that remains the sovereign moral decision of the consumer. Nevertheless, insofar as market forces have a determining influence over human choices, the market ceases to be purely instrumental and comes to occupy the religious space where human ends are determined.

What is especially striking here is the way in which objective market forces have to be explained in terms of human subjectivity. The basis of any notion of a market mechanism is that the balance of market forces, including such factors as supply and demand, is measured by its resolution in terms of a price, which then impacts upon human preferences until an equilibrium price is approached. If the price is too high, then consumers will look elsewhere; if it is too low, then vendors will raise it to increase profits. Unfortunately, the main source of information that vendors and consumers have about market forces is found in the price itself, and the price is determined by vendors and/or consumers. How, then, are prices to be determined? Experience of the transactions that take place is clearly a guide. But a guide to what? Participants in 'the market' have no better super-computer for resolving the complex equations of global market forces than do economists, so the basis upon which they have to do their calculations is the rather strange 'back of an envelope' found in the form of their own 'preferences', their sense of 'marginal utility', their 'rational self-interest'. Economic forces reveal themselves through the balance of costs and benefits weighed up in decisions on where and when to buy and sell. The objective market mechanism is enacted through the human subject. Here, economists have to take human nature as a given, and as consistent: even if subjective preferences have been formed by tradition, habit and persuasion, by religion, ethics and politics, they are at least formed before individuals enter 'the market', wherever that is. Moreover, even if they are entirely reformed the subsequent day by further religious, ethical and political influences, they remain consistent once the individuals again reveal their new preferences through subsequent acts of purchase or sale. Of course, an individual who is dissuaded from pursuit of a religious, ethical or political end because the cost is just too high, from a sense of marginal disutility, may be suspected of lacking devotion, virtue or commitment. Yet where persuasion is a political act, purchase is an economic one. The 'market mechanism', if it exists, is ultimately to be found in the human soul in the form of a tendency to calculate and reveal preferences.

Here, again, the individual has no privileged way of surveying the relative balance of their preferences, given certain perceived costs and benefits, other than their own actual behaviour. The wealth of experimental and historical evidence, as well as theoretical counter-arguments, against the view of human nature required for a consistent distribution of preferences is overwhelming (see, for example, Altvater 1993; Goodchild 2009; Hutchinson, Mellor, and Olsen 2003; Lawson 1997; McCloskey 1998; Mirowski 1991; Ormerod 1994). For example, one simple requirement of consistency over preferences is transitivity: if people prefer Coca-cola to Pepsi, and Pepsi to lemonade, then they will prefer Coca-cola to lemonade. Experimental evidence shows that this is not the case (cited in Ormerod 1994, 111). If people do not even exhibit transitive behaviour, then no careful comparison of the marginal utility of competing choices can be regularly taking place. Indeed, as Alfred Marshall emphasised: "It cannot be too much insisted that to measure directly, or *per se*, either desires or the satisfaction which results from their fulfilment is impossible, if not inconceivable" (cited in Robinson 1964, 49). If this is true for economists, then surely it is also true for rational actors. One knows only one's experience, not what one might have gained or lost. Indeed, as Robinson explained, "*Utility* is a metaphysical concept of impregnable circularity; *utility* is the quality in commodities that makes individuals want to buy them, and the fact that individuals want to buy commodities shows that they have *utility*" (Robinson 1964, 48).

In what sense is the utility-maximising individual rational, if such a person is unable to measure utility? How can one have rational freedom without knowledge, where there is only the guess, the impulse and the hunch? How do people determine their preferences, except through the limitations of what they pay attention to, and what they take as real? The only measure that substitutes for desire, satisfaction and utility is money. The only way of comparing preferences and their marginal costs and benefits is on a single quantitative scale, the scale of money. The only way of revealing such preferences is to purchase with money. The real economic calculus does not take place in the soul, but in account books. The only way to maximise one's utility or self-interest, therefore, is to maximise one's ability to acquire money, whether through asset values, income, or credit. The supposedly rational actor is therefore one who postpones religious, ethical or political ends and preferences in favour of the acquisition of wealth.

In short, participation in economic behaviour requires participation in the 'utility fiction', a variant on Marx's 'commodity fetishism': one behaves as if goods and services have a determinable use-value; one behaves as if that determinable use-value is measurable in terms of exchange-value; one behaves as though that determinate exchange-value in expressed in terms of money. In reality, by contrast, one merely purchases for a determinate price that is normally set by manufacturers and retailers, where price itself is the main indicator of the quality of positional goods in comparison to others. Where other information is lacking, price itself becomes an indicator of quality or utility. The forces that drive economic behaviour are not expressed in terms of preferences, but in terms of effective demand, the money that is actually paid for goods and services (Hutchinson 1998). Here we meet a curious phenomenon: each revealed preference expresses a choice between the imagined utility of some good or service as against the choice for money, or a liquidity preference. Such a liquidity preference is an instance of a delayed satisfaction for the sake of a wider choice of future satisfactions. But there is also the possibility that such a delay may enable the acquisition of more money, through capital investment or asset appreciation. Indeed, *since preferences are only revealed to the extent that they are backed up by money as effective demand, and more money enables one to reveal one's preferences more strongly, the most powerful and effective preferences will, over the long term, be those that aim at profit.* The economy, as is widely known to all who work in business (even if not to all economists) is driven by the profit motive. Profits are always earned in the form of money.

3. The Preference for Money

So if the 'market mechanism' consisting of shifting preferences coordinated through prices is a fiction, we can at least consider the money mechanism that is real. Since the invention of stamped coinage by the ancient Greeks for the purposes of taxation, but more especially since the founding of the Bank of England that introduced reliable paper currency, and most especially in an electronic economy where sight deposits are records of the liabilities of others, money itself has been composed of credit (Ingham 2004). Money itself is a promise, and that promise consists in its acceptability by some issuing authority (Wray 1998, 24). Money is acceptable in our banks because it is the unit they use to record credits and debits. In the contemporary global economy, the money base of notes and coins in circulation is expanded many times over by the capacity of banks to lend in excess of reserves; yet even the notes and coins themselves are mere promises of value. Every monetary transaction, therefore, consists in a transfer of promises–both promises made by central issuing authorities and promises made by those who take out loans, and whose promises themselves then bear the promise of value. This value consists simply in the belief or credit that is invested in money, a social or collective value that can vary both in relation to other currencies and in relation to itself over time. It is a belief that cannot be read off from the soul–how much do you believe in your nation's currency?–but is formed by those who trade on the currency markets, especially the major banks that act as market makers. It is a product of the record of the actual transactions that take place. The agreement of exchanges and contracts is made possible by credit, by the transfer of liabilities. An economy operates through people taking on obligations, agreeing contracts, and taking out loans, renouncing ease and pleasure–no longer in the service of a transcendent God–but in the expectation that in the future they might be compensated by having more liabilities of others transferred to them than they have undertaken. That is to say, they believe they might make a profit. The system of obligations and liabilities becomes an immanent system with clear boundaries insofar as there is a common measure and means of payment for all liabilities: money itself. It is therefore important to analyse the implicit theology present in the creation and use of money itself.

In the first place, the value of money is transcendent: it is a promise, taken on faith, and only realized to the extent that this faith is acted out in practice in exchange. One cannot hold the value of money in one's hand, even if one can use that value to pay for things. 'The eye has never seen, nor the hand touched a dollar. All that we can touch or see is a promise to pay or satisfy a debt due for an amount called a dollar.' (Innes 2005, 358)

In the second place, money is both a means of payment and a measure of prices. As a measure of prices, money endows all things with a universal value: the price is the same, whoever is the buyer. Yet as a means of payment, money only grants the power of effective demand to those with money. In order to achieve what one values, one must value money first as the means of access to what one desires. Once must participate in the immanent system, otherwise one has no effective demand within that system. Since it is the means by which all other social values may be realized, it posits itself as the supreme value. Nothing is more liquid, more exchangeable, more valuable than money. Whatever one's own values, one must value money first as the means of access to all other values (Goodchild 2002, 127–29).

In the third place, money is only 'value in motion': one cannot achieve profitability without investing that money. The value of assets is determined not by their intrinsic worth but by their expected yield, their anticipated rate of return. The value of assets is determined by speculative projections. Moreover, even if these anticipations prove misguided, at every stage the value of assets is determined by the next wave of anticipations about the future. Thus this future never comes: it is purely ideal. Financial value is essentially a degree of hope, expectation, trust, or credibility. Just as paper currency is never cashed in, so the value of assets is never realized. It is future or transcendent. Being transcendent to material and social reality, yet also being the pivot around which material and social reality is continually reconstructed, financial value is essentially religious.

In the fourth place, the entire monetary system has its own intrinsic logic of growth. This drive for growth is a separate engine of the global economy in addition to the individual acquisition of necessities and the individual pursuit of self-interest. There are three relevant components here:

- A logic of natural selection: wealth brings access to power, both extrinsically, through military superiority, access to information, shaping public consciousness, political influence, and selective funding, and intrinsically, through investments, profits, growth, negotiating favourable contracts, and bringing liberation from the constraints of natural necessity and social responsibility that limit the economic freedom of those without wealth.
- A logic of appropriation: speculative profits can only be made on the basis of profits extracted from production and consumption, and to achieve this, an increasing quantity of the world's physical resources

must be appropriated for production, exchange and consumption, in a colonization and commodification of the world.

– A logic of intensification: increased production and profits require increased investment, credit and debt. While production is of goods and services, debts and interest are repaid in the form of money. Increased production can only lead to the repayment of debts if there is more money to pay for them; yet money can only be created in the form of further loans, or else it is inflationary. The result is that, since the founding of the Bank of England, the nascent global economy has been progressively enslaved to an increasing spiral of debt. The entire global economy is driven by a spiral of debt, constrained to seek further profits, and always dependent on future expansion.

An anthropological judgement on the nature of modernity would identify the value of money as the modern religion, the transcendent principle of the social order. The market is not divine: its corrections are unjust, inefficient, and untimely. Yet every market correction reinforces the need for money. Since the value of money is a purely ideal construct, the religion of money has its own theology. Its principles are fourfold: money is the promise of value upon which actual value may be advanced; money is the supreme value against which all other values may be measured; money is a speculative value whose intrinsic worth waits to be demonstrated; and money is a debt or social obligation that requires that social activity be continually re-ordered around increasing profit and the repayment of debt, while also continually expanding the debt and the obligation. Money fulfils the practical and social functions of religion. Economic globalization is the universalization of this religion through its drive for growth and power, its progressive colonization of all dimensions of life, and its commitment to growing debt. A theology of money is required to explain the distinctive nature of this spectral power in the modern world, and subject it to critical evaluation.

People engage in economic activity for three reasons: to fulfil their needs and desires, to gain positional advantage over others, and to repay their debts. The latter factor is obscured when economic activity is reduced to the mythical scene of a village market exchange based on barter. In practice, money has to be used for the payment of taxes, rent, wages and interest, in addition to purchasing commodities. More fundamental than the institutions of private property and instantaneous exchange (which promote the illusion that a synchronic map of distribution of property is an accurate description of the economy) are the practices of entering into contracts and obligations that endure over time. It is not sufficient to count one's assets; it is necessary to consider one's income, debts and obligations in order to determine one's overall financial position. Each reason for economic activity only becomes effective in conjunction with the others. There would be barely any trade without money, and barely any money without investment, credit, debt and obligation.

What we call 'market forces', therefore, are driven by the impersonal system required to maintain financial value. To stand outside the modern economic system with its drive for growth is to risk being crushed. For since wealth can only grow if it devotes its demands toward making profits and paying back debts, then it necessarily depletes the resources required to meet natural necessities and social responsibilities–in particular, the needs of subsistence and sustainability. Since it is the condition for all social activity, the demands of sustaining the money system and wealth creation take priority over the demands for sustaining the environment, population, or the social order.

Overall, then, the fact that economic transactions are measured and conducted through the medium of money as debt has a significant effect on the preferences revealed in any transaction. For money will be required in the future for the payment of rents, wages, interest, and taxation, as well as repayment of the principal for any loan. All economic agents must seek money under such conditions, and so must seek to engage in some activity that will reward them with an income. Just as it is necessary to acquire the basics of life in order to survive in the physical order, it is necessary to acquire a basic income in order to survive in the economic order. Instead of regarding a delay in consumption as a sacrifice of satisfaction in the name of a future gratification, it is necessary to regard the act of consumption as a sacrifice of profits in the name of needs and desires. If revealed preferences express a sacrifice of other utilities, the general equivalent against which all other utilities can be measured is the possibility of gaining income and profits to meet further obligations.

4. The Nature of Social Causation

The 'market mechanism' would appear to require supplementation by intentional human behaviour in at least three respects: in generating the political structures that maintain the markets, enforcing property rights and contracts, determining and regulating appropriate conduct; in enabling the trust that facilitates the establishment of contracts and exchanges by means of the integrity and goodwill of market participants; and, at the level of individual choice, in the purposeful reasoning and self-determination that establishes preferences. Without the latter, there is a direct contradiction between the mechanics of market forces and individual freedom. The needs of economic modelling require the elimination of such purposeful reasoning, for if choice is real, the future is uncertain. Some, such as Pareto, seem content to eliminate individual freedom, acknowledging that, 'The individual can disappear, provided that he leaves us with this photograph of his tastes' (cited in Hodgson 1993, 218). If preferences are to be more than programmed responses to circumstances, though, some degree of intentional action is necessary that entirely undermines the market mechanism insofar as preferences are self-caused, rather than a response to market conditions. Insofar as intentions and purposes are invoked, then some kind of non-economic evaluation, together with the political resolution of competing forces, has a direct influence over the course of economic conduct.

Nevertheless, humanistic categories of explanation are not complete in themselves. Economic conduct cannot be explained in terms of intentionality alone. For there are real economic forces which operate through money. Just as a person is obliged to fulfil basic physical needs in order to continue to live, a person is also obliged to pursue basic economic survival. An analogy with physics is inappropriate here: there is no compulsion as to how one spends or acquires money. The choice of economic failure remains an indispensable component of economic freedom. Nevertheless, there is a degree of constraint placed upon the choices of individuals, businesses and nations alike insofar as they are to maintain their credibility. One does not simply employ efficient means to achieve determinate preferences or ends. Such a model of human conduct ignores the social element that is the distinctive feature of market relations: preferences are only known insofar as they are *revealed*. They are performed for an audience; they are made public; they are recorded in transactions. Human rationality is not merely instrumental but also communicative. Human conduct draws attention to some matters and draws attention away from others. Instead of the public nature of economic action being incidental to its conduct, it is the means through which preferences are formed, expressed, and validated.

It has been a common theme to berate the unrealistic nature of the atomic individualism required for the theory of neo-classical economics (e.g. Lawson 1997). Human behaviour is reflexive: it responds to macro-level information such as stock index prices (Soros 2008). Levels of human ignorance over the state of the market and imperfections in competition are sufficient to ruin equilibrium equations, leading to perpetual movement far from equilibrium (Nelson 2001, 61). There are exceptions to marginal utility, such as positional goods, for there is no limit to displays of wealth and power, and no limit to the desire for wealth. Free markets are unsuitable for the efficient allocation of positional goods (such as money), which tend to accumulate in the hands of intermediaries. The rates of profits from finance are above the rates of profits from industry, leading to a perpetual imbalance and instability. Moreover, economies are not composed of individuals as economic agents alone, and certainly not of mathematical continua, but instead are composed largely of major institutions such as states, local governments and transnational corporations (Ormerod 1994, 48). Labour is not a commodity that can be easily bought and sold, since it is inalienable from persons, and persons cannot be easily disembedded from their networks of social and educational relationships. The hypothetical 'market' is entirely dependent on an external environment, which includes geological, ecological, social, political, and historical features that have their own logic not explicable by market forces, however much 'economics imperialism' lays claim to psychology (Fine and Milonakis 2009; Carrette 2007). Economic growth is exponential, in fundamental contradiction with ecological finitude which is cyclical, and geological finitude which is entropic (Altvater 1993, 198 ff.). Finally, the proactive role of money as debt and therefore obligation introduces perpetual instabilities that abolish any stable equilibria. Each of these factors refers to 'externalities', in other words, the real world, as opposed to the imaginary world called 'the market'.

Nevertheless, even if one takes all such externalities as given, economic behaviour involves an *externalization*. Contracts, the elementary unity of economic interaction, are public documents, enforceable in law, that record obligations and duties. They cannot possibly represent all the other 'external' conditions necessary for the contract to be fulfilled, nor can they represent all the internal reflections in the human soul that feature as factors influencing decisions. Only a small aspect of the situation is recorded in an agreement. Similarly, exchanges lead to the recording of the agreed price, not all the prior hopes or negotiations regarding possible prices. Account books record the transactions that have taken place, not all the factors that make such transactions possible, or the transactions that might have happened but were refused. In short, if economic conduct reveals preferences, then it does not reveal 'externalities', but it externalizes that aspect of economic conduct that can be recorded in contracts and accounts. Atomic individualism is not merely some bizarre predilection of economic theorists, even if it does mask certain economic and political interests. Individual preference is simply the only aspect of economic conduct that is revealed in contracts and accounts. It is the form of representation through which such conduct can be disclosed. What is imagined as 'the market' is simply a set of records, a set of contracts and accounts. Atomic individualism is imposed upon economists by their data: only preferences are externalized and revealed.

This has immense consequences for human conduct. As we have noted, market participants have no access to their own preferences until these are externalized in decision and action. While much of human life may be shaped by external geological, ecological, historical and social realities, among other factors, and much of human conduct may be guided by religious, ethical and political persuasions, human conduct that involves cooperation through money requires no such agreement on ends. In such human relations, only the contracts and accounts are recorded–and this is why they will be deemed 'market relations'. The pursuit of the satisfaction of human needs, of the competition for positional goods, and the repayment of debts that drives economic behaviour, as well as the pursuit of religious, ethical or political ends, can only be effective through market relations when such conduct aims at the acquisition of money. The acquisition of money is the criterion of effectiveness. Effective human conduct is that which considers decisions and actions in relation to money. In other words, free human self-determination takes place by regulating conduct in line with what has been recorded in contracts and accounts. People are obliged to behave as if they are atomic individualists in order to be effective, even if they subsequently wish to regulate their conduct in accordance with traditional religious, ethical or social norms and practices, which have separate means of recording.

It is important to understand the mode of social causation at work here. The categories of means and ends, or instrumental and purposive reason, or economics and politics, are inadequate. Instead, social possibilities are delimited by the scope of attention. One can only respond to what one sees, and what one takes as significant. The keeping of contracts and accounts is a technology designed to regulate human conduct by recording the obligations that have lasting significance. Of course, the use of such technologies can be considered a means, and the virtue of maintaining public credibility by fulfilling obligations can be considered an end. Nevertheless, human self-determination by directing attention to what is publicly recorded as real and significant–in this case, revealed preferences–is an ongoing modulation of behaviour. Instead of activity being directed towards specific projects and goals that come to an end at a particular time, activity is perpetually regulated through ongoing vigilance and self-discipline. Instead of socially-sanctioned norms providing the standards that guide behaviour, such behaviour is an individual responsibility that takes care to ensure that social obligations are met. Instead of choices being driven by mechanical necessity, there is a certain 'economic necessity', a need to acquire money, to make demands effective, that drives human choices. This is the mode of social causation that is operative in 'the market', through money.

5. Conclusion

Is the market a god? No, the market has no existence outside of the collection of contracts, accounts, and banking institutions that constitute its transactions. Is money a god? No, money has no existence outside of the collection of contracts, accounts, and banking institutions that constitute its transactions. Yet this very collection determines what is revealed as significant, focuses attention, and expresses the obligations that shape human conduct. The market is best considered neither as a means towards human fulfilment, nor as the end of human fulfilment. It does, however, regulate human life through self-determination. In terms of social function, perhaps the best category to describe it is the religious category of asceticism (Flood 2004). For religious life is that which regulates time and the conduct of time, through rituals, festivals and seasons. Religious life prescribes how time is to be spent, and how life should be conducted. Religious life provides the rituals and technologies that allow us to record, repeat and remember; it provides the spiritual practices through which life is perpetually reconstructed; it provides the collective goals of human behaviour. The economy is heir to ascetic life.

Moreover, the economy discloses the mode of social causation that has been present in religious life all along. This has considerable metaphysical and theological significance. It is possible to regard both God and the market as cognitive illusions produced by the mechanical operation of evolutionary forces. It is possible, by contrast, to regard the world as the creation of a purposeful God, the market as an illusion produced when a pure means is taken as an end. Each of these worldviews derives from taking one mode of social causation as final and ultimate: instrumental or purposive causation. Each of these worldviews only pays attention to that which it records as real. Each of these worldviews derives from the implications of a particular mode of representation. Each of these worldviews focuses on a set of relations–linear in the case of mechanical causality, organic in the case of purposive causality–that are too narrow to explain the range of externalities and the strategies of self-determination present in economic life. For reflexive self-determination in response to ongoing external relations, through the medium of some strategy of recording that focuses attention, detaches itself from the predictable or moral forms of behaviour required by instrumental or purposive reason.

In practice, as the philosopher of religion Michael McGhee explains:

> All we see of the world is what our attention is focused on and, *a fortiori*, we don't see the underlying reasons for this. We take the focus of our attention to reveal the state of things, but it only reveals what it reveals, and what is outside the focus is not apparent to us, so that we don't even know what someone is talking about who points to things outside its scope. And we take our perceived world to be a ground of judgement, whereas it is only the present *scope* of our judgement … (McGhee 2000, 85).

If this is the way in which economic and intellectual life is determined, then it will remain blind to its limitations, and its path will be guided by its blindness. What matters most, if philosophy is to be a practice contributing to human freedom, is that we discover means of recording that enable us to pay attention to that which matters, and that which is decisive. For the way in which we pay attention to things, and the way in which we focus on what we take as decisive, will ultimately determine the destiny of human life. For this, a certain amount of ascetic practice may be required.

References

Altvater, Elmar. (1993). *The future of the market: An essay on the regulation of money and nature after the collapse of 'Actually Existing Socialism'*. Tr. By Patrick Camiller. London: Verso.

Atherton, John. (2008). *Transfiguring capitalism: An enquiry into religion and global change*. London: SCM Press.

Carrette, Jeremy. (2007). *Religion and critical psychology: Religious experience in the knowledge economy*. London: Routledge.

Collingwood, R.G. (1926). Economics as a philosophical science. *International Journal of Ethics* 26 (2), 162–85.

Fine, Ben, & Dimitris Milonakis. (2009). *From economics imperialism to freakonomics: The shifting boundaries between economics and other social sciences*. London: Routledge.

Flood, Gavin. (2004). *The ascetic self: Subjectivity, memory, tradition*. Cambridge: Cambridge University Press.

Fukuyama, Francis. (1995). Trust: The social virtues and the creation of prosperity. London: Hamish Hamilton.

Goodchild, Philip. (2002). *Capitalism and religion: The price of piety*. London: Routledge.

Goodchild, Philip. (2009). *Theology of money*. Durham, North Carolina: Duke University Press.

Hodgson, Geoffrey M. (1993). Economics and evolution: Bringing life back into economics. Cambridge, Polity Press.

Hutchinson, Frances. (1998). *What everyone really wants to know about money*. Charlbury: Jon Carpenter.

Hutchinson, Frances, Mary Mellor, & Wendy Olsen (2003). *The politics of money: Towards sustainability and economic democracy*. London: Pluto Press.

Ingham, Geoffrey. (2004). *The nature of money*. Cambridge: Polity Press.

Innes, Mitchell. (2005/1910). The credit theory of money. In Geoffrey Ingham (Ed.), *Concepts of money*. Cheltenham: Edward Elgar.

Lawson, Tony. (1997). *Economics and reality*. London: Routledge.

McCloskey, Deirdre. (1998). *The rhetoric of economics*. Second Edition. Madison, Wisconsin: University of Wisconsin Press.

McGhee, Michael. (2000). *Transformations of mind: Philosophy as a spiritual exercise*. Cambridge: Cambridge University Press.

Mirowski, Philip. (1991). More heat than light: Economics as social physics, physics as nature's economics. Cambridge: Cambridge University Press.

Nelson, Robert H. (2001). *Economics as religion: From Samuelson to Chicago*. University Park, Pennsylvania: Penn State University Press.

Ormerod, Paul. (1994). *The death of economics*. London: Faber and Faber.

Robinson, Joan. (1964). *Economic philosophy*. Harmondsworth: Penguin.

Soros, George. (2009). *The crash of 2008 and what it means*. New York: Public Affairs.

Weil, Simone. (1956). *Notebooks. Volume 2*. Tr. By Arthur Wills. London: Routledge.

Wray, L.R. (1998). *Understanding modern money*. Cheltenham: Edward Elgar.

Contributors

Bulbulia, Joseph, PhD, Senior Lecturer, Victoria University of Wellington, New Zealand

Goodchild, Philip, PhD, Professor of Religion and Philosophy, University of Nottingham, UK

Grüne-Yanoff, Till, PhD, Fellow of the Helsinki Collegium for Advanced Studies, Finland

Gwin, Carl R., PhD, Associate Professor of Economics, Graziadio School of Business and Management, Pepperdine University, USA

Kamppinen, Matti, PhD, Senior Lecturer, Department of Religious Studies, University of Turku, Finland

Nelson, Robert H., PhD, Professor of Environmental Policy, School of Public Policy at the University of Maryland, USA and Senior Fellow, The Independent Institute

North, Charles M., PhD, Associate Professor, Department of Economics, Baylor University, USA

Pyysiäinen, Ilkka, PhD, Academy Research Fellow, Helsinki Collegium for Advanced Studies, Finland

Schjoedt, Uffe, PhD, Aarhus University, Denmark

Schmaus, Warren, PhD, Professor of Philosophy, Illinois Institute of Technology, USA

Index